T0291150

Emerging Issues and Trends in Indian Business and Management

Volume 3

FRESH PERSPECTIVES ON INDIA'S ORGANIZATIONAL DIMENSION

Emerging Issues and Trends in Indian Business and Management

Series Editors: Vipin Gupta *(California State University San Bernardino, USA)*
Samir Ranja Chatterjee *(Curtin University, Australia)*
Alka Maurya *(Amity University, India)*

Published

Emerging Issues and Trends in Indian Business and Management

Volume 3

FRESH PERSPECTIVES ON INDIA'S ORGANIZATIONAL DIMENSION

Editors

Vipin Gupta
California State University, USA

Samir Ranjan Chatterjee
Curtin University, Australia

Alka Maurya
Amity University, India

World Scientific

NEW JERSEY · LONDON · SINGAPORE · BEIJING · SHANGHAI · HONG KONG · TAIPEI · CHENNAI · TOKYO

Published by

World Scientific Publishing Co. Pte. Ltd.

5 Toh Tuck Link, Singapore 596224

USA office: 27 Warren Street, Suite 401-402, Hackensack, NJ 07601

UK office: 57 Shelton Street, Covent Garden, London WC2H 9HE

British Library Cataloguing-in-Publication Data
A catalogue record for this book is available from the British Library.

Emerging Issues and Trends in Indian Business and Management — Vol. 3
Fresh Perspectives on India's Organizational Dimension

ISBN 978-981-12-9643-7 (hardcover)
ISBN 978-981-12-9644-4 (ebook for institutions)
ISBN 978-981-12-9645-1 (ebook for individuals)

For any available supplementary material, please visit
https://www.worldscientific.com/worldscibooks/10.1142/13938#t=suppl

Desk Editors: Soundararajan Raghuraman/Nicole Ong

Typeset by Stallion Press
Email: enquiries@stallionpress.com

About the Editors

Vipin Gupta is a professor, author, truth seeker, and motivator at the Jack H. Brown College of Business and Public Administration, California State University San Bernardino, USA. He has a PhD in managerial science and applied economics from the Wharton School of the University of Pennsylvania. He is a gold medalist from the post-graduate program of the Indian Institute of Management, Ahmedabad, India. Professor Gupta has authored more than 180 journal articles and book chapters and published 30 books, including the co-edited *Culture, Leadership, and Organizations: The GLOBE Study of 62 Societies.* Besides delivering lectures and keynotes, he has presented at international academic conferences in more than 60 nations. He has been on the governing board and organizing committee of several international conferences. As a 2015–2016 American Council of Education fellow, he visited 62 universities, colleges, and higher education institutions in nine European nations, the USA, and India. In his most recent project, he has self-published 12 self-authored books under the series "Vastly Integrated Processes Inside Mother Nature" in 2021 and 2022. His homepage is Drvipingupta.com.

Alka Maurya is a professor of international business at Amity International Business School, Amity University, India. She is a computer science graduate and has received her master's in international business from the Indian Institute of Foreign Trade, New Delhi, India, and her PhD in international business from Jiwaji University, Gwalior, India. She has over 27 years of experience in teaching, research, and consulting. Before coming into academics, she worked with various export promotion bodies in India as well as preparing strategies for promoting exports from India. She has presented her research work in various national and international forums on various topics related to international business. She has published 10 books and several research papers/case studies in her area of specialization. She is also invited as a speaker/resource person for various international conferences and seminars in the area of international business. Teaching is her passion, and she is shaping young minds to take up the challenges in this dynamic and competitive environment.

Samir Ranjan Chatterjee is an emeritus professor renowned for his role as a university academic, research scholar, and international trainer and consultant for more than five decades. Besides his home base at Curtin University in Australia, he has lived and worked for extended periods in India, China, the US, the UK, France, former Yugoslavia, Japan, Singapore, Mongolia, Malaysia, Indonesia, and Hong Kong. During 1994–1995, he lived in Mongolia for a year as the United Nations Adviser in the development of management education in the country, and he worked there until 1999 as the director of large capacity-building programs funded by the United Nations Development Program. During 1999–2003, he was an international expert reviewer with the Asian Development Bank on a US$250 million higher education sector reform project in Indonesia. From 2013 to 2015, he was the project adviser for a "Pro-Poor Capacity-Building" program for senior public sector executives in Mongolia, funded by the Australian government. He has been a fellow of the Australian Institute of Management and the Australian Society of CPAs. He has authored and co-authored 11 books, including a book on Indian management published by Sage, 35 book chapters, and about 200 scholarly journal publications and refereed international conference papers. He is on the editorial boards of many international scholarly journals. He serves as the doctoral thesis examiner for many Australian and Asian universities. He was the president of the Society for Global Business and Economic Development (SGBED) and currently chairs the organization's board of trustees. Professor Chatterjee was a national shortlisted nominee for the "2017 Australian of the Year" award.

Contents

Prologue: Performing for Both Profiting and Development

Shrirang Ramdas Chaudhari[*,§]**, Sasmita Palo**[†,¶]**,**
Moitrayee Das[†,††]**, and Vipin Gupta**[‡,‡‡]

[*]*School of Management and Labor Studies, Tata Institute of Social Science, Mumbai, India*

[†]*Department of Psychological Sciences, School of Liberal Education, FLAME University, Pune, India*

[‡]*Center for Global Management, The Jack H. Brown College, Business and Public Administration, California State University, San Bernardino, CA, USA*

[§]*shrirangchaudhary@gmail.com*

[¶]*spalo@tiss.edu*

[††]*moitrayee.das@flame.edu*

[‡‡]*vipin.gupta@csusb.edu*

India offers a fresh context for research into the organizational dimension of management. The twin criteria of profit and development are complementary to the performance of organizations in India. This prologue sets the context for the volume using a case study of Bandhan Bank. This case study highlights how the planning of organizations in India makes developmental profiting integral to their performance and how planning is adapted through evolutionary programming in dynamic correlation with the environment. A great example of the need for adaptation is the effects of the COVID-19 pandemic on how organizations operate in a post-COVID-19 environment. The COVID-19 pandemic has impacted microfinance institutions worldwide. The story of Bandhan Bank is about organizing with a hyperactive focus on grassroots to become a transformative force at the national level in a very short period with very limited resources. Bandhan Bank is a microfinance institution that has successfully transitioned into a commercial bank. It has a strong focus on financial inclusion, with over 15 million female customers. Established in 2001 as a microfinance institution, Bandhan Bank primarily serves the unbanked and underbanked sections of society, including low-income individuals, small businesses, and women entrepreneurs. It has a robust presence in rural and semi-urban areas, where access to financial services is limited. With its strong foundation, customer-centric approach, and commitment to financial inclusion, Bandhan Bank is a beacon of hope for millions of individuals and businesses traditionally excluded from formal financial systems. Bandhan Bank has been able to achieve this success by focusing on women's empowerment and financial literacy. The bank has also been able to provide access to organized finances to millions of rural unbanked and underbanked individuals. In recent years, Bandhan Bank has implemented various strategies to enhance its asset quality and improve its standing in the banking sector. The bank has shifted its focus from microfinance to retail lending by successfully moving clients from micro enterprises to small and medium enterprises. It has also strengthened its risk management framework and upgraded its technology infrastructure to better monitor loans and identify risks. The bank has also prioritized hiring local staff to better understand the needs of rural and semi-urban markets. Bandhan Bank's response to the COVID-19 crisis includes providing financial assistance to customers, collaborating with local governments, and offering educational support. The bank has strengthened its digital banking platform and increased its focus on customer service, adopting a flexible approach to lending during these challenging times.

About the Founder

Mr. Chandra Shekhar Ghosh, a skilled statistician with a vision of socioeconomic equity, encountered a life-changing event during his stay in West Bengal, further propagating the idea of today's most prominent microfinance institution in India. After education from Dhaka University and social work experience in Bangladesh, Ghosh started working with the Village Welfare Society in West Bengal and was actively engaged in the socioeconomic development of ruler eastern India.

Mr. Chandra Shekhar Ghosh was born in 1960 into a refugee family from Bangladesh. It was clear that the family was not financially well off. Ghosh's father owned a small sweet shop. Despite the family's hardships, Ghosh's father ensured his son received a good education and somehow sent him to study statistics at Dhaka University. Ghosh started working in 1985, and his training and work experience as a field officer in Bangladesh Rural Advancement Committee (BRAC) (an international development agency based in Bangladesh) led him to work with several Non-Governmental Organizations (NGOs) to uplift the economically backward in West Bengal. That was a crucial period in Ghosh's life because he was exposed to the world of microfinance, eventually leading to the formation of Bandhan Bank in West Bengal. Ghosh's work in NGOs began in 2001, giving small loans to those in need in Kolkata's Konnagar. Interestingly, no commercial bank was willing to lend money to him. Hence, his capital came from a local money lender, from whom he borrowed Rs. 1.75 lakh at an interest rate of 7.5, and his sister and brother-in-law supported him with Rs. 25,000 in his venture.

His work started with only two staff members — Partha Samanta and Fatik Bera. They began their work in and around Konnagar and Bagnan areas in the Kolkata suburbs by lending small loans (Rs. 1,000) to poor borrowers. One fine morning, Mr. Ghosh saw women laborers gathering at a local shop, where the owner used to lend money to them for their daily household expenses. With the spontaneity of zestful exploration of his social cause, Ghosh approached the women and tried to understand their money-lending mechanism and its technicality.

Mr. Ghosh found that the women borrowed Rs. 100 from the local lender daily in the morning and returned Rs. 110 at the end of the day. He was stunned by the hardworking woman repaying 10% interest on such a small loan. Surprised, Ghosh curiously asked those women about it. What he heard next significantly influenced his vision. The women said they were offering the Rs. 10 to the lender in goodwill for tea and snacks, not as interest on a loan.

Ghosh realized the laboring potential of those women and the need for a systematic venture to develop their socioeconomic lives. He quit his job at the Village Welfare Society and independently started crafting a socio-economic welfare system for women. In 2001, Mr. Ghosh established an NGO named Bandhan-Konnagar in Kolkata, West Bengal.

With Rs. 2 lakh of initial capital and three employees' help, Mr. Chandra Shekhar Ghosh paved a path for the socioeconomic development of women in socioeconomically vulnerable strata. Bandhan-Konnagar started providing a micro-finance service to small and marginalized women entrepreneurs who need formal banking assistance of any kind. The growth story of Bandhan Bank is the story of Mr. Chandra Shekhar Ghosh. "*Bandhan*" translates to the bond of togetherness. Thus, Ghosh's connection with the economically deprived community of rural eastern India rural led to the foundation of Bandhan Financial Services Ltd., which expanded into a private bank in less than 15 years.

Strategy and the Success Story of the Bank

The success story of Bandhan Bank is rooted in women's liberation from gender norms and discrimination in rural India. Bandhan Bank's 71% of banking outlets are rural and semi-urban. In rural India, women are denied most of the emerging opportunities in the labor market, such as trade, transport, storage, and services, that are stereotypically reserved for men. The reason is the need for more education.

The emerging livelihood opportunities for women without discrimination required Bandhan Bank to help them acquire the necessary skills. The first step was to facilitate the elimination of discrimination in education and simplify banking operations. In doing so, as a preliminary step, the rural women's mindset of "dependency" had to change. Bandhan Bank helped rural women become conscious of their abilities to change themselves, their families, and their community through their outreach program.

Bandhan Bank started the socioeconomic upliftment of women by emphasizing gender equality through financial literacy programs, and by 2021, the program had educated 995,214 rural women. With a belief in community development, the bank has created millions of entrepreneurs who, in turn, employ others. The bank provides around Rs. 25,000–30,000 per family spread over 24 months to help them create a livelihood. Until 2017, the bank had supported about 56,000 families. A research study in the Gorakhpur region found that 90% of the women agree that microfinance Bandhan Bank has helped improve their overall socioeconomic status by allowing them to generate extra income, which is helpful for their families.

Today, Bandhan Bank has more than 15 million female customers, making up two-thirds of the bank's total customer base of 22 million.

Bandhan Bank has also supported millions of rural unbanked and underbanked individuals in some of India's lowest-income segments by giving them access to organized finances. For Bandhan Bank, emphasis on responsible financing and sensitization to the virtues of saving are the key drivers in promoting financial literacy nationwide. The results of the financial literacy program have historically positively impacted the lives of its customers. In 2019, a study report by Bandhan Bank suggested that the households of beneficiaries of the program have more assets, the food security in the region is higher, and women started earning more.

More than 50% of the small credit customers have remained with Bandhan Bank for a period ranging from 4 years to 19 years (right since Bandhan's inception in 2001). They have had multiple credit cycles with the bank, clearly reflecting their trust in the Bandhan brand and the role the bank has played in uplifting their lives.

The Concept of Alms

The concept of alms was something other than what Ghosh believed. He would say, "Give work instead to the destitute." Bandhan Bank also worked in community development and shared huge corporate responsibility toward society. By March 2020, through various programs, Bandhan Bank had 28,366 families moved out of poverty, extreme hunger, and malnutrition, and about 13,49,690 families enjoyed nutritional food every day and were freed from hunger. Around 14,66,661 families accessed good healthcare and well-being.

Ghosh has many success stories to share: one such story is that of a woman from Murshidabad who used to beg for a living, and who now lives in a four-storied building. She could achieve her permanent livelihood by making and selling puffed rice through the program offered by Bandhan Bank. She recently met Ghosh and offered him some of her puffed rice. The whole gesture touched Ghosh deeply, and he expressed, "If someone says our work has changed their lives, it inspires me to do more."

Ghosh has a long-term vision to lead India's human development index meaningfully and sustainably. He is very motivated by his team and says, "Together, we can move mountains."

A noble cause propensity of Bandhan Bank resulted in a considerable micro-finance giant networked in 34 out of 36 states and union territories of India, facilitating 5,310 banking outlets and more than 2.63 crore customers. In the last 5 years, Bandhan Bank's loan book served Rs. 74,300 crore and provided deposits of Rs. 60,600 crore to its customers.

With a growing customer base, Bandhan Bank attracted investments from global investors, including the International Finance Corporation, the Abu Dhabi Investment Authority, and Singapore's Caladium. In the growth of Bandhan Bank, only one thing has remained unchanged — its foundational framework as a micro-credit business. In its total customer base of 2.63 crores, 1.23 crore (nearly 47%) are micro banking customers holding Rs. 47,5000 crore, or around 64% of the total loan book of Rs. 74,300 crore. This includes an individual loan portfolio amounting to Rs. 2,200 crore.

Bandhan Bank understands its customers well due to its distributed on-field community networks. The bank has made history by transforming into a universal bank that serves all socioeconomic sections across the country. Though Bandhan Bank has expanded over the years, its mission remains the same, i.e. to build a financially inclusive India.

Trust as Resilience in MFIs

The impact of external forces on micro-credit financing has become an increasing concern globally. Especially during the pandemic, micro-finance institutes faced new challenges. The COVID-19 pandemic in early 2020 has exposed several challenges and considerations for Bandhan Bank. The pandemic and lockdown caused visible economic distress across the country. In particular, people availing micro-finances for their small businesses could not earn enough for the loan repayments.

In March 2020, an Agra resident, Gajendra Sharma, filed a petition with the Supreme Court of India for a loan waiver. Under the Supreme Court's direction, on March 27 2020, seeking to ease the borrowers' pain, the Reserved Bank of India (RBI) issued a circular allowing banks and lending institutions to grant a moratorium on the payment of term loan installments between March 1 and May 31, 2020, which was further extended for the period till August 31, 2020, due to the prolonged pandemic situation in the country.

In an interview with *The Economic Times* on May 14, 2020, the CEO and MD of Bandhan Bank, Mr. Chandra Shekhar Ghosh, said, "We are in constant touch with our customers. Nearly 95% of its customer base has said they are ready to pay, and its assets have not been impacted. The difficulty in collection/repayment was due to the lockdown as they couldn't come to the branch to deposit that amount."

In the same interview, Mr. Gosh admitted that the impact of natural calamities on microcredits is short-lived, lasting for a minimum of 3 months and a maximum of 6 months. But if it is politically motivated, it could last longer as the intent to repay is impacted.

India faced the most brutal hit of COVID-19, the second wave, in terms of the number of deaths and the economy's downfall. For Bandhan Bank, the vicious second wave of the pandemic and the emerging political challenge of the Assam and West Bengal elections created a dangerous storm.

The state assembly passed legislation aiming to protect and relieve economically vulnerable individuals from undue hardship of interest rates and coercive means of recovery by Micro-Finance Institutes (MFI). This emerged as a poll plank on the threshold of the 2021 Assam assembly election; BJP and Congress, both competing political parties, promised a loan waiver of different degrees to the voters. While 16% of Bandhan Bank's microloans originate from Assam, borrowers refused to repay the loan installments amidst the hope and confusion triggered by political competition.

Earlier in the pandemic, CEO and MD Chandra Shekhar Ghosh told the press that their customers were keen to repay the loan interest. However, natural calamities and political gambling affected the business of the bank. A year later, due to the second wave, the collection efficiency of the Bandhan Bank is potentially reduced, especially in its largest market in eastern India. There was a dip of 83% from 88% in the December quarter during the first quarter in the collection efficiency in Assam. Bandhan Bank is a microfinance institute where many repayments happen through cash. Considering 75% of microfinance loans booked under the moratorium, around 71,847 crores were at stake. The Bandhan Bank stock seems to be flowing downward per its historical valuation. But Bandhan Bank kept serving the masses. It expanded its advances by as much as 21% during the January–March quarter in the pandemic-hit FY21 compared with the figures in the corresponding quarter of FY20. Mr. Ghosh said, "As the country is going through a difficult phase again, we are committed to supporting our valued customers in whichever way we can."

Despite the uncertainty and financial risks, constant backing and trust of Bandhan Bank for their customers helped them recover from losses during the pandemic. Bandhan Bank's loan book rose 16% in Q4; the bank's total loan stood at Rs. 101,359 crore during Q4 of FY22. Similarly, at the end of December 2022, Bandhan Bank's collection efficiency ratio increased to 98% from 95%. Bandhan Bank's total business (deposits and advances) grew 16% year-on-year to reach Rs. 200,070 crore as of December 31, 2022. The bank's financial results for the quarter/year ended March 31, 2023, reported a profit after tax of Rs. 2,195 crore while reaching a customer base of 3 crore.

Moreover, today, Mr. Ghosh is more optimistic than ever. While speaking in Ahmedabad earlier this year, he said that with the GDP growth estimate of over 7%, moderately high inflation (in India), and credit offtake growth of 15.1%, the state of the micro-finance industry in India appeared promising. The bank plans to expand beyond the eastern region by increasing the number of branches from 5,640 to 8,000 by 2025, mainly in western states, south India, and some parts of the north. Indeed, the high stake in micro-credit is both a strength and a weakness for banks, but Bandhan Bank has made history by transforming into a universal bank that serves all socioeconomic sections across the country. This exponential growth of Bandhan from a foundation to a universal bank is the result of an unparallel micro-finance strategy and socially grounded vision. This case further highlights the key developmental imperative embodied by Bandhan Bank to survive and thrive in the changing contemporary world.

Bandhan at a Last Mile

Bandhan Bank has taken several steps to improve its asset quality over the past 3 years. These include:

- **Focusing on retail lending:** Bandhan Bank has shifted its focus from microfinance to retail lending. This has helped to reduce the risk of default, as retail loans are generally less risky than microfinance loans.
- **Strengthening its risk management framework:** Bandhan Bank has strengthened its risk management framework by implementing new systems and processes.
- **Upgrading its technology infrastructure:** Bandhan Bank has upgraded its technology infrastructure to improve its ability to collect

data and monitor loans. This has helped to improve the bank's ability to identify and manage risks.

As a result of these steps, Bandhan Bank's asset quality has improved significantly over the past 3 years. The bank's gross non-performing assets (GNPAs) ratio has declined from 10.8% in March 2019 to 7.2% in March 2022. The bank's net non-performing assets (NPAs) ratio declined from 3.0% in March 2019 to 1.9% in March 2022.

Bandhan Bank's asset quality is now comparable to that of other banks of similar nature in India. For example, the GNPAs ratio of the State Bank of India (SBI) was 7.5% in March 2022, and the net NPAs ratio of SBI was 2.3% in March 2022. Bandhan Bank is a relatively new bank in India, receiving its banking license in 2015. However, it has quickly become one of the most successful banks in the country.

Bandhan Bank has implemented several systems and processes to identify and mitigate risks. These systems and processes include:

- **A comprehensive credit scoring system:** Bandhan Bank uses a comprehensive credit scoring system to assess each loan applicant's default risk. The credit scoring system considers several factors, including the applicant's income, employment history, and credit history.
- **A robust loan monitoring system:** Bandhan Bank has a robust loan monitoring system in place to track the performance of its loans. The loan monitoring system helps identify loans at risk of default and take early action to prevent default.

Bandhan Bank has attracted customers and proliferated due to a strong focus on retail lending. Bandhan Bank has focused on lending to individuals and small businesses, which traditional banks underserve. This has helped Bandhan Bank reach a broader range of customers and grow its loan book. With the help of a robust risk management framework and innovative technology, it has kept interest rates and fees lower in markets where traditionally all customers were clubbed as high-risk.

Bandhan Bank has also been innovative in its use of technology. The bank has used technology to improve its efficiency and reduce its costs. For example, Bandhan Bank uses a mobile banking app to allow customers to access their accounts and make transactions from anywhere. The bank also uses a digital lending platform to approve loans quickly and easily. Bandhan Bank's specific strategies have helped it become one of India's most successful banks. The bank's focus on retail lending, its robust risk management framework, and its innovative use of technology have helped it to grow its loan book, improve its asset quality, and reach a broader range of borrowers.

One of the critical strategies that Bandhan Bank has used to operate in rural and semi-urban markets is to hire local staff. The bank believes that local staff can better understand the local community's needs and build relationships with customers. In addition to providing customer service, local branch officers at Bandhan Bank are also responsible for the following:

- **Providing financial education to customers:** Local branch officers at Bandhan Bank are responsible for providing financial education to customers. This includes teaching customers about the different types of financial products and services available and how to use them to improve their financial situation.
- **Providing credit counseling to customers:** Local branch officers at Bandhan Bank are also responsible for counseling customers. This includes helping customers understand their credit scores and how to improve them.
- **Providing referrals to other financial services providers:** Local branch officers at Bandhan Bank are also responsible for providing referrals to other financial services providers. This service includes referring customers to lawyers, accountants, and other professionals who can help them with their financial needs.

As of March 2023, 70% of branches of Bandhan Bank were in rural and semi-urban markets, focused on agriculture, microlending, and micro, small, and medium enterprises. Supported by the bank's services, about 25% of the bank's microcredit customers graduated to small and medium enterprise loans after the pandemic. According to Chandra Shekhar Ghosh, Founder, and Managing Director of Bandhan Bank, "[t]he average ticket size for loans has increased from around [Rs.] 55,000 to [Rs.] 1.15 lakh [between 2020 and 2022]." The Bank plans to expand beyond the eastern region by increasing the number of branches from 5,640 to 8,000 by 2025, mainly in western states, south India, and some parts of the north.

Bandhan Bank responds to the needs of rural and semi-urban markets in several ways. These include:

- **Providing financial services to people whom banks have traditionally underserved:** Bandhan Bank provides a wide range of financial services to people in rural and semi-urban areas, including savings accounts, loans, and insurance. This service has helped to improve financial inclusion in these areas.
- **Using a locally focused approach:** Bandhan Bank firmly understands the needs of people in rural and semi-urban areas. The bank's employees are from these areas and are familiar with the challenges people face. This service has helped Bandhan Bank to develop products and services that meet the needs of these customers.
- **Providing affordable financial services:** Bandhan Bank is committed to providing affordable financial services to people in rural and semi-urban areas. The bank's fees are lower than those of many other banks, and the bank offers a variety of products that are designed to meet the needs of people with limited income.
- **Providing convenient access to financial services:** Bandhan Bank has an extensive network of branches in rural and semi-urban areas. This service makes it easy for people to access financial services, even those living in remote areas. The bank also offers various digital banking services, making it possible for customers to access their accounts and conduct transactions from anywhere.

Bandhan Bank's efforts to respond to the needs of rural and semi-urban markets have been successful. The bank has a large customer base in these areas, which has helped improve financial inclusion in these areas.

Bandhan Bank has used a locally focused approach to navigate the COVID-19 crisis in many ways. These include:

- **Providing financial assistance to customers:** Bandhan Bank has provided financial assistance to customers affected by the COVID-19 crisis. This service includes waiving late fees and interest charges on loans and providing additional credit to customers who need it.
- **Working with local governments:** Bandhan Bank has worked with local governments to provide financial assistance to people affected by the COVID-19 crisis. This service includes loans to small businesses and financial assistance to people who have lost their jobs.

- **Providing educational support:** Bandhan Bank has provided educational support to children affected by the COVID-19 crisis. This service includes scholarships for students affected by the crisis and online learning resources for students who cannot attend school in person.

In addition to the above, Bandhan Bank has also taken the following measures to navigate the COVID-19 crisis:

- **Strengthened digital banking platform:** Bandhan Bank has strengthened its digital banking platform to make it easier for customers to access their accounts and conduct transactions online. This service has been especially important for customers unable to visit branches due to the pandemic.
- **Increased focus on customer service:** Bandhan Bank has increased its focus on customer service to ensure that customers are able to get the help they need during this difficult time. The bank has launched a number of new customer service initiatives, including a 24/7 customer care helpline and a new customer service portal.
- **Adopted a flexible approach to lending:** Bandhan Bank has adopted a flexible approach to lending to help customers struggling financially due to the pandemic. The bank has waived late fees and interest charges on loans and has provided additional credit to customers who need it.

Bandhan Bank's efforts to navigate the COVID-19 crisis have been praised by customers, government officials, and community leaders. The bank's locally focused approach and its focus on customer service have helped it provide much-needed financial assistance to people affected by the pandemic.

Bandhan Bank's organizational culture is a crucial factor in its success. The bank's employees are committed to providing excellent customer service, operating ethically and transparently, and innovating to improve the bank's products and services. Here are some examples of how Bandhan Bank's organizational culture is reflected in its day-to-day operations:

- **Customer focus:** Bandhan Bank's employees are always willing to go the extra mile to meet the needs of their customers. If a customer has a problem with their account, Bandhan Bank's employees will work with the customer to resolve the problem as quickly as possible.

- **Integrity:** Employees are not allowed to accept customer bribes or gifts.
- **Innovation:** Bandhan Bank was the first bank in India to offer a mobile banking app.

Bandhan Bank is different from other microcredit-focused banks in the following ways:

- **Loan size:** Bandhan Bank offers loans that are larger than the loans offered by most other microfinance banks. This consideration allows Bandhan Bank to reach a broader range of borrowers, including those who need larger loans to start or expand their businesses.
- **Loan terms:** Bandhan Bank offers longer-term loans than most microfinance banks. This facility allows borrowers to repay their loans over extended periods, making managing their finances easier.
- **Repayment options:** Bandhan Bank offers a variety of repayment options, including weekly, biweekly, and monthly payments. This service allows borrowers to choose a repayment option that fits their budget.
- **Customer support:** Bandhan Bank offers 24/7 customer support. This service allows borrowers to get help with their loans whenever needed.

These differences make Bandhan Bank a more attractive option for borrowers than most other microfinance banks. Within a short period, it has become the largest microfinance bank in India.

Bandhan Bank's entry into rural and semi-urban markets has positively impacted the availability of credit in these areas. The bank's loans have helped people improve their livelihoods and build a better future for themselves and their families. These loans have helped people to start or expand their businesses, improve their homes, and send their children to school. The entry of Bandhan Bank into a rural or semi-urban market increases the total amount of credit disbursed in that market by 15%. Bandhan Bank's loans are more likely to be used for productive purposes, such as starting or expanding a business, than loans from other banks.

Further, Bandhan Bank's loans are typically at a lower interest rate than loans from other banks. The annual interest rate on a personal loan from Bandhan Bank is typically around 10%, while a standard bank charges around 12%. This suggests that Bandhan Bank's presence is helping to make credit more affordable for borrowers in these areas.

There has been growth in women-run businesses in markets where Bandhan Bank is operating. Bandhan Bank's entry into the market is estimated to increase the number of women-run businesses by 15%. Further, Bandhan Bank's loans are more likely to be repaid on time than loans from other banks, suggesting the positive contribution of these loans to upgrading the financial capacity of its borrowers to start new businesses and expand existing ones.

A study by the National Association of Bank Officers found that 70% of banks surveyed said Bandhan Bank's entry into the market forced them to reconsider their lending strategies. The study also found that 60% of banks said they were now more willing to lend to borrowers with low credit scores.

According to the bank's annual report for 2022, women make up 95.7% of Bandhan Bank's borrowers. The bank has a strong outreach program that targets women borrowers. The bank's outreach program includes door-to-door visits, group meetings, and workshops. Bandhan Bank's focus on women borrowers has positively impacted the lives of millions of women in India. The bank's loans have helped women start and grow businesses, improve their homes, and send their children to school. Bandhan Bank's work is helping to empower women and improve their economic opportunities.

For instance, a 2019 survey (Singh & Ugrasen, 2019) of the Gorakhpur region in the state of Uttar Pradesh found that a third of women borrowers were engaged in labor work earning less than Rs. 4,500 (US$60) per month. They became aware of the microcredit option through ads from Bandhan Bank and word-of-mouth from their friends. 90% of the surveyed borrowers reported improved socioeconomic status after receiving the loan from Bandhan Bank.

At the end of March 2023, Bandhan Bank had deposits of Rs. 1.08 trillion, with over 6,000 banking outlets spread across 34 out of 36 states and union territories in India. It had 30 million customers.

Select Case Studies of Bandhan Bank's Life-Transforming Impact

Case study 1: Alpana, driven by her determination to support her family and achieve self-sufficiency, recognized the importance of standing on her own two feet and contributing to her husband's income as a schoolteacher. Understanding her household responsibilities, she decided to embark on a small-scale venture that would allow her to maintain a part-time commitment. Her initial step involved sourcing sarees from a trusted supplier and selling them within her local community. As she progressed in her entrepreneurial journey, Alpana swiftly grasped the significance of a consistent influx of capital and a diverse inventory in her industry.

During this juncture, Alpana came across the opportunity presented by Bandhan Bank and secured her first loan of Rs. 5,000 in 2006. She allocated these funds toward expanding her stock and inventory. Over the subsequent years, Alpana continued to avail herself of loans from Bandhan Bank, utilizing them to fuel the growth of her business. Presently, she has obtained a loan of Rs. 150,000. Additionally, she contacted manufacturers in Phuliya, a district in West Bengal and Kolkata, and established direct business relationships with them. With unwavering support from Bandhan Bank, Alpana successfully established a profitable saree shop, enabling her to flourish in her entrepreneurial endeavors.

Case study 2: Shardaben Bhavsar, a resident of Ahmedabad, led a humble and industrious existence until she seized control of her destiny with a little assistance from Bandhan Bank. Her family relied solely on her husband's cloth printing machine for income, but their profits steadily declined as demand dwindled. It became evident that their business needed a reinvention to overcome this challenge. Fueled by a determination to secure the future of their enterprise, Shardaben turned to Bandhan Bank for a loan to establish their manufacturing unit.

In 2012, she borrowed Rs. 15,000 to purchase a sewing machine for her son, who worked as a tailor. Within 2 years, they kick-started their manufacturing business, with women's leggings as their inaugural product. Gradually, with the aid of an additional loan of Rs. 40,000, Shardaben acquired three more machines. As the tailoring business gained significant momentum, the cloth printing venture took a back seat, along with its losses. They adapted their products to align with industry and market demands. They own 14 tailoring machines and have created job opportunities for 15 individuals.

In their seventh loan cycle of Rs. 150,000, the Bhavsars aspire to expand into other sectors. They are securing a larger space to accommodate 25 machines, thus enhancing their production capacities. Shardaben firmly believes that her association with Bandhan Bank has been transformative for her business and her family, instilling a sense of profound change and growth.

Case study 3: Nilam's journey embodies a tale of unwavering determination. She has become a catalyst for change, not only for her family but also for the women in her community. In a household where her husband, a farmer, was the sole breadwinner struggling to make ends meet, Nilam recognized the pressing need to augment their financial income. Unfortunately, mainstream financial institutions proved unattainable due to their daunting list of complex documentation requirements. However, a glimmer of hope emerged when she discovered Bandhan Bank.

With a streamlined application process, Nilam successfully obtained her inaugural loan of Rs. 10,000 from the bank. This financial support enabled her to establish her costume jewelry store, breathing new life into her family's prospects. She expresses her heartfelt appreciation and affirms, "Bandhan Bank has empowered me to step into the realm of entrepreneurship, transforming me from a job seeker to a job provider." Moreover, she credits her newfound financial independence for enabling her to champion her children's education. Today, her son is pursuing engineering studies while her daughter thrives in Grade 12.

Case study 4: Sumathi's husband produced plain white cloth, catering to traders as a small-scale manufacturer. However, their family of five struggled to make ends meet with his meager earnings. The situation worsened when their cloth-making machine malfunctioned, dealing a severe blow to their business.

In this challenging predicament, Sumathi turned to Bandhan Bank and secured a loan of Rs. 35,000. This timely support proved a godsend, enabling them to purchase a new machine and rejuvenate their business. Since then, their progress has been unstoppable. Sales skyrocketed, and the increasing demand prompted them to hire three workers to operate two machines.

Their fruitful association with Bandhan Bank remains steadfast. Sumathi is on her fifth loan cycle, receiving Rs. 130,000, which she reinvested in expanding their business. She joyfully shares that her two sons are now pursuing higher studies, all made possible by the invaluable financial assistance they received from Bandhan Bank.

Bandhan Bank's strategy revolves around people centrality. Simplifying banking, and serving customers at their doorstep. Bandhan

Bank's extensive on-field community networks have enabled it to understand its customers' needs and build trust (Palo & Chaudhari, 2023). As a result, the bank has evolved into a universal financial institution, catering to all socioeconomic sections across the country while staying true to its mission of building a financially inclusive India.

During the pandemic, external forces posed challenges to Bandhan Bank's micro-credit operations. Many borrowers, particularly those running small businesses, struggled to repay their loans due to economic distress caused by the lockdown. The Supreme Court's intervention led to a moratorium on loan repayments, providing temporary relief to borrowers. Legislative measures to protect economically vulnerable individuals and political promises of loan waivers created confusion among borrowers, impacting loan repayments. Like other banks in India, the collection efficiency of Bandhan Bank suffered, particularly in its largest market in eastern India. However, Bandhan Bank remained in constant touch with its customers during this period and expressed confidence that most would resume loan repayments once the situation improved.

A report[1] by Goldman Sachs highlighted risks such as geographic and industry concentration, diverse customer demographics, and the need to offer different financial products to attract customers. Bandhan Bank is addressing the risks highlighted in the Goldman Sachs report by taking several steps. These include:

- **Expanding its geographic reach:** Bandhan Bank is expanding by opening new branches in new areas. The bank also focuses on expanding its reach in rural and semi-urban areas.
- **Diversifying its lending portfolio:** Bandhan Bank is diversifying its lending portfolio by lending to a broader range of industries, including government businesses and housing loans. The bank also focuses on lending to small- and medium-sized businesses, as many of its clients have grown from micro-enterprises to small- and medium-sized operations.
- **Attracting new customers:** Bandhan Bank attracts new customers by offering a wider range of financial products. The bank is also focusing on marketing its products to a broader range of customers, in line with

---

[1]Report by Goldman Sachs on Bandhan Bank Limited. Retrieved from https://www.goldmansachs.com/worldwide/india/ipo/bandhan-bank-prospectus.pdf.

the improving credit profile of its previously low-income bottom-of-the-pyramid customers.

Bandhan Bank has been depicted in several television shows, serials, and movies in India. In most cases, the bank is portrayed as a positive force that is helping to improve the lives of people in India.

- For example, in the television show "Yeh Rishta Kya Kehlata Hai," Bandhan Bank is a bank helping a young woman start her own business. The bank provides her with a loan and business advice, and she can start her business successfully.
- In the movie "Piku," Bandhan Bank is shown as a bank helping a young woman take care of her aging father. The bank provides her with a loan to pay for her father's medical expenses, and she is able to provide him with the care that he needs.
- In the 2023 Hindi movie "Jhund," Bandhan Bank is shown as a bank that is helping a group of slum children start their football team. The bank provides the children with loans to buy equipment and travel to tournaments. The children are able to use the bank's assistance to achieve their dream of becoming professional footballers.

Here are some of the ways in which Bandhan Bank has been depicted in popular culture:

- **As a bank helping to improve financial inclusion:** In the Telugu movie "Rangasthalam," Bandhan Bank is shown as a bank helping a young man fight for the rights of his village. The bank provides him with a loan to start a business, and he is able to use the business to help his village.
- **As a bank helping to support small businesses:** In the Kannada serial "JotheJotheyali," Bandhan Bank is shown as a bank providing loans to small businesses. The loans help the businesses grow and create jobs.
- **As a bank committed to social responsibility:** In the Bengali movie "Bela Seshe," Bandhan Bank is shown as a bank supporting education. The bank provides scholarships to students from rural areas. In the Tamil serial "Vaani Rani," Bandhan Bank is shown as a bank supporting healthcare. The bank provides free medical care to people from rural areas. In the Malayalam movie "Odiyan," Bandhan Bank is shown as a bank that supports environmental protection. The bank provides loans to businesses that are working to protect the environment.

Bandhan Bank has very rightly created a stable name in the market for helping the rural population with unemployment, healthcare, education, nutrition, and financial illiteracy. Their motto to help the poorest of poor has been seen in every activity and program undertaken by the bank. Today, Bandhan Bank has seen the pinnacle of success, but its motto of building a financially inclusive India remains unchanged.[2] This is an example and a journey of the man who came and saw the plight of the people, truly immersed himself in their pain, and worked tirelessly to improve their lives bit by bit.

This volume is based on the insights gleaned from many stories like that of Bandhan Bank. We hope you will benefit from it in the same way we have as we examined how India offers a fresh perspective on the organizational dimension.

References

Singh, V. & Ugrasen. (2019). Study on Role of Bandhan Bank Microfinance in Women Entrepreneurship with Reference to Gorakhpur Region. In *Proceedings of 10th International Conference on Digital Strategies for Organizational Success.* http://dx.doi.org/10.2139/ssrn.3309292.

Palo, S. & Chaudhari, S. R. (2023). Bandhan Bank's Strategic CSR: Building Knowledge and Experience of Rural Microfinance. *NHRD Network Journal,* 16(2), 138–152.

---

[2]Bandhan Bank. Homepage. Our Story. Bandhan Bank Limited. Retrieved from https://bandhanbank.com.

Part I

FRESH Approach

Chapter 1

A FRESH Perspective on India's Organizational Dimension

Vipin Gupta[*,§], Alka Maurya[†,¶], and Samir Chatterjee[‡,||]

California State University, San Bernardino, USA

†Curtin University, Bentley, Perth, Australia

‡Amity University, Noida, India

§vipin.gupta@csusb.edu

¶amaurya@amity.edu

||Samir.Chatterjee@cbs.curtin.edu.au

Abstract

The chapter sets the context for the book and the contributions of the chapters that follow. It articulates an urgent need for a fresh perspective on India's organizational dimension. Globalization, technological advancements, and shifting market dynamics are leading to significant functional reforms in India, which is changing the very core of the organizational dimension. To develop a FRESH perspective, five elements are key: Functional, Responsibility, Ecosystem, Subaltern, and Historical. Culturally, different industries and sectors in India have their own specific organizational structures and practices. The Indian business ecosystem is characterized by diverse factors such as government policies, regulatory frameworks, and infrastructure. Subaltern opportunities emerge for followership so that each member of the nation enjoys the benefits of globalization. A fresh perspective which recognizes these five elements is critical to foster innovation, inclusivity, adaptability, and sustainability.

Keywords: Functional, responsibility, ecosystem, subaltern, historical.

Introduction

This book calls for a fresh perspective on India's organizational dimension. A FRESH approach is one that functions technologically in the context of India, recognizes the responsibility of the organizations, and is sensitive to the potential of the organizations to transform their ecosystem for advancing their leadership. As the organizations strive for leadership, subaltern opportunities emerge for followership so that each member of the nation enjoys the benefits of the globalization of the organizations through the unique values they add. Co-leadership of members creates history as the nation grows and becomes a magnate for the aliens for trading to co-create wealth as well as exchange of leadership wealth through a variety of manipulations.

A FRESH perspective recognizes the role of globalization, technological advancements, and shifting market dynamics in functional reforms. As functions reform, organizations become more engaged in taking responsibility for inclusive approaches. In fact, grassroots initiatives, local communities, and small-scale businesses are at the heart of India's development model. History is propelling the members to recognize the value of building grassroots alliances around the world using the power of technology, organization, and markets.

Existing approaches do not fully leverage the opportunities presented by new technologies, hindering organizational growth and competitiveness. They do not sufficiently include diverse stakeholders, local communities, and marginalized groups in the decision-making process. Rooted in traditional perspectives, they impede organizational agility and responsiveness in a fast-changing business environment. In this light, a fresh perspective is critical to foster innovation, inclusivity, adaptability, and sustainability.

In the organizational dimension of India, the FRESH perspective plays a crucial role in shaping the way businesses, industries, and value chains are organized. The FRESH perspective includes functional, responsibility, ecosystem, subaltern, and historical aspects:

First, functional aspect: Different industries and sectors in India have their own specific organizational structures and practices. For example, the IT and outsourcing industry has embraced a globalized and networked organizational model, leveraging India's strengths in software development and service leadership. On the other hand, traditional industries like textiles or handicrafts follow more decentralized and artisanal approaches to production and value chains.

Second, responsibility aspect: In recent years, there has been a growing emphasis on corporate social responsibility (CSR) and sustainable business practices in India. Organizations are increasingly expected to go beyond profit-making and contribute positively to society and the environment. This includes initiatives focused on environmental conservation, community development, employee welfare, and ethical supply chains.

Third, ecosystem aspect: The Indian business ecosystem is characterized by diverse factors such as government policies, regulatory frameworks, infrastructure, and market dynamics. The presence of a mixed economy, with both private and public enterprises, influences how businesses and industries are organized. Government initiatives, such as the "Make in India" campaign, aim to promote domestic manufacturing and create a conducive ecosystem for businesses to thrive.

Fourth, subaltern aspect: India's vast and diverse population, with its regional and cultural variations, influences organizational practices at the grassroots level. Local communities, artisanal clusters, and self-help groups play a significant role in organizing small-scale businesses and industries. This includes cooperatives, microenterprises, and community-based initiatives that prioritize social and economic development at the grassroots level.

Fifth, historical aspect: India has a rich history that influences its organizational practices. Traditional forms of organization have shaped the indigenous managerial culture. The hierarchical and patriarchal nature of leadership, as well as the emphasis on collective decision-making and loyalty, can still be observed in many Indian organizations today.

Overall, the organizational dimension in India is shaped by a combination of functional requirements, responsibility imperatives, ecosystem factors, subaltern initiatives, and, last but not least, the continuity of historical traditions in new and dynamic forms. Understanding and integrating these aspects are crucial for businesses and industries operating in the Indian context, as they navigate the complexities and opportunities presented by the diverse and dynamic Indian market.

This introductory chapter highlights the key elements of these five aspects in relation to the organizational dimension of India. It also outlines how the next 15 chapters, organized in five parts of three chapters each, enlighten the dynamics of these elements.

Functional Aspects

Functional aspects shape both intra-organizational and inter-organizational value systems.

First, operations and production: Excellence in production processes, quality control, supply chain management, inventory management, and logistics is vital for competitive advantage. Maruti Suzuki has used lean manufacturing to streamline production processes, supply chain networks, and robust dealer networks.

Second, marketing and sales: Market research, branding, product positioning, pricing strategies, distribution channels, and customer relationship management are essential for organizational success. Hindustan Unilever Limited (HUL) has leveraged deep market insights from their consumer goods business to craft localized marketing strategies which cater to diverse consumer preferences across regions and demographics.

Third, human resources: Talent acquisition, employee training and development, performance management, compensation and benefits, and fostering a positive work culture are also crucial. Infosys has developed HR initiatives, such as "Campus Connect" and "Leadership Institute," to advance their talent acquisition, employee training, and development.

Fourth, finance and accounting: Financial planning, budgeting, financial analysis, risk management, and financial reporting are also necessary.

HDFC Bank is known for its prudent risk management, efficient capital allocation, and technological innovations as the building blocks for consistent financial performance and industry leadership.

Fifth, research and development (R&D): R&D activities, technological advancements, product innovation, and process improvement are also significant elements. Biocon has been a leader in investing in R&D to develop innovative and affordable medicines, establishing a strong position in the global pharmaceutical industry.

Sixth, information technology (IT): IT infrastructure, software systems, data analytics, and cybersecurity measures have become very important. Flipkart has developed a robust e-commerce platform, advanced data analytics, and supply chain management systems for e-commerce marketplace leadership.

Seventh, legal and regulatory compliance: Compliance with legal and regulatory requirements helps organizations mitigate risks and build trust with stakeholders. Reliance Industries (RIL), known for pushing the boundaries of possibility, prioritizes legal and regulatory compliance in all functions of business, including labor laws, taxation, intellectual property rights, environmental regulations, and industry-specific requirements, ensuring ethical practices and sustainable growth.

Eighth, strategic management: A well-defined strategy helps organizations adapt and grow in a dynamic market. The Tata Group has grown sustainably to become a diversified conglomerate with businesses spanning industries such as automotive, steel, and IT services, supported by initiatives such as Tata Sustainability Group and Tata Social Enterprise Challenge.

By effectively leveraging functional elements, organizations in India enhance their competitiveness, adapt to market dynamics, and drive sustainable growth. The interplay and integration of various functional areas ensure coherence, efficiency, and strategic alignment across different organizational dimensions, contributing to the success and resilience of businesses, industries, and value chains in India.

Part II of this book includes three chapters on the functional approach to the organizational dimension in India.

In Chapter 2, "Talent Inbreeding: The Case of Indian Academic Institutions as Organizations," Shalini Shukla and Ram Singh investigate talent inbreeding in Indian educational institutes and develop the Talent Inbreeding Index (TII) to measure its extent. The research focuses on 67 institutes of eminence, analyzing faculty profiles from official websites to assess academic inbreeding. The findings reveal that specialized sciences-focused institutes have the highest talent inbreeding scores compared to management-focused and applied sciences-focused institutes. The study emphasizes the implications for government, educational organizations, and policymakers in managing talent effectively and enhancing research and education outcomes. It also discusses the factors contributing to talent inbreeding, such as academic focus, research orientation, pedagogical continuity, tradition, and legacy. The study highlights the need for diversity, merit-based hiring, and accessibility to outside talent in Indian academia and suggests measures to address talent inbreeding, including transparent job postings, open competition, collaboration, and international exchange programs. The study's implications are significant in the context of India's focus on quality education, innovation, and outcome-based learning, as outlined in the New Education Policy (NEP) 2020 of India.

In Chapter 3, "Digital Transformation of Supply Chains in Indian Organizations," Prakash Agrawal, Rakesh Narain, and Mayank Agarwal underline how the digital transformation of supply chains is driven by emerging technologies and has disrupted traditional business practices. They observe that the adoption of digital supply chains in Indian organizations has been slow. To understand the factors affecting digital transformation in India, they surveyed the current status and issues related to the implementation of digital supply chains. The survey findings indicate that digital transformation enhances both processes and products in the supply chain. Factors such as flexibility, automation, operational improvements, real-time visibility, customization, innovation, and recognition of customers' needs contribute to process and product enhancement. The study also tested hypotheses related to these factors and found significant support for them. The results highlight the importance of embracing digital technologies in supply chain management to improve profitability and customer experience.

In Chapter 4, "Paths to Digital Transformation in Service Marketing," Sasmita Kant Maurya explores the digital transformation strategies of service companies in India by analyzing multiple case studies. It emphasizes the unique characteristics of the services sector, such as heterogeneity, intangibility, inseparability, perishability, and demand fluctuation. The companies deployed various strategies to embrace digital transformation. Kotak Mahindra Bank launched digital services, like KayPay and Keya, to enhance the customer experience. Yash Raj Films digitized their films and utilized social media to promote new releases and monetize their content. Decathlon focused on customer-centricity through their Phygital stores, leveraging technology and data for real-time insights. Nightingales Health Services adopted an app-based approach for efficient operations and improved customer convenience. The chapter draws on Indian ethos, emphasizing relationship building, morality, teamwork, personal connections, and trust in conducting business. It provides insights and strategies for companies to navigate this transformative journey effectively.

Responsibility Aspects

Responsibility aspects focus on ethical practices, social impact, and environmental sustainability. Here are some examples:

First, CSR: With both cultural and legal imperatives, all companies in India allocate resources toward social and environmental projects that benefit communities. Tata Group's CSR initiatives focus on education, healthcare, rural development, and sustainable livelihoods, making a positive impact on society.

Second, sustainable supply chains: As the organizations in India have sought to play in the global market, they are working to implement responsible sourcing practices, promote fair trade, and ensure environmental sustainability. The global players operating in India have also played a leadership role in propelling Indian organizations to dig deeper into their indigenous values. HUL contributes to responsible sourcing and a sustainable value chain by working with smallholder farmers, providing training and support to adopt sustainable agricultural practices.

Third, environmental stewardship: Businesses in India are organizing for environmental sustainability through practices such as waste management, energy efficiency, and conservation. Infosys, an IT services company, has implemented several green initiatives, including renewable energy adoption, water conservation, and carbon footprint reduction, reflecting their commitment to environmental responsibility.

Fourth, inclusive business models: Organizations in India are creating business models that benefit marginalized communities. For example, the SELCO Foundation promotes inclusive access to clean energy by providing solar solutions to underserved rural populations, addressing energy poverty, and improving livelihoods.

Fifth, human rights and ethical labor practices: Organizations in India are working to ensure fair and ethical labor practices, respecting workers' rights, and promoting safe working conditions. The Fairtrade movement, represented by brands such as Fabindia and Amar Biotech, emphasizes fair wages, fair trade practices, and worker empowerment.

Sixth, social impact investments: Impact investment firms, such as Aavishkaar, are investing in businesses that address social and environmental challenges while generating sustainable financial returns, contributing to the organization of impact-driven industries.

Seventh, diversity and inclusion: Organizations in India recognize the importance of diversity and inclusion in their organizational dimensions. The Godrej Group focuses on gender diversity and inclusion through initiatives such as the Godrej Gender Parity Accelerator.

Eighth, stakeholder engagement: Organizations actively engage with stakeholders to seek input, address concerns, and build trust. ITC Limited's e-Choupal initiative engages farmers, empowering them with market access, information, and fair prices, strengthening stakeholder relationships.

Ninth, social entrepreneurship: Organizations like Aravind Eye Care Systems provide affordable eye care services to underserved populations, blending social impact with sustainable business models.

Tenth, voluntary initiatives: Organizations in India go beyond compliance and voluntarily engage in initiatives that address societal challenges. The CII-ITC Centre of Excellence for Sustainable Development works with businesses to promote sustainable practices, encourage responsible business conduct, and drive industry-wide change.

Eleventh, responsible marketing and advertising: The Advertising Standards Council of India (ASCI) sets guidelines for fair advertising practices and monitors advertisements to ensure they are honest and socially responsible.

Twelfth, sustainable packaging and waste management: Businesses in India are increasingly adopting sustainable waste management systems. Hindustan Coca-Cola Beverages (HCCB) has introduced eco-friendly packaging solutions to reduce plastic waste and promote recycling.

Thirteenth, access to essential goods and services: Organizations in India work toward ensuring access to essential goods and services in underserved areas. Lifebuoy, a brand under HUL, runs the "Help a Child Reach 5" campaign, focusing on promoting handwashing with soap to improve public health and reduce preventable diseases.

Fourteenth, transparency and accountability: Indian organizations are increasingly prioritizing transparency and accountability in their operations. This helps build trust and ensure responsible practices throughout the organization.

Responsible practices not only contribute to societal well-being but also enhance competitiveness, reputation, and long-term sustainability.

Part III of this book includes three chapters on the responsibility approach to the organizational dimension in India.

Chapter 5, "Social Responsibility in Indian Organizations: Developments Since Independence," Syed Mohammad Akrama Ali Rizvi, Chayan Poddar, and Iqra Fatima examine the social responsibility measures undertaken by Indian organizations, focusing on the Social Responsibility in Companies Act, 2013. They discuss the social contributions of Indian organizations, the parallel between economic development and social responsibility, and emerging trends and challenges in stakeholder responsibilities. They also explore the implementation of CSR budgets and the role of different sectors, such as banking, in fulfilling social responsibilities. They raise questions about the effectiveness and genuineness of mandated CSR spending and highlight the unique role of family firms in CSR activities. They conclude by addressing the need for better monitoring, reporting, and assessment of CSR projects to ensure the benefits reach the intended beneficiaries.

In Chapter 6, "Social Responsibility in Indian Organizations: The Way Forward for Sustainable Development," Nivedeeta Thombare and Moitrayee Das analyze how the concept of CSR has evolved in India, extending beyond large organizations to include small and medium enterprises (SMEs). Research on CSR in SMEs is limited, and the focus has primarily been on large organizations. This chapter highlights the role of CSR and corporate governance in SMEs, the challenges they face, and the benefits they can derive from these practices. It emphasizes the importance of CSR and corporate governance for sustainable development. Several examples of CSR initiatives by organizations in India are provided, showcasing their contributions to society. The chapter concludes by emphasizing the need for a stronger CSR framework and better implementation practices to ensure sustainable development in India. Additionally, the chapter suggests that CSR and corporate governance should be tailored to suit the unique characteristics and challenges of SMEs.

In Chapter 7, "Green Organization and Strategies Toward Sustainability," Seema Garg and Namrata Pancholi investigate the role of green organizations in sustainability strategies as part of CSR. Green organizations, ranging from environmental NGOs to eco-friendly businesses, play a vital role in addressing environmental challenges and shaping sustainable practices. They safeguard ecosystems, advocate for climate action, influence policies, and raise public awareness. Local green community groups also contribute to sustainable living at the grassroots level. India's growth in green organizations is evident, driven by government initiatives and corporate sustainability efforts. Several prominent organizations in India, including Infosys, Tata Motors, and Wipro, have implemented sustainability initiatives. The future of green organizations holds potential for innovation, global collaboration, and stakeholder involvement at the ecosystem level.

Ecosystem Aspects

Ecosystem aspects encompass the broader economic, social, technological, and environmental factors that shape the organizational landscape, as noted in the following:

First, market dynamics: The Indian market is characterized by diverse consumer preferences, regional variations, and evolving trends. FMCG companies in India tailor their product offerings and marketing strategies to cater to diverse consumer preferences and regional variations.

Second, regulatory framework: Policies related to taxation, foreign direct investment, intellectual property rights, labor regulations, and environmental sustainability impact organizational dimensions such as market entry, competition, investment decisions, and compliance requirements. The Goods and Services Tax (GST) implementation in India restructured supply chains and prompted organizations to reassess their distribution networks and compliance processes.

Third, supportive infrastructure: India's vast and diverse geography presents logistical challenges, but it also offers opportunities for innovative supply chain solutions. Businesses must navigate the infrastructure gaps and develop efficient transportation and distribution networks to connect production centers with markets and consumers across the country. E-commerce companies, such as Flipkart and Amazon India, invest in building robust logistics networks to ensure timely delivery of goods across the country.

Fourth, technological advancements: The rapid growth of digital technologies, internet connectivity, and mobile penetration is unleashing new business models, digital platforms, and e-commerce ecosystems. Indian fintech start-ups, such as Paytm and PhonePe, are using digital payment solutions to transform the way financial transactions are conducted.

Fifth, innovation and R&D ecosystem: Government initiatives like the Atal Innovation Mission and Start-up India support entrepreneurship and provide platforms for innovative ideas to flourish, shaping the organizational dimensions of start-ups and technology-driven industries. The Indian pharmaceutical industry is actively investing in research and development to develop new drugs and therapies, leading to breakthrough innovations.

Sixth, skill development and talent pool: India's large and diverse talent pool offers a range of specialized skills, particularly in sectors such as information technology, engineering, and services. Indian IT services companies, including Infosys and Tata Consultancy Services (TCS), invest in training programs to enhance the skills of their workforce and stay competitive in the global market.

Seventh, collaboration and partnerships: Collaborative initiatives, such as industry-academia partnerships, research collaborations, and public-private partnerships, foster knowledge exchange, innovation, and the sharing of best practices. The Indian automotive industry collaborates with academic institutions to foster research on electric vehicle technology and develop sustainable mobility solutions.

Eighth, social impact: Increasingly, ecosystem elements related to social impact are influencing how businesses and industries organize themselves. Responsible sourcing, social responsibility, and inclusive business practices are gaining importance. Companies like Tata Group focus on corporate social responsibility initiatives, such as providing healthcare services and education, to uplift underprivileged communities.

Ninth, environmental sustainability: Organizations are increasingly adopting sustainable practices, renewable energy sources, waste reduction measures, and responsible supply chain management. Renewable energy companies, such as Suzlon Energy and ReNew Power, contribute to India's goal of achieving a greener economy by investing in wind and solar energy projects.

Tenth, geographic factors: India's diverse geography, including its varied landscapes, climate, and natural resources, influences the organization of businesses and industries. For instance, industries related to agriculture, such as tea plantations in the hilly regions of Darjeeling, are organized around the natural suitability of the terrain. Similarly, coastal areas are hubs for industries like fisheries and shipping due to their proximity to ports and marine resources. Geographic factors shape the location, distribution, and specialization of industries within the Indian ecosystem. Tea plantations in Darjeeling, West Bengal, are organized around the region's hilly terrain and favorable climatic conditions for tea cultivation.

Eleventh, industrial clusters: India has several industrial clusters that bring together businesses operating in related sectors or specializing in specific products or services. These clusters provide a supportive ecosystem where companies can collaborate, share resources, access skilled labor, and benefit from shared knowledge and infrastructure. Examples include textile clusters in Surat, diamond cutting and polishing clusters in Gujarat, and software technology parks in cities such as Bengaluru and Hyderabad.

Twelfth, financial and investment ecosystem: Initiatives like the "Make in India" campaign and the establishment of industrial corridors attract domestic and foreign investments, shaping the organizational dimensions of industries in specific regions. The establishment of the National Investment and Manufacturing Zones (NIMZs) attracts both domestic and foreign investments in manufacturing sectors, promoting industrial growth in specific regions of the country.

By considering and aligning with the various ecosystem elements, businesses and industries in India can navigate the dynamic landscape, capitalize on opportunities, and address challenges. Collaboration with government agencies, industry associations, research institutions, and local communities fosters an ecosystem that supports innovation, competitiveness, and sustainable growth. Adapting to ecosystem dynamics and leveraging the strengths of India's diverse ecosystem elements is essential for organizational success and long-term sustainability.

Part IV of this book includes three chapters on the ecosystem approach to the organizational dimension in India.

In Chapter 8, "Start-ups in Smaller Cities of India: Ecosystem Challenges and Unique Opportunities," Kumar Mukul, Monoo John, Amit N. Angadi, Jayadatta S., and Preethi M. investigate how smaller cities and towns must find entrepreneurial solutions to overcome challenges to their participation in the booming Indian start-up ecosystem. These challenges include a lack of access to resources, a weak entrepreneurial ecosystem, and the impact of COVID-19. The opportunities for solving these challenges are the rise of digital technologies and the growing demand for innovative solutions. Start-ups in smaller cities and towns need to be creative and problem-solving, and they need to focus on building a strong ecosystem.

In Chapter 9, "Frugal Innovation with Bricolage Mindset for Organizational Evolution," Geo P. Jose explores the effectiveness of community engagement through frugal innovation. The author selects three illustrative cases to explore how community engagement has enhanced the diffusion and commercialization strategy of frugal innovations. The cases show that community engagement helps identify and understand local needs, build trust and relationships with stakeholders, get feedback on prototypes and products, and promote the adoption of frugal innovations. For instance, Prarabda Multi-Business Corporation (PMBC) worked with local leaders, such as the village head or Sarpanch, to install water

ATMs in their communities. This has helped to build trust and support for the project. It also provided employment opportunities to members of the community, such as ex-military soldiers, unemployed youth, women, widows, and physically disabled people. It also provided training and education to members of the community on how to use and maintain the water ATMs. This has helped to ensure that the project is sustainable. Similarly, Rain T. A. P. has formed partnerships with industry, trade bodies, and management associations to promote its product. This has helped to raise awareness of the product and its benefits.

In Chapter 10, "Entrepreneurial Organization of Social Innovations in the Diverse Indian Culture," Preeti Aagneya, Soumitro Chakravarty, and Umesh Prasad investigate how social entrepreneurship as an organizational solution for social innovations is deeply rooted in India's cultural values, with a historical tradition of emperors and religions emphasizing social welfare. These cultural values emphasize optimism, quality focus, karma, long-term relationships, environmental care, and acceptance of diversity, all essential for achieving social development goals. The evolution of social responsibility in Indian businesses has gone through phases, from philanthropy to strong civil society engagement. India's pressing social issues, including poverty, unemployment, environmental challenges, and gender disparity, necessitate the presence of more social entrepreneurs. They can create inclusive societies, tackle environmental issues, innovate for social impact, build sustainable businesses, and inspire change.

Subaltern Aspects

Subaltern aspects represent the grassroot voices and needs of local communities, workers, and small-scale enterprises. They shape the organizational landscape in several ways:

First, local community engagement: Businesses in India often engage local communities, seeking community support, addressing concerns, and incorporating local preferences and cultural sensitivities into organizational strategies. It is common for companies operating in the tourism sector to involve local communities in designing experiences and promoting local art, craft, and culture. The Taj Group of Hotels collaborates with local communities to incorporate traditional art forms, cuisine, and cultural experiences into their hospitality offerings, showcasing the local heritage and engaging with the community.

Second, skill development and empowerment: Organizations in India frequently collaborate with local institutions, NGOs, and government programs to provide skill training to the local workforce, enhancing their employability and contributing to the growth of industries such as textiles, handicrafts, and agro-based sectors. TCS runs the TCS Rural IT Quiz to promote digital literacy and skill development among students in rural areas, empowering them with technological knowledge and enhancing their employability.

Third, micro, small, and medium enterprises (MSMEs): MSMEs often operate in clusters, which connect with larger organizations for access to markets, technology, and resources, strengthening value chains. Marico Ltd., a consumer goods company, collaborates with local coconut farmers in Kerala, providing them with training, resources, and access to markets, while sourcing raw materials for their products, contributing to the development of the coconut-based industry.

Fourth, farmer producer organizations (FPOs): In agricultural-based industries, Indian FPOs enable farmers to aggregate their produce, access markets, negotiate better prices, and enhance their bargaining power. ITC Limited works with FPOs in the agriculture sector, such as the ITC e-Choupal initiative, which connects farmers to information, markets, and fair prices, transforming the organization of agricultural supply chains.

Fifth, self-help groups (SHGs): Indian SHGs empower women by providing access to credit, training, and livelihood opportunities. They are particularly active in textiles, handicrafts, and food processing. Fabindia, a retail company promoting traditional crafts, collaborates with SHGs of rural artisans, providing them with design inputs, training, and market access, enabling women artisans to create sustainable livelihoods.

Sixth, informal sector integration: The informal sector, comprising street vendors, small traders, and home-based workers, enables Indian organizations to enhance their supply chains, tap into local markets, and promote sustainable livelihoods. Flipkart, an e-commerce platform, partners with local small-scale sellers and artisans, enabling them to reach a wider customer base and participate in the formal retail ecosystem, integrating informal sector workers into value chains.

Seventh, bottom-up innovation: Grassroots innovators and social entrepreneurs in India bring novel solutions to local challenges, particularly in sectors such as renewable energy, affordable healthcare, and rural development. SELCO Foundation promotes grassroots innovations in renewable energy by collaborating with rural innovators, facilitating the development and deployment of affordable solar solutions to address energy poverty.

Eighth, social enterprises: Social enterprises operate at the grassroots level, addressing specific social issues and creating economic opportunities for marginalized communities. Aavishkaar Group, an impact investment firm, supports social enterprises such as Husk Power Systems, which electrifies rural communities using biomass gasification technology, combining business objectives with social impact.

Ninth, participatory decision-making: Grassroots elements encourage participatory decision-making processes to gain local insights, improve transparency, build trust, and ensure the alignment of organizational strategies with community needs. Arghyam, a water-focused foundation, involves local communities in decision-making processes for water resource management, empowering them to actively participate in planning and implementation and ensuring sustainable water solutions.

Tenth, local entrepreneurship: Indian local entrepreneurs, often from rural or marginalized communities, drive economic activities by identifying local needs, creating innovative solutions, and organizing their businesses accordingly. The Kudumbashree Mission in Kerala promotes local entrepreneurship among women by providing training, access to microfinance, and business support, fostering a vibrant network of women-led enterprises.

Eleventh, cluster development: Grassroots-level industrial clusters in India bring together a concentration of small-scale enterprises specializing in a particular industry to facilitate cooperation, knowledge sharing, resource pooling, and collective bargaining power. Examples include Tiruppur's textile cluster and Moradabad's brassware cluster. The Coimbatore Textile Cluster brings together textile manufacturers, dyeing units, and accessory suppliers in the region, fostering collaboration, shared infrastructure, and knowledge exchange and enhancing the competitiveness of the textile industry.

Twelfth, cooperative societies: Grassroots-level cooperative societies, such as dairy cooperatives (e.g. Amul) and agricultural cooperatives (e.g. NAFED), have transformed the organization of industries in India. These member-driven organizations facilitate collective decision-making, resource sharing, market access, and the fair distribution of benefits. Amul, operated by the Gujarat Cooperative Milk Marketing Federation, empowers dairy farmers through collective ownership and decision-making, transforming the dairy industry and ensuring fair returns to farmers.

Grassroot elements bring diversity, inclusivity, and community engagement to the organization of businesses, industries, and value chains in India. They foster local entrepreneurship, create sustainable livelihoods, and address the unique needs of different regions and communities. By recognizing and incorporating grassroots perspectives, organizations can foster social cohesion, achieve inclusive growth, and build a resilient and sustainable business ecosystem.

Part V of this book includes three chapters on the grassroots approach to the organizational dimension in India.

In Chapter 11, "Digital Revolution in Indian SMEs and a Regenerative Managerial Mindset," Manu Shukla and Purvi Pujari focus on the role of SMEs in India's inclusive economic growth and the challenges they face, particularly in light of the COVID-19 crisis. It highlights the importance of digitization for the future prospects of SMEs and proposes a framework that combines managerial mindset and policy intervention to achieve sustainable economic growth. The integration of smart technologies and tools into SMEs' business models and processes has proven beneficial, reducing costs and improving access to information, resources, innovation, and government services. The chapter emphasizes the need for SMEs to upgrade their technological infrastructure to remain competitive in the global market. It also discusses the mindset shift required for SME owners to embrace digitalization and the importance of teamwork and innovation in this process. Further research is needed to explore the relationship between a growth mindset and other factors such as education, motivation, creativity, and risk-taking propensity and their impact on SME performance.

In Chapter 12, "Digital Technologies for Sustaining SME Growth in India," Namrata Pancholi, Seema Garg, Madhu Khurana, and Vinita Sharma investigate factors supporting the ability of SME's in India to survive and thrive through the adoption of digitization. Despite challenges in technological upgrading and innovation, SMEs benefit from their close connection to Indian culture and their contribution to sustainable development goals. The authors investigate the integration of new technologies, the role of government and other institutions, and the impact of traditional practices on SMEs. The government has introduced various programs and initiatives to support and empower SMEs, such as the National Rural Livelihood Mission, self-help groups, and panchayats. Success stories and examples from different states demonstrate the positive impact of these initiatives. The chapter concludes by emphasizing the need to address infrastructure, technology, and skill gaps to facilitate the sustained growth of SMEs and harness the cultural diversity of India as an opportunity for local business development.

In Chapter 13, "Catalyzing SME Growth in India," Rachetty Hariprasad and D Ashok further elaborate on the government initiatives supporting SMEs in India, such as the Credit Guarantee Trust for Micro and Small Enterprises (CGTMSE) and the Aatma Nirbhar Bharat Package to provide financial support during the COVID-19 pandemic. Entrepreneurship and Skill Development Program (ESDP) and Procurement and Marketing Support (PMS) schemes aim to promote innovation, skill development, and marketing support for SMEs. They conclude that the government's support in technological, financial, infrastructural, and marketing aspects is crucial for SMEs to overcome operational difficulties and thrive.

Historical Aspects

Understanding and appreciating the historical elements in Indian business and industry is crucial for navigating the unique organizational landscape. It helps organizations contextualize their practices, adapt to local customs, and leverage historical wisdom while innovating for the future. By acknowledging and integrating historical elements, businesses can build stronger relationships with stakeholders, foster sustainable growth, and contribute to the socioeconomic development of India.

First, organizational structures: Historical traditions and cultural practices influence the organizational structures prevalent in India. Many traditional Indian businesses, such as the professions of priests, black-smiths, and farmers, follow hierarchical structures with clearly defined roles and responsibilities. The ancient hierarchical social system influences divisions of labor and authority within businesses and industries.

Second, leadership styles: India's traditional forms of leadership, such as *guru–shishya parampara* (teacher-disciple tradition), emphasize respect, mentorship, and the passing down of knowledge from one generation to another. Leaders in Indian organizations often embody the guru (teacher) role, nurturing and guiding their subordinates with wisdom and experience.

Third, family businesses: In India, historical norms and cultural values have shaped the way family businesses are organized, with an emphasis on kinship, loyalty, and maintaining the family legacy. Prominent examples include the Tata Group, Bajaj Group, and Reliance Industries, where family ties and succession planning play a significant role in organizational decision-making.

Fourth, entrepreneurial traditions: India has a long history of successful business communities and entrepreneurial families who continue to shape the organizational dimensions of Indian businesses, including family-owned enterprises, corporate conglomerates, and start-up ecosystems. Prominent examples include the Ambani family (Reliance Industries), the Birla family (Aditya Birla Group), and the Murthy family (Infosys), who have built successful conglomerates and inspired generations of entrepreneurs.

Fifth, artisanal and craft traditions: India's historical practices of skill development and craftsmanship have strong influences. Artisanal clusters and guilds have emerged over time, with a focus on apprenticeship, intergenerational knowledge transfer, and maintaining the quality and uniqueness of traditional crafts. The organization of industries such as handloom weaving in Varanasi, pottery in Khurja, and jewelry-making in Jaipur is deeply rooted in intergenerational knowledge transfer and artisanal guilds.

Sixth, traditional business systems: India's traditional corporate system, the "Shreni system," was a guild-based organizational model that promoted collective decision-making, skill development, and mutual support among artisans. These historical business models have left imprints on the organization of industries like textiles, handicrafts, and jewelry, where craft clusters and artisanal networks continue to thrive. The Shreni system still influences the organization of industries, including silk weaving in Kanchipuram and carpet weaving in Mirzapur.

Seventh, trade routes and commerce: India's historical position as a hub of trade and commerce on ancient trade routes, such as the Silk Road and the spice trade, led to the establishment of trading communities and mercantile practices. Historical trading centers such as Surat, Kolkata, and Kochi continue to have a strong presence of industries organized around domestic and international trade.

Eighth, colonial influence: The period of British colonial rule in India (1757–1947) shaped the establishment of large-scale industries, the adoption of Western organizational models, and the emergence of corporate governance structures. Companies like the East India Company and the Indian Railways, established during British colonial rule, have shaped the organizational dimensions of industries such as shipping, railways, and tea plantations.

Ninth, institutional framework: India's historical experiences with colonialism and the struggle for independence have shaped the country's institutional framework. Organizations must navigate complex bureaucratic processes, legal frameworks, and governance structures influenced by historical events and political developments. The establishment of institutions like the Reserve Bank of India, the Securities and Exchange Board of India, and the Ministry of Corporate Affairs has influenced the organizational dimensions of businesses in terms of governance and compliance.

Tenth, traditional knowledge systems: India's ancient knowledge systems, such as Ayurveda (traditional medicine) and Yoga, continue to exert influence. The organization of healthcare, wellness, and alternative medicine industries often incorporates traditional knowledge systems. These industries have unique organizational structures, with a focus on holistic approaches, traditional practitioners, and community participation. Organizations in the Ayurveda and Yoga sectors follow unique organizational structures that incorporate traditional practitioners, holistic approaches, and community involvement.

Eleventh, independence movement: The Indian independence movement led to the rise of a new class of entrepreneurs who were committed to building businesses that would benefit all Indians, regardless of their economic class or social status. The Swadeshi movement during India's struggle for independence fostered the growth of indigenous industries, such as textile mills and khadi (handspun cloth) production, which continue to shape organizational dimensions.

Twelfth, economic reforms: India's liberalization policies of the 1990s led to the emergence of multinational corporations, such as Tata Motors, Infosys, and Hindustan Unilever Limited (HUL), which introduced new organizational practices and reshaped industries in sectors such as automotive, IT, and fast-moving consumer goods (FMCG).

Understanding and appreciating the historical elements in Indian business and industry is crucial for navigating the unique organizational landscape. It helps organizations contextualize their practices, adapt to local customs, and leverage historical wisdom while innovating for the future. By acknowledging and integrating historical elements, businesses build stronger relationships with stakeholders, foster sustainable growth, and contribute to the socioeconomic development of India.

Part VI of this book includes three chapters on the historical approach to the organizational dimension in India. Ancient India had many corporate organizations, such as Jati, Sangha, Shreni, Puga, and Gana. The concept of Jati, often misconstrued as caste, functioned like a modern-day business organization. It was composed of people who shared a common occupation or profession, and it provided them with a forum for cooperation and collaboration. Sangha was a form of association or assembly that fostered cooperation and collaboration among various groups or communities. Shreni was a guild or professional association that facilitated cooperation and collective endeavors within specific trades or professions. Puga was a cooperative society or collective group that worked together for common goals, comparable to modern-day associations of persons. Gana was an organized group or community that functioned with shared objectives. These corporate bodies played a vital role in the economic and social life of ancient India. They helped to ensure that the various trades and professions were well organized and that the needs of the community were met. They were based on the principles of dharma, which emphasize duty rather than focusing solely on rights and privileges. These bodies were self-governing and democratic, with members having a say in how they were run. They played a vital role in the transmission of knowledge and skills, as well as in the provision of social welfare. The principles of cooperation and harmony that were embodied in these corporate bodies remain imprinted in the DNA of modern Indian organizations.

In Chapter 14, "Corporate Organization in Ancient India — The Shreni System," Alka Maurya, Veenus Jain, and Pallavi Mohanan delve into the Shreni system as an association of traders, merchants, and artisans. The chapter examines the historical references to Shreni dating back to the 8th century BC and how some became wealthy custodians and bankers of religious endowments. It also explores how Shreni played a pivotal role in governing various economic activities and crafts. The study concludes that the Shreni system was integral to ancient Indian society, significantly influencing the economy and social structure. Each Shreni was dedicated to a specific vocation or activity, regulating manufacturing standards, trade, ethical codes, prices, and craftsmanship quality.

In Chapter 15, "Corporate Governance in Shreni System: Glimpses from Ancient India," Veenus Jain and Pallavi Mohanan explain how the Shreni were self-governing organizations that regulated the quality and pricing of goods, provided markets for the sale of manufactured items, and procured raw materials for manufacturing. The Shreni were responsible for setting standards for the quality of goods and services produced by their members, and they also played a role in regulating prices.

In Chapter 16, "The Management and Organizational Paradigm of Chaitra Parva and Its Role in the Sustenance of Chhau," Nitin Mane, Ruhi Lal, and Satyabrata Rout investigate the holistic nature of organization in ancient India and its resilience through modern times in the context of art and culture. Chhau is a folk-dance form that originated in the Chhota Nagpur Plateau of eastern India. The dance is associated with the Chaitra Parva festival, which is celebrated in the spring. The association of Chhau with Chaitra Parva has helped to sustain the dance form over the centuries. The festival provides a platform for Chhau performances, and it also helps to promote the dance form to a wider audience. The dance form has evolved over time, and it now incorporates elements of tribal culture, martial arts, and religious symbolism. Chhau is a highly stylized dance form that is characterized by its intricate footwork, graceful movements, and elaborate costumes. The dance is performed to the accompaniment of drums, cymbals, and other traditional instruments. Chhau performances typically depict stories from Hindu mythology, folk tales, and the lives of historical figures. The study finds that the efforts made by the local populace and the royal families in organizing the Chaitra Parva and managing the rehearsal and training process of the dance troupes helped in the growth, development, and sustenance of Chhau. It highlights the importance of audience support, careful planning, financial assistance, encouragement, artistic exchange, innovation, and socio-cultural integration in the growth and sustenance of Chhau.

Conclusions

In conclusion, a FRESH perspective on the organizational dimension of India is shaped by various factors. The functional aspect recognizes different industries and sectors with their specific organizational structures, such as the globalized and networked model in the IT industry. The ecosystem aspect considers government policies, regulatory frameworks, infrastructure, and market dynamics, including initiatives like "Make in India," to promote domestic manufacturing. The responsibility aspect highlights the increasing emphasis on corporate social responsibility and sustainable practices. The subaltern aspect acknowledges the grassroots role of local communities, cooperatives, and self-help groups in organizing small-scale businesses and industries. Lastly, the historical aspect reflects traditional forms of organization and indigenous managerial culture, emphasizing hierarchy, collective decision-making, and loyalty.

The inclusion of these aspects offers a fresh approach to the organizational dimension in India by bringing new perspectives, priorities, and considerations into the fold. Here's how each aspect contributes to this fresh approach:

Functional aspect: A fresh approach recognizes the specific organizational structures and practices within different industries. It helps businesses tailor their organizational strategies and operations accordingly, ensuring a better fit with the industry's unique needs and challenges.

Responsibility aspect: The fresh emphasis on corporate social responsibility and sustainable practices encourages businesses to consider their impact on society, the environment, and stakeholders beyond shareholders. Organizational goal alignment with broader societal well-being and sustainability fosters a more balanced and responsible approach.

Ecosystem aspect: A fresh perspective acknowledges the influence of various factors, such as government policies, regulations, infrastructure, and market dynamics. It enables organizations to adapt and respond effectively to the ever-changing ecosystem, leveraging opportunities and mitigating risks.

Subaltern aspect: The fresh recognition of the role played by local communities, artisanal clusters, and self-help groups values the contributions and potential of grassroots initiatives. A more inclusive and diverse approach harnesses local knowledge, skills, and resources for sustainable development.

Historical aspect: A fresh understanding of the historical traditions that have shaped organizational practices enables organizations to leverage the strengths and lessons of the past. Incorporating innovative practices to address modern challenges fosters a balance between tradition and progress.

Overall, the inclusion of these aspects offers a fresh perspective by bringing forth new insights, priorities, and considerations, thereby enabling organizations to navigate the complexities of the organizational dimension in India more effectively. It encourages a dynamic and adaptive mindset that incorporates diverse perspectives and aligns organizational practices with the evolving needs of society, the economy, and the environment. The subsequent chapters in the book further explore these elements to provide a comprehensive understanding of the organizational dynamics in India.

Part II

Functional Approach

https://doi.org/10.1142/9789811296444_0002

Chapter 2

Talent Inbreeding: The Case of Indian Academic Institutions as Organizations

Shalini Shukla[*,‡] **and Ram Singh**[†,§]

Department of Management, Sikkim University, Gangtok, India

†*Department of Business Administration, University of Lucknow, Lucknow, India*

‡*shuklashalini@ymail.com*

§*kamboj.ram5@gmail.com*

Abstract

The current study explores talent inbreeding in Indian educational institutes as organizations. The study develops the talent inbreeding index (TII), which measures the extent of talent inbreeding in educational organizations using a sample from India. A total of 67 institutes (13 IIMs, 23 IITs, and 31 NITs) have been taken into consideration for the sample. To measure the extent of talent (academic) inbreeding, the faculties' profiles of every institution have been explored and obtained from the official websites. Finding highlights that technical institutes have more academic inbreeding compare to management and other social science institutes. The study also presents many implications for the government, educational organizations, and policymakers for managing talent effectively and improving research and education-based outcomes.

Keywords: Talent inbreeding, talent inbreeding, educational organizations, Institutes of National Importance, India, IIM, IIT, NIT.

Introduction

Talent inbreeding in educational organizations is a recent concept in the field of social sciences. However, the literature on the impact of talent inbreeding on the productivity and effectiveness of institutes is growing (Soler, 2001; Sivak & Yudkevich, 2009; Horta *et al.*, 2010; Inanc & Tuncer, 2011; Horta *et al.*, 2011; Horta, 2013; Yudkevich *et al.*, 2015; Horta & Yudkevich, 2016; Tavares *et al.*, 2019). A few inter-regional organizations (e.g. The Organisation for Economic Co-operation and Development (OECD)) have surveyed the talent inbreeding and inward-looking tendencies of many universities in different countries. Surveys and reports have indicated a high level of talent inbreeding in countries like Portugal (Tavares *et al.*, 2019).

Talent inbreeding, also referred to as academic inbreeding, is one of the important factor influencing research productivity and educational effectiveness (Tavares *et al.*, 2019). Although no unanimous definition of talent inbreeding has evolved, many research studies have agreed that it is the practice of hiring their own graduates for teaching positions by institutes/universities. Much of this literature is concentrated on the impact of talent inbreeding on research productivity, outside collaborations, educational effectiveness, and many more (Dutton, 1980; Sivak & Yudkevich, 2009; Yudkevich *et al.*, 2015; Seeber & Mampaey, 2022; Singh, 2020). Little focus has been given to the extent of talent inbreeding, especially in countries like India. However, research productivity and educational effectiveness in India are much-discussed issues nowadays. The government is all set to implement the New Education Policy (NEP, 2020) to bring about drastic reforms in the educational sector. Diversity in terms of skills and expertise among the teaching fraternity is one of the focus areas in the NEP (2020). Thus, research on talent inbreeding, its extent, and its impact on the performance of academic institutions becomes imperative in the contemporary scenario.

Apart from this, being one of the densest populated countries in the world, providing equal and fair job opportunities is as important as providing education. India is a country where unemployment is always a concern, even after higher education. Inequalities in job opportunities in terms of nepotism and favoritism are much discussed in the research literature. However, literature is less available in the context of talent inbreeding among Indian institutions. Considering the importance of talent inbreeding in the context of India, the current study attempted to explore talent inbreeding in Indian institutes of national importance. The study also explores the organizational dimensions of talent inbreeding from the viewpoint of technical and social science institutes.

The chapter is organized as follows: The first section is a review of the literature and theoretical framework, which details the conceptual literature, types, and impact of talent inbreeding. Next, we present the rationale of the study, and the subsequent section describes the data, variables, and model used in the study to calculate the extent of talent inbreeding and variation across institutes in terms of discipline and experience. We then present the statistical results, elaborate on the results, and explore the significance of the study. Further, the last three sections include the implications, limitations, future directions, and conclusions of the research.

Review of Literature and Theoretical Framework

Talent inbreeding in the educational industry is identified as an important factor influencing research productivity, teaching effectiveness, innovation, etc. However, it has not attracted much attention from policymakers as well as researchers. In discussions and policy papers, inbreeding has been rarely mentioned as an academic menace. Talent inbreeding has a long tradition in a number of countries. However, a number of researchers are also of the opinion that talent inbreeding does not hamper research productivity or teaching effectiveness. Recruiting their own students after their terminal degree is generally not considered malpractice in many countries and academic systems (Altbach *et al.*, 2015). Basically, in a number of universities, it is considered a matter of pride to retain their own intellectual talent. In this study, talent inbreeding is considered detrimental to the efficiency and productivity of higher educational institutes in India. Talent inbreeding may promote the malpractices of favoritism and nepotism and violate the fundamental rights of Indian citizens to get equal employment opportunities. From an institutional point of view, talent inbreeding restricts educational institutes from recruiting the best available talent on the market. Padilla (2008) argued that talent inbreeding entrenches the same culture in institutes and makes reform implementation more difficult than otherwise. On the other hand, it also affects the power relationship within the department and promotes power dynamics rather than coordination (Godechot & Louvet, 2008). Additionally, the practice of talent inbreeding may also be detrimental to the marginalized sections of society that were traditionally not allowed to participate in the teaching profession (Wyer, 1980; Pan, 1993). Apart from the above discussion, talent inbreeding hampers the infusion of new ideas and thought processes into the system. Hiring their own graduates may lead to the development of a monotonous culture and a restricted learning environment.

Berelson has given the most accepted definition of talent inbreeding in the 1960s. The last 60 years have seen substantial changes in higher education, and the emergence of different disciplines has led to changes in academic careers as well (Hessels & Lente, 2008; Frank & Gabler, 2006; Altbach, 2000, 2003). Thus, conceptual reformation is required to study talent inbreeding in the present context (Horta, 2013). Several studies have attempted to distinguish between inbred, silver-corded, and non-inbred professors. The term "silver-corded" is used to denote those inbreds who have moved only once from the university where they obtained the doctorate to the university where they were recruited (Horta, 2013).

Talent inbreeding and performance: The increasing importance of higher education in India also signals the emerging significance of the academic profession. The government and policymakers are also paying heed to the contribution of India to global research and innovation. For a strong research environment, quality higher education is one of the important pillars. Infrastructure, diverse and competent faculty, a learning environment, facilitative administration, and a student-supportive culture are among the parameters that decide the future and effectiveness of any higher education institute.

Several studies (Gorelova & Lovakov, 2016; Alipova & Lovakov, 2018) have confirmed that this phenomenon is global in nature. A few developed countries are also witnessing the trend of talent inbreeding in their higher educational institutes. The impact of talent inbreeding on research productivity (Gorelova & Lovakov, 2016; Alipova & Lovakov, 2018), learning, networking (Shin et al., 2016), training (Shin et al., 2016), culture, research information exchange (Horta, 2013), and effectiveness (Inanc & Tuncer, 2011; Mora, 2015) has been investigated by a few studies. Although researchers have adopted somewhat diverse approaches to measuring the effect of talent inbreeding, there is an approximate consensus on the negative impact of this practice on the performance of institutes, faculty, and students.

However, the study conducted by Horta *et al.* (2011) on Japanese universities concluded that talent inbreeding assured organizational stability and institutional identity. Talent inbreeding also influences the academic research careers of individuals. The study conducted by Horta *et al.* (2013) found that mobility in the early research career is decisive and that less mobile academics have more inward-oriented information exchange and lower scientific productivity. Moreover, it was also revealed that the information exchange and scientific productivity of academics who changed institutions only once do not differ substantially from those of "mobile inbred academics." Contradictorily, the study conducted by Alipova *et al.* (2018) indicated that there is no significant effect of talent inbreeding on publication productivity. Further, the research conducted by Smyth and Mishra (2013) on faculty employed at Australian law schools revealed that silver-corded faculty outperform other faculty in publication in top journals.

However, some studies have argued that talent inbreeding can lead to lower research quality, as it limits exposure to diverse perspectives, methodologies, and ideas. Abramo *et al.* (2009) examined Italian universities and found that higher levels of talent inbreeding were associated with lower scientific productivity and impact. In line with this, another study conducted by Niederle and Vesterlund (2007) on gender differences in academic hiring found that talent inbreeding could perpetuate gender imbalances by reinforcing existing male-dominated networks. Talent inbreeding can reduce diversity within institutions by perpetuating certain biases, preferences, and traditions.

Inbreeds and organizational perspective: Many organizations have recognized the potential drawbacks of talent inbreeding and have implemented policies to promote diversity and mitigate its effects. Other studies, such as Tavares *et al.* (2015), found that talent inbreeding is harmful to the recognition and impact of research. In line with this, according to Morichika and Shibayama (2015), this may blunt scientific creativity, lower scientific production, diminish knowledge sharing, and reduce faculty mobility. Many empirical researches (e.g. Banks, 2006; Cruz-Castro & Sanz-Menéndez, 2010; Hargens & Farr, 1973; Horta *et al.*, 2013; İnanç & Tuncer, 2011; Morichika & Shibayama, 2015; Yudkevich, 2015;

Horta *et al.*, 2021) indicated that candidates who are later employed as faculty members at a university in which they studied exhibit less scientific productivity. These findings are in line with those of Smyth and Mishra (2014), who emphasize that faculty mobility between institutions or countries improves research creativity. Furthermore, talent inbreeding practices may constrain faculty members and compel them to stay in a certain setting for an extended period of time. It can also limit potential faculty experiences in diverse locations, requiring them to work at the same university for the duration of their careers and prohibiting investment in external credentials, activities, and products (Altbach *et al.*, 2015). According to research conducted by de la Torre *et al.* (2021), university systems with a high level of talent inbreeding are less open to attracting and prioritizing the retention of human resources in the institution.

There are a number of reasons why talent inbreeding may be a problem at IIMs. First, it can lead to a lack of diversity of thought. When faculty members are all from the same institution, they are more likely to share the same views and perspectives. This can stifle creativity and innovation. Ultimately, talent inbreeding can lead to a decline in the quality of teaching and research. When faculty members are not exposed to new ideas and perspectives, they may become less engaged in their teaching and research. This can lead to a decrease in the quality of education and research at the institution. Further, talent inbreeding can make it difficult for institutions to attract and retain top talent. When faculty members know that they are likely to be hired, promoted, and tenured based on their relationships with existing faculty members, they may be less likely to leave for other institutions. This can limit the institution's ability to bring in new ideas and perspectives.

Further, the study conducted by Horta *et al.* (2022) concluded that there are significant differences between indigenous and silver-corded academics, and the latter type of academics should not be recognized as part of the talent inbreeding process. Additionally, another study carried out by Horta *et al.* (2022), revealed that career regulations intended to ensure quality may have unexpected consequences in terms of talent inbreeding, according to some researchers. First and foremost, habilitation procedures provide significant hurdles to international candidates and frequently result in increased barriers between specialties. Language requirements play a significant role in the inbreeding of academics in specific subjects and geographical areas (Sabeer & Mampey, 2022).

talent inbreeding require a proper framework to measure it. The current study attempted to provide such a framework so that talent inbreeding can be identified, measured, and removed.

Following the above discussion, the study attempts to address the following research questions (RQs):

RQ1: How are institutes of national importance indulging in talent inbreeding?

RQ2: What is the extent of talent inbreeding among the different institutes of national importance?

RQ3: How can different institutes be ranked on the talent inbreeding index (TII)?

RQ4: How do organizational dimension shape talent inbreeding in India?

Data and Method

For this study, institutes of national importance (in higher education) have been selected as samples. Institutes of national importance have been selected owing to the reason that these institutions represent the best practices in the industry. Some institutes are even conferred as "Centres of Excellence" in their fields. A total of 61 Indian institutes have been considered for analysis, of which 12 were Indian Institutes of Management (IIMs), 21 were Indian Institutes of Technology (IITs), and 28 were from the National Institutes of Technology (NIT). To measure the extent of talent inbreeding, an index has been prepared for every sampling unit, named the TII. The following indicators have been used to measure TII:

(1) establishment year of the institution (Experience),
(2) total numbers of departments (Size),
(3) total number of student seats (Size),
(4) total number of faculties,
(5) number of faculties from their same IIM/IIT/NIT,
(6) number of faculties from different IIMs/IITs/NITs,
(7) number of faculties from other universities/institutions (Other than IIMs/IITs/NITs).

To ensure the authenticity of the information, the official website of every institution has been explored to get relevant and required information. Almost every institute has maintained proper disclosure of their teaching staff and the number of students. However, information about a few teaching staff was not updated and completed; therefore, those faculties have been placed under a separate category ("information not given").

Talent Inbreeding Index Calculation

To quantify talent inbreeding, experts from various academic fields were consulted to assign the weightage for calculating the TII. Finally, each variable was assigned weightage as follows:

(1) 0.5 for the total number of faculty from the same institute.
(2) 0.4 for the total number of faculty from other branches of the same institute.
(3) 0.1 for the total number of faculty from another institute.

To assess the validity of the above weightage, unstructured interviews were conducted with senior faculties of the government institutes (directors, deans, and heads of departments), as they are involved in the planning and implementation of academic strategies in institutions.

Finally, the TII was computed using the formula

Talent inbreeding index (TII) = 0.5 ∗ (Total number of faculty from the same institute)
+ 0.4 ∗ (Total number of faculty from other branches of the same institute)
+ 0.1 ∗ (Total number of faculty from another institute).

Data Analysis

Sample Profile

Different institutions of national importance have been considered for the sample. The following tables depict that, in the case of management institutions, 50% have experience of less than 20 years. Whereas, in the case of technical institutions, 61.9% of IITs and 42.9% of NIT have experience of fewer than 20 years. In the case of technical institutes (IITs/NITs), a few have experience of more than 60 years, whereas none of the management institutes have experience of more than 60 years. These figures show homogeneity in terms of the experience of institutions (See Tables 1 and 3).

Department size has been used as a proxy of the organization size. The following table indicates that 50% of management institutions have 5–10 departments, whereas 46.4% of the technical institutes, IITs and NITs, have 5–10 departments. Thus, the management and technical institutes have the same size in terms of the number of departments.

The TII has been calculated for the management and technical institutes (IITs/NITs) and can be deciphered from Table 4.

Table 1. Sample characteristics: IIMs.

Experience	Frequency	Percent
Less than 20 years	6	50.0
21–40 years	3	25.0
41–60 years	3	25.0
Total	12	100.0

No. of departments (size)	Frequency	Percent
Less than 5	4	33.3
5–10	6	50.0
10–15	2	16.7
Total	12	100.0

Table 2. Sample characteristics: IITs.

Experience	Frequency	Percent
Less than 20 years	13	61.9
21–40 years	1	4.8
41–60 years	2	9.5
More than 61 years	5	23.8
Total	21	100.0

No. of departments (size)	Frequency	Percent
Less than 5	1	3.6
5–10	13	46.4
10–15	10	35.7
More than 15	4	14.3
Total	28	100.0

Table 3.   Sample characteristics: NITs.

Experience	Frequency	Percent
Less than 20 years	12	42.9
21–40 years	2	7.1
41–60 years	13	46.4
More than 61 years	1	3.6
Total	28	100.0
No. of departments (size)	**Frequency**	**Percent**
Less than 5	1	3.6
5–10	13	46.4
10–15	10	35.7
More than 15	4	14.3
Total	28	100.0

Table 4.   Talent inbreeding index.

Institutes	No.	Total faculty	Total faculty from the same institute (inbred)	Total faculty from other branches of the same institute	Number of faculty from other institutes	Talent inbreeding index (score)
IIMs	12	770	44	210	507	156.7
IITs	21	3,862	633	1,719	2,170	1,221.1
NITs	28	4,133	748	1,022	1,917	974.5

Table 5.   Ranking of the institutes (types).

Institutes	Rank
IIM	I
IIT	III
MNIT	II

The institute with a higher talent inbreeding score was assigned a lower rank, and vice versa. The overall performance of the institutes based on the TII is shown in Table 5.

It can be seen from Table 5 that IIMs are ranked first in terms of talent inbreeding, indicating that IIMS have faculties from other institutions and exhibit low talent inbreeding. On the other hand, IITs were found to have a high TII, which indicates that IITs employed faculties who received education from IITs only.

Variation in Talent Inbreeding

Experience of the institute: To assess the variation in talent inbreeding based on experience, the one-way ANOVA test was employed. This clarifies the variations within the same institute and across all institutes. The results are discussed as follows:

(i) Variation in talent inbreeding based on experience in the same types of institutes

Table 6 shows the descriptive statistics, and it is evident that there is significant variation in talent inbreeding across IIMs based on experience ($p = 0.011 < 0.05$).

Table 7 shows the descriptive statistics, and it is evident that there is significant variation in talent inbreeding across IITs ($p = 0.006 < 0.05$).

Table 8 shows the descriptive statistics, and it is evident that there is significant variation in talent inbreeding across NITs ($p = 0.010 < 0.05$).

Table 6. Variation in talent inbreeding in IIMs based on experience in the same institute: ANOVA test.

	Sum of squares	d*f*	Mean square	*F*	Sig.
Between groups	202.021	2	101.010	7.731	0.011
Within groups	117.588	9	13.065		
Total	319.609	11			

Table 7. Variation in talent inbreeding in IITs based on experience: ANOVA test.

	Sum of squares	d*f*	Mean square	*F*	Sig.
Between groups	42114.068	3	14038.023	5.829	0.006
Within groups	40938.724	17	2408.160		
Total	83052.792	20			

Table 8. Variation in talent inbreeding in NITs based on experience: ANOVA test.

	Sum of squares	df	Mean square	F	Sig.
Between groups	10011.419	3	3337.140	4.752	0.010
Within groups	16854.251	24	702.260		

Table 9. Variation in talent inbreeding across all institutes based on experience: ANOVA test.

	Sum of squares	df	Mean square	F	Sig.
Between groups	52760.519	3	17586.840	13.596	0.000
Within groups	73733.844	57	1293.576		
Total	126494.363	60			

(ii) Variation in talent inbreeding based on experience across all institutes

To assess the variation in talent inbreeding based on experience, the one-way ANOVA test was again employed. This shows us the variations within the same institute and across all institutes. It can be seen from Table 9 that there are significant variations in talent inbreeding across all institutions ($F = 13.596$, $p = 0.000$).

Later, a *post hoc* test, Tukey's Honestly Significant Difference (HSD), also indicated that in terms of the within-group comparison, the institutes with less than 20 years of experience are significantly different from those with more than 61 years of experience, while there is difference between the variation in TII between institutes with less than 20 years and those with experience of 21–40 years and 41–60 years. There are significant variations in the TII between the institutes with 21–40 years of experience and those with more than 61 years of experience. The results are shown in Table 10.

Size of the Institute

Table 11 shows the descriptive statistics, and it is evident that there is no significant variation in talent inbreeding across IIMs ($p = 0.391$).

Table 10. *Post hoc* test.

Experience		Mean difference (I–J)	Std. error	Sig.	95% confidence interval Lower bound	Upper bound
Less than 20 years	21–40 years	−9.08656	16.04133	0.942	−51.5395	33.3664
	41–60 Years	−27.08100	10.65803	0.064	−55.2872	1.1252
	More than 61 years	−100.45323*	16.04133	0.000	−142.9062	−58.0003
21–40 years	Less than 20 years	9.08656	16.04133	0.942	−33.3664	51.5395
	41–60 years	−17.99444	16.95469	0.714	−62.8646	26.8757
	More than 61 years	−91.36667*	20.76516	0.000	−146.3211	−36.4122
41–60 years	Less than 20 years	27.08100	10.65803	0.064	−1.1252	55.2872
	21–40 years	17.99444	16.95469	0.714	−26.8757	62.8646
	More than 61 years	−73.37222*	16.95469	0.000	−118.2424	−28.5021
More than 61 years	Less than 20 years	100.45323*	16.04133	0.000	58.0003	142.9062
	21–40 years	91.36667*	20.76516	0.000	36.4122	146.3211
	41–60 years	73.37222*	16.95469	0.000	28.5021	118.2424

Note: *Significant values below 0.05.

Table 11. Variation in talent inbreeding in IIMs based on size: ANOVA test.

	Sum of squares	df	Mean square	F	Sig.
Between groups	60.268	2	30.134	1.046	0.391
Within groups	259.341	9	28.816		
Total	319.609	11			

Table 12. Variation in talent inbreeding in IITs based on size: ANOVA test.

	Sum of squares	df	Mean square	F	Sig.
Between groups	51010.222	3	17003.407	9.021	0.001
Within groups	32042.570	17	1884.857		
Total	83052.792	20			

Table 13.   Variation in talent inbreeding in NITs based on size: ANOVA test.

	Sum of squares	df	Mean square	F	Sig.
Between groups	10011.419	3	3337.140	4.752	0.010
Within groups	16854.251	24	702.260		
Total	26865.670	27			

Table 14.   Variation in talent inbreeding across overall institutes based on size: ANOVA test.

	Sum of squares	df	Mean square	F	Sig.
Between groups	52760.519	3	17586.840	13.596	0.000
Within groups	73733.844	57	1293.576		
Total	126494.363	60			

Table 12 indicates the descriptive statistics, and it is evident that there is significant variation d in talent inbreeding across IITs ($p = 0.001$).

Table 13 shows the descriptive statistics, and it is evident that a significant variation is observed in talent inbreeding across NITs ($p = 0.010$).

(i)   Variation in talent inbreeding based on size across all institutes
Table 14 shows the descriptive statistics, and it is evident that there is significant variation in talent inbreeding across all institutes understudy based on size ($p = 0.000$).

The *post hoc* test, Tukey's HSD, also indicated that in terms of the within-group comparison, the institutes with less than 5 and 5–10 numbers of departments and 10–15 numbers of departments are significantly different from the institutes with more than 15 departments (see Table 15).

Table 15. *Post hoc* analysis: multiple comparisons.

Dependent variable: TII2 Tukey HSD

(I) Dept cat		Mean difference (I–J)	Std. error	Sig.	95% confidence interval	
					Lower bound	Upper bound
Less than 5	5–10	-5.77857	13.39651	0.973	-41.2321	29.6749
	10–15	-17.74286	14.23698	0.600	-55.4206	19.9349
	More than 15	-102.39841*	15.97627	**0.000**	**-144.6792**	**-60.1176**
5–10	Less than 5	5.77857	13.39651	0.973	-29.6749	41.2321
	10–15	-11.96429	9.74739	0.612	-37.7605	13.8319
	More than 15	**-96.61984***	**12.14748**	**0.000**	**-128.7678**	**-64.4719**
10–15	Less than 5	17.74286	14.23698	0.600	-19.9349	55.4206
	5–10	11.96429	9.74739	0.612	-13.8319	37.7605
	More than 15	**-84.65556***	**13.06853**	**0.000**	**-119.2411**	**-50.0700**
More than 15	Less than 5	102.39841*	15.97627	0.000	60.1176	144.6792
	5–10	96.61984*	12.14748	0.000	64.4719	128.7678
	10–15	84.65556*	13.06853	0.000	50.0700	119.2411

Note: *Significant values below 0.05.

Results and Discussion

The main purpose of the study was to assess and compare the extent of talent inbreeding among institutes of national importance in India. The results of the study indicate that there is a prevalence of talent inbreeding practices in Indian institutes. However, several national institutes have adopted the practice of moderating talent inbreeding by placing a restriction on the hiring of candidates who immediately graduated from the very same institution. The study found that IIMs have low talent inbreeding, whereas premier technology institutes (IITs) were found to have high talent inbreeding, which indicates that IITs employed faculties with degrees from IITs. Leveraging and utilizing domain expertise to maintain continuity in research work may be one of the probable reasons for high inbreeding in technical institutes. Interestingly, cross-institute exchange of faculties and students through different programs can reduce this practice of talent inbreeding in technical institutes. However, talent inbreeding is not peculiar to technical institutes; management institutes are also exposed to this practice. However, lateral entries in the teaching profession from different industries and expertise can help the management institutes maintain diversity and reduce talent inbreeding.

The **experience of the institutes** plays a vital role in talent inbreeding. Less experienced institutes were different from the experienced ones in terms of hiring inbred teachers. There are significant variations in the TII between the institutes with 21–40 years of experience and those with more than 61 years of experience. Further, while making a comparison within the group, the study found significant variation in talent inbreeding across IIMs and IITs based on experience. Thus, experienced educational institutes were found to have more inbreds than new ones. As far as **the size of the institutes** is concerned, the study indicated significant variations in talent inbreeding across all institutions. The study found significant variation in talent inbreeding across NITs in terms of size. However, no significant variation is observed in talent inbreeding across IIMs based on size. Further, while making a comparison within IITs with different sizes, a significant variation is observed in talent inbreeding across IITs and NITs. Thus, the experience and size of the institute were found to be important factors influencing talent inbreeding in India.

There are a number of measures that IIMs can take to address the problem of talent inbreeding. They can make a concerted effort to hire faculty members from a wider range of institutions. This will help to ensure that there is a diversity of thought within the faculty. IIMs can provide faculty members with opportunities to collaborate with researchers from other institutions. This will help expose faculty members to new ideas and perspectives. IIMs can create a more competitive environment for faculty promotions. This will encourage faculty members to publish in top journals and produce high-quality research. This can also address the problem of talent inbreeding and ensure that they continue to produce high-quality education and research.

Why Academic Institutions as Organizations are Nurturing Inbreds?

There are several factors such as academic focus, research orientation, pedagogical continuity, tradition, and legacy that may be responsible for talent inbreeding in educational institutes in India. Technical institutes nurture inbreds for continued research focus and advancement in similar fields. Shared values and belief systems help the faculties pursue their research interests for longer durations and generate more substantive outcomes. Similar to organizations, educational institutes have a brand image based on various educational parameters. Hiring inbreds helps them maintain their legacy and image through continuity. However, balance of perspective, quality and competence, innovation and collaboration, diversity and inclusivity, long-term vision, and succession planning are a few points that need consideration before deciding on an academic feeding strategy. Because both sources of hiring have their own limitations and benefits, educational organizations need to decide which source/strategy is aligned with their long-term pursuit and vision.

In Indian academics, the need for diversity, merit-based hiring, and accessibility to outside talent is becoming more and more apparent. Some universities and organizations have begun to work on encouraging more inclusive recruiting practices and reducing talent inbreeding. These initiatives are motivated by the need to raise academic and research standards, promote teamwork, and recruit from a broad talent pool. To encourage variety and prevent talent inbreeding, the UGC, the top regulatory authority for higher education in India, has formed rules and regulations. They stress the value of transparent job postings, open competition, and global partnerships. There are various measures that educational institutions are taking to tackle the issue of talent inbreeding, such as faculty recruitment policies, open advertisements, competitive selection, external peer review, collaboration and research networks, international exchange programs, and incentives for diversity.

Implications of the Study

The study is important in the present context of India, when government and policymaking agencies have started focusing on quality, innovation, and outcome-based learning in the education system. From a practical point of view, the study gives impetus to educational institutes to look inward to find out the solutions for deteriorating quality and ranking on global indices. Inbreeding in academics has detrimental effects on research productivity, information exchange, and other output-related parameters (Horta, 2011). Thus, such an understanding of talent inbreeding among national institutes brings forth insights into probable reasons for low-quality research and information exchange. Institutes of national importance can use their goodwill and expertise to reduce this menace in central, state, and other educational institutions.

India is on the verge of implementing NEP (2020) and major reforms in the education sector. Skill diversity, capability-building, research productivity, and teaching effectiveness are key areas where policy interventions are pending. Thus, removing talent inbreeding, allowing faculty exchange, lateral entries, etc., could provide a possible solution for existing challenges associated with research productivity and teaching effectiveness.

Moreover, providing equal employment opportunities to every candidate is one of the mandates of the Indian Constitution. Favoritism at any stage of employment is deemed a violation of fundamental rights. Thus, understanding the intensity of inbreeding is the first step to ensuring fair and just employment opportunities for appearing candidates. Further, this study has developed the TII, which measures the extent of talent inbreeding in any institution. Recognition and measurement are the primary steps for removing any menaces and malpractices. Thus, this TII can be used to list and index institutions and universities based on talent inbreeding.

Limitations and Future Directions

A few limitations of the study are important to discuss here. First, the study is based on faculty information disclosures on the official website of the respective institute. Due to this data collection process, a few sampling units were missed due to the unavailability of the information on the website. Using a primary questionnaire-based data collection process in future studies may provide a clearer picture of talent inbreeding. Second, for the current study, silver-corded academicians have been taken into consideration instead of pure-inbred academicians (Caplow & McGee, 1958; Berelson, 1960; Hargens & Farr, 1973; Dutton, 1980; Horta, 2013; Smyth & Mishra, 2013). In this study, the time gap (experience) after the terminal degree is not considered, and candidates have been categorized as breeders even if they have earned their terminal degree from other institutes and have previous work experience in a different organization. Thus, future studies in this direction can give better insights into the intensity of silver-corded and pure-inbred in these institutes. Moreover, the TII can be computed for various institutes across the globe and various countries to assess the status of talent inbreeding in institutes around the world. Future research studies can be channeled toward validation on this scale as well as the development of a more comprehensive scale as an improved measure of talent inbreeding.

Conclusion

The study concludes that excessive talent inbreeding is one of the long-standing menaces in higher education in India. Research has also indicated the negative impact of talent inbreeding on the education system. The current study concluded that even in the higher education system of India, the practice of talent inbreeding is prevalent. The existence of this phenomenon in institutes of national importance becomes more significant owing to their role in the progression and development of other educational institutes and universities.

The study also proposed a scale for talent inbreeding that can be further validated in future studies. However, there are organizational dimensions of talent inbreeding precipitated through the cultural roots and educational system of India that also reflect through different forms of arts and expression. In the end, whether to hire an academic in-bred applicant or an external candidate should be based on a thorough assessment of individual qualifications, the institution's special needs, and the desired organizational culture. Striking a balance and taking into account the aforementioned elements can assist institutions in making sound decisions that encourage excellence, diversity, and long-term viability in academia.

References

Abramo, G., D'Angelo, C. A., & Di Costa, F. (2009). Research collaboration and productivity: Is there correlation? *Higher Education*, 57, 155–171.

Alipova, O. & Lovakov, A. (2018). Academic inbreeding and publication activities of Russian faculty. *Tertiary Education and Management*, 24(1), 66–82.

Altbach, P. G. (2000). *The Changing Academic Workplace: Comparative Perspectives*. Boston: Center for International Higher Education.

Altbach, P. G. (2003). *The Decline of the Guru: The Academic Profession in Developing and Middle-Income Countries*. New York: Palgrave.

Altbach, P. G., Yudkevich, M., & Rumbley, L. E. (2015). Academic inbreeding: Local challenge, global problem. *Asia Pacific Education Review*, 16(3), 317–330.

Banks, M. G. (2006). An extension of the Hirsch index: Indexing scientific topics and compounds. *Scientometrics*, 69(1), 161–168. https://doi.org/10.1007/s11192-006-0146-5.

Berelson, B. (1960). *Graduate Education in the United States*. New York: McGraw Hill.

Balyer, A. & Bakay, M. E. (2022). Academic inbreeding: A risk or benefit for universities? *Journal of Education and Learning*, 11(1), 147–158.

Caplow, T. & McGee, R. (1958). *The Academic Marketplace*. New York: Doubleday.

Cruz-Castro, L. & Sanz-Menéndez, L. (2010). Mobility versus job stability: Assessing tenure and productivity outcomes. *Research Policy*, 39, 27–38. https://doi.org/10.1016/j.respol.2009.11.008.

de la Torre, E. M., Perez-Esparrells, C., & Romero-Madrid, T. (2021). Academic inbreeding in the Spanish public university system: A review of its institutional and context determinants. *Culture and Education*, 33(2), 229–258. https://doi.org/10.1080/11356405.2021.1904658.

Dutton, J. E. (1980). *The Impact of Inbreeding and Immobility on the Professional Role and Scholarly Performance of Academic Scientists*.

Frank, D. J. & Gabler, J. (2006). *Reconstructing the University: Worldwide Shifts in the 20th Century*. Stanford: Stanford University Press.

Godechot, O. & Louvet, A. (2008). Academic inbreeding: An evaluation. Laviedesidees.fr. Retrieved from http://www.book sandideas.net/Academic-Inbreeding-An-Evaluation.html.

Gorelova, O. & Lovakov, A. (2016). Academic inbreeding and research productivity of Russian faculty members. Higher School of Economics Research Paper No. WP BRP, 32.

Hargens, L. L. & Farr, G. M. (1973). An examination of recent hypotheses about institutional inbreeding. *American Journal of Sociology*, 78(6), 1381–1402.

Hessels, L. K. & Lente, H. (2008). Re-thinking new knowledge production: A literature review and a research agenda. *Research Policy*, 37(4), 740–760.

Horta, H. (2013). Deepening our understanding of academic inbreeding effects on research information exchange and scientific output: New insights for academic based research. *Higher Education*, 65, 87–510. https://doi.org/10.1007/s10734-012-9559-7.

Horta, H. & Yudkevich, M. (2016). The role of academic inbreeding in developing higher education systems: Challenges and possible solutions. *Technological Forecasting and Social Change*, 113, 363–372.

Horta, H., Meoli, M., & Santos, J. M. (2022). Academic inbreeding and choice of the strategic research approach. *Higher Education Quarterly*, 76(1), 76–101.

Horta, H., Sato, M., & Yonezawa, A. (2011). Academic inbreeding: Exploring its characteristics and rationale in Japanese universities using a qualitative perspective. *Asia Pacific Education Review*, 12(1), 35–44.

Horta, H., Veloso, F. M., & Grediaga, R. (2010). Navel gazing: Academic inbreeding and scientific productivity. *Management Science*, 56(3), 414–429.

Horta, H., Tavares, O., Amaral, A., & Sin, C. (2022). New perspectives and analytical approaches to better understand academic inbreeding. *Higher Education Quarterly*, 76(1), 3–7.

Inanc, O. & Tuncer, O. (2011). The effect of academic inbreeding on scientific effectiveness. *Scientometrics*, 88(3), 885–898.

Mora, J. G. (2015). Academic inbreeding in Spanish universities: Perverse effects in a global context. In *Academic Inbreeding and Mobility in Higher Education* (pp. 206–227). London: Palgrave Macmillan.

Morichika, N. & Shibayama, S. (2015). Impact of inbreeding on scientific productivity: A case study of a Japanese university department. *Research Evaluation*, 24, 146–157. https://doi.org/10.1093/reseval/rvv002.

National Education Policy (NEP) (2020). Ministry of Human Resource Development, Government of India. https://www.mhrd.gov.in/sites/upload_files/mhrd/files/nep/NEP_Final_English.pdf referred on 10/08/2020.

Niederle, M. & Vesterlund, L. (2007). Do women shy away from competition? Do men compete too much? *The Quarterly Journal of Economics*, 122(3), 1067–1101.

Padilla, L. E. (2008). How has Mexican faculty been trained? A national perspective and a case study. *Higher Education*, 56(2), 167–183.

Pan, S. (1993). A Study of Faculty Inbreeding at Eleven Land-Grant Universities. Doctoral Dissertation, Iowa State University.

Seeber, M. & Mampaey, J. (2022). How do university systems' features affect academic inbreeding? Career rules and language requirements in France, Germany, Italy and Spain. *Higher Education Quarterly*, 76(1), 20–35.

Shin, J. C., Jung, J., & Lee, S. J. (2016). Academic inbreeding of Korean professors: Academic training, networks, and their performance. In *Biographies and Careers Throughout Academic Life* (pp. 187–206). Cham: Springer.

Singh, D. (2020). Academic inbreeding in Indian Institutes of Technology (IITs): A case study. *The Wire*. https://thewire.in/education/indias-best-universities-must-discard-practice-academic-inbreeding.

Sivak, Y. & Yudkevich, M. (2009). Academic inbreeding: Pro and contra. *Educational Studies*, (1), 170–187.

Smyth, R. & Mishra, V. (2014). Academic inbreeding and research productivity and impact in Australian law schools. *Scientometrics*, 98, 583–618.

Soler, M. (2001). How inbreeding affects productivity in Europe. *Nature*, 411(6834), 132.

Tavares, O., Sin, C., & Lança, V. (2019). Inbreeding and research productivity among sociology PhD holders in Portugal. *Minerva*, 57(3), 373–390.

Tavares, O., Cardoso, S., Carvalho, T., Sousa, S. B., & Santiago, R. (2015). Academic inbreeding in the Portuguese academia. *Higher Education*, 69, 991–1006. https://doi.org/10.1007/s10734-014-9818-x.

Wyer, J. C. (1980). Institutional origin: Labor market signaling in higher education. Doctoral dissertation, The College of William and Mary.

Yudkevich, M., Altbach, P. G., & Rumbley, L. E. (2015). *Academic Inbreeding and Mobility in Higher Education: Global Perspectives*. Palgrave Macmillan London.

Chapter 3

Digital Transformation of Supply Chains in Indian Organizations

Prakash Agrawal[*,§], Rakesh Narain[†,¶], and Mayank Agarwal[‡,||]

**Department of Mechanical Engineering,
Rewa Engineering College, REWA, India*

*†Department of Mechanical Engineering, Rewa Engineering
College, REWA, India*

*‡Institute of Engineering and Technology,
Dr. RML Avadh University, Ayodhya, India*

§prakashagrawal2308@gmail.com

¶amitdotiitg@gmail.com

||mayankres@gmail.com

Abstract

Recent technological trends have changed how people live, consume, and interact. New emerging technologies have disrupted the way of doing business. The "digital transformation of supply chain (SC)" refers to complex organizational changes using emerging digital technologies to create new forms of revenue and business value through a customer-centric platform that captures and maximizes the utilization of real-time information emerging from various sources, enabling performance optimization and risk minimization. Companies are under common pressure to reform as new technological trends continue to emerge, but their pace of transformation is slow, especially in Indian organizations. Owing to the slow adoption rate of digital SC in India, this chapter attempts to identify the transformation factors pertinent to expanding their implementation in India. In view of this, a questionnaire-based survey has been conducted to assess the current status of the digital transformation of SC in Indian organizations and other issues related to it. Several hypotheses have also been developed and tested, which present valuable insights to organizations in digitalizing their SCs.

Keywords: Digital disruption, customer-centricity, Indian ethos, artificial intelligence, case studies.

Introduction

The rapid pace of technological innovations is influencing almost every part of our day-to-day lives, both in business and leisure. It has changed the way people live and communicate with their surroundings. Besides, new digital technologies, such as the Internet of Things (IoT), Big Data analytics (BDA), artificial intelligence (AI), and blockchain, have disrupted business processes and industries (Nasiri *et al.*, 2020). Almost every organization's key business function, i.e. supply chain (SC) management, finds itself at the center of this disruption. These recent technological developments have rationalized supply chain processes (Da Silva *et al.*, 2019), forcing organizations to re-evaluate how they design their SCs as business as usual will not work anymore (Schrauf & Berttram, 2016). Digital transformation of the SC (DTSC) is emerging as one of the most relevant strategies that can revolutionize traditional SCs, facilitating organizations in developing new capabilities that would be essential for surviving in the current global market (Table 1 shows a comparison between traditional and digital SCs). The digital transformation of SCs can be considered a means of converting recent technological advancements, global market uncertainties, and rising customers' demands into a source of competitive advantage through the creative deployment of new emerging technologies into various SC operations that will convert

Table 1. A comparison between traditional and digital supply chain.

Attributes	Traditional supply chain features	Digital supply chain features
Purpose	Was designed to manage operational and logistics activities	In addition to managing operational and logistics activities, it is designed to have more intense information about customers' needs to fulfill their expectations through quality and service they want
Communication	Have a linear and hierarchical interaction among all the members of supply chain	Create a nonlinear and circular interaction among all the functions inside the digital supply chain with real-time connectivity
Processes	Processes and activities are stable	Adaptable processes are there to address any unpredictable change
Products	Focused on standardized products to enhance efficiency	It is all about customization and delivering unprecedented customer experiences
Information flow	Information flow delayed as it passes through every member of supply chain	Information available to all the elements of supply chain simultaneously
Demand forecasting	Blind forecasting which totally depends on past demand data	Intelligent forecasting, which includes additional customer data and market trends, allows for predictive analytics
Responsiveness	Number of planning cycles resulting in delays and unsynchronized responses across different levels	Real-time data to demand changes across all the tiers during planning and execution empowers to react quickly to demand
Transparency	Limited visibility to supply chain	Complete view of supply chain
Flexibility	Changes in end customer demand get distorted	Changes in end customer demand are quickly assessed by effectively utilizing the data collected
Scalability	Organizations often struggle to scale capacity.	Scaling up or down supply chain capacity just as needed prospects is not an issue

organizational resources into differentiated capabilities (Panda & Rath, 2021). Digital transformation of SCs will drive growth, unprecedented customer experience, competitive advantage, optimize costs, and mitigate risks. Yet, the pace of transformation is slow, especially in Indian organizations.

When compared to organizations in developed nations, the progress of digitalization in Indian businesses seems to be slower than expected. The reasons behind this sluggish implementation are the absence of clear and specific guidelines, a lack of digital skills in the present workforce, high investment, cyber security issues, etc. However, before taking any digital transformation initiatives, organizations must assess prevailing market conditions, evaluate their current state where they fall in digitization, establish a new set of business and SC objectives that need to be attained in the future, and assess its enablers and barriers. It is against this background that a survey of Indian organizations has been carried out to assess the status of the adoption of the digital SC by Indian organizations and its related issues.

Literature Review

DTSC is one of the trending business movements of the present time. It is proclaiming the next era of the Supply chain management (SCM), where each member of the SC comes together in a completely new manner, breaking the walls between the digital and physical worlds and eradicating the traditional boundaries. Digital transformation is an inevitable revolution driven by a confluence of several technologies, such as BDA, IoT, AI, 3D printing, blockchain, augmented reality (AR), and advanced robotics. (Tjahjono et al., 2017; Koh et al., 2019; Fatorachian & Kazemi, 2021). The transformation is driven by two trends. On one side, digital technologies, such as IoT, AI, AR, cloud computing, and BDA, are propelling into the market. On the other side are the challenges of meeting the more customized demands of consumers and appropriately responding to competitors' moves. Horvath and Szabo (2019) have identified major drivers of this transformation: the leading driver is about satisfying the ever-increasing demands of customers; it is followed by the diminishing product life cycles; the next is maintaining product/service flexibility; and the last is about responding to competitors' actions. Digital transformation comprises three categories: digital transformation within an organization, digital transformation between organizations and their customers, and digital transformation between organizations and their partners (Dougados & Felgendreher, 2016).

Digital Supply Chain

The concept of Digital supply chain (DSC) is still developing (Kayikci, 2018). There is no universally accepted definition of the digital SC, yet various definitions of DSC are available in the literature; for example, Kinnet (2015) defined DSC as "a smart, data-driven network that leverages analytics and new technologies to generate new forms of returns, through a centric platform that catches and augments the usage of live data arising out of multiple sources." DSC is an agile, customer-driven, and productive way to fulfill the changing demands of customers and offer differentiated services to them (Büyüközkan & Göçer, 2018). The digital transformation of SC refers to the process of adopting new technologies to redefine and reshape present business processes to create a remarkable competitive advantage across the enterprise. Industry 4.0 lies behind the incredible capabilities of DSC.

Both scholars and practitioners have realized the importance of DSC. There is a plethora of articles available in the literature discussing the concept of DSC, its features, and its importance in the present scenario. Agrawal and Narain (2018) have given an overview of the term digital SC. Calatayud *et al.* (2019) discussed significant changes that can be realized by adopting new digital technologies in SCM and presented how developments in information and communication technologies (ICTs) will help address key SC challenges and opportunities. Büyüközkan and Göçer (2018), Garay-Rondero *et al.* (2019), Tiwari (2020), and Zekhnini *et al.* (2021) presented a literature review on DSC, discussing the concept of DSC, its features, benefits, impact on SC functions, and its role in meeting the requirements of the current global marketplace. Several articles in the literature have discussed critical success factors (Moeuf *et al.*, 2020; Pozzi *et al.*, 2021), barriers (Raj *et al.*, 2020; Jones *et al.*, 2021), and enablers (Attaran, 2020; Agrawal & Narain, 2023) of DSC. Ghadge *et al.* (2020) highlighted 16 barriers that act as intimidating resisting forces for implementing the digital transformation of the SC. Agrawal *et al.* (2019) proposed an ISM-MICMAC (Interpretive structural modelling-Matrix multiplication cross impact applied to classification) model, depicting the hierarchical levels of the identified barriers. Agrawal and Narain (2023) proposed an ISM model, depicting a sequence in which various technological enablers of DSC should be implemented. Sony and Naik (2019), through thematic analysis of the literature, identified 10 critical success factors essential for the successful implementation of Industry 4.0 in organizations. Though several articles have discussed various aspects of DSC and Industry 4.0, few articles have conducted a survey among the organizations to gauge the perceptions of industry personnel regarding the in-depth story of the digital transformation of SC. Besides, the review of the literature has revealed that very few studies have been conducted in the context of Indian organizations. Owing to the lack of DSC research in India, this chapter attempts to identify the transformation factors pertinent to expanding the implementation of DSC in India by conducting a questionnaire-based survey to assess the current status of DTSC in Indian organizations and other issues related to it.

Methodology: Survey Design and Sampling

For the purpose of the survey, a questionnaire has been prepared through an extensive review of existing literature to know the opinions of experts. The questions were framed on a 5-point Likert scale. A total of 434 respondents were invited to participate in an online survey, and the link for filling out the online questionnaire was sent to them, out of which 19 were not delivered because of errors in email addresses, and 22 consultants refused to fill out the questionnaire as they considered the data requested classified. Subsequently, the sample size decreased to 393, out of which a total of 122 responses were received, which gives an effective response rate of 31.04%, complying with the response rate of surveys available in the literature (Chiou *et al.*, 2002; Singh *et al.*, 2006). The statistical analysis of the data has been carried out using SPSS (version 16) and MS Excel. A factor analysis has also been done to get a more focused view of the variables. To check the reliability of the data, Cronbach's coefficient, alpha (a), has been calculated.

The questionnaire was divided into two parts. The first part aimed to collect organizational demographics containing questions such as the organization's name, its type and size, business sector, and annual turnover. The second aimed to collect detailed information about current market conditions and the challenges of SCM, digital SC management and current status, its enablers, barriers, critical success factors, and expected benefits.

Reliability Analysis

To check the consistency of the data, a reliability test has been performed. The results are shown in Table 2. For data to be decisive, the value of

Table 2. Reliability analysis of the survey data.

S. No.	Constructs	Cronbach's alpha (α)
01	Market conditions	0.791
02	Supply chain challenges	0.873
03	Enablers of DSC	0.795
04	Critical Factors	0.844
05	Barriers to DSC	0.817
06	Expected benefits of DSC in processes	0.931
07	Expected benefits of DSC in products	0.906

Cronbach's alpha (α) should be more than 0.7 (Leech *et al.*, 2005). It can be observed from the table that all the scales have high reliability.

Findings of the Survey

The survey findings are presented in the following sections.

Demographic Profile of the Organizations

Figure 1 shows the characteristics of the respondent organizations. It can be observed that about 98% of the respondents are from the private sector, and only 1.7% are from the public sector. A majority of respondents (91.52%) are from large-scale organizations; 6.77% are from medium-scale organizations and 1.7% are from small-scale organizations. One of the possible reasons for the massive participation from large-scale organizations could be that digital transformation requires enormous investment to be made, and it is therefore considered a deterrent by medium- and small-scale enterprises. About 42% of respondents belong to the IT sector, followed by the automobile sector (23.9%). The remaining responses are from the fast moving consumer goods (FMCG) sector (13.55%), the e-commerce sector (10.16%), and others (10.09%) that include a few responses from the tourism and construction sectors.

Prevalent Market Conditions

Figure 2 schematically represents the prevailing market conditions ranked by the respondent organizations. The top four prevailing market

Sample Characteristics	Classification	Percentage
Organization size	Large Scale Enterprise	89.70%
	Medium Scale Enterprise	8.60%
	Small Scale Enterprise	1.70%
Organization type	Private Sector	98.30%
	Public Sector	1.70%
Business type	Software and Consultancy	42.30%
	Automobile Sector	23.90%
	FMCG Sector	13.55%
	E-Commerce	10.16%
Respondent Position	Senior management level	28.90%
	Middle management level	40.80%
	Lower management level	20.30%
Annual turnover	Over 1000 Crores	89.70%
	100 to 500 Crores	8.60%
	Upto 10 Crores	1.70%

Figure 1. Demographic profile of the surveyed organizations.

conditions (with a mean of 4 and above) as stated by respondents are: the use of the Internet changes customers' buying behavior; the growth of the business world has created tighter market competition; technology in our industry is changing rapidly; and today's customers have unique demands and preferences. These variables can be considered drivers of digital transformation (Ellis *et al.*, 2017). Penthin and Dillman (2015) advocated that about 75% of the world's total population is now able to use the Internet. This high Internet penetration has changed customers' buying habits, enabling them to access all the alternatives across the globe, which increases volatility in demand. The rapid globalization of the business world has created tighter market competition that has heightened the need to extend the SCM into a multi-tier SCM, which facilitates the sourcing and selling of products and components worldwide (Farahani *et al.*, 2017). The SC technology is developing more rapidly than ever. Dolgui and Ivanov (2022) advocated that emerging technologies can potentially transform companies' existing processes in terms of speed, efficiency, and flexibility. The high ratings for the four market conditions suggest the need for the digital transformation of the SC so that organizations can offer a better customer experience through relevant products/services and survive in the business.

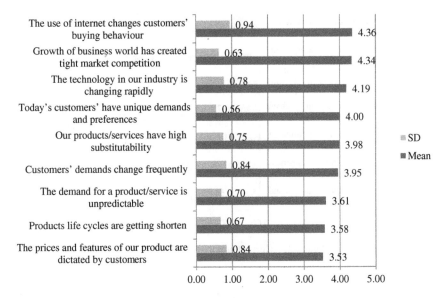

The use of internet changes customers' buying behaviour — 0.94 — 4.36

Growth of business world has created tight market competition — 0.63 — 4.34

The technology in our industry is changing rapidly — 0.78 — 4.19

Today's customers' have unique demands and preferences — 0.56 — 4.00

Our products/services have high substitutability — 0.75 — 3.98

Customers' demands change frequently — 0.84 — 3.95

The demand for a product/service is unpredictable — 0.70 — 3.61

Products life cycles are getting shorten — 0.67 — 3.58

The prices and features of our product are dictated by customers — 0.84 — 3.53

SD ▪ Mean

0.00 1.00 2.00 3.00 4.00 5.00

Figure 2.   Prevailing market conditions.

Current Supply Chain Challenges

The challenges associated with the current SC are shown in Figure 3. The four most rated challenges are: achieving flexibility in the SC, improving SC visibility, mass customization, and improving collaboration with SC partners. The other challenges with relatively lower ratings include: the standardization and automation of processes, volatility in demand and supply, and developing a new business model. Farahani *et al.* (2017) also identified these challenges of the SC, which would become a matter of concern in the 2020s. These challenges of the current SC are actually the goals of the future SC. Transforming the traditional SC into DSC will help in mitigating these challenges and achieving the desired goals (Raab & Griffin-Cryan, 2011; Schrauf & Berttram, 2016). DSC drives higher integration within the SC processes by leveraging Industry 4.0 technologies that bring about greater collaboration among SC partners, enabling an efficient flow of material, information, and finance (Tiwari, 2020). The cloud allows for greater collaboration as it enables seamless communication and sharing of information and data within the SC and with trading partners. Blockchain technology helps increase transparency throughout

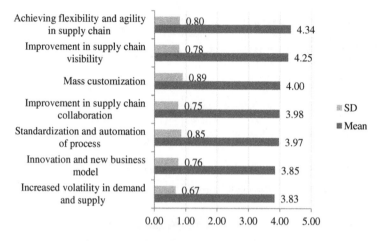

Figure 3.   Current supply chain challenges.

the SC. With 3-D printing, manufacturing will become more agile and better capable of reacting to changes in customers' demand. It also enables companies to offer customized products to individual customers at reasonable rates.

Digital Supply Chain and Current Status

The questionnaire inquired about the status of digital SC among the surveyed organizations. About 59% of respondents said that in the current market situation, digital transformation of the SC is very important, while 37% of respondents rated it as important.

Further, respondents were asked about their progress so far in their efforts toward this transformation. It is observed from Figure 4 that about 50% of respondents replied that they are struggling to develop a suitable implementation strategy or framework for the implementation of DSC. Following that, 33.8% of respondents answered that they are planning to start implementation in the near future. About 10% of respondents replied that the digital transformation strategy is well defined and is being implemented, and 6.8% respondents replied that they do not want to transform as they like where they are, which reveals that the progress of organizations is not very satisfactory. It can be inferred that most of organizations

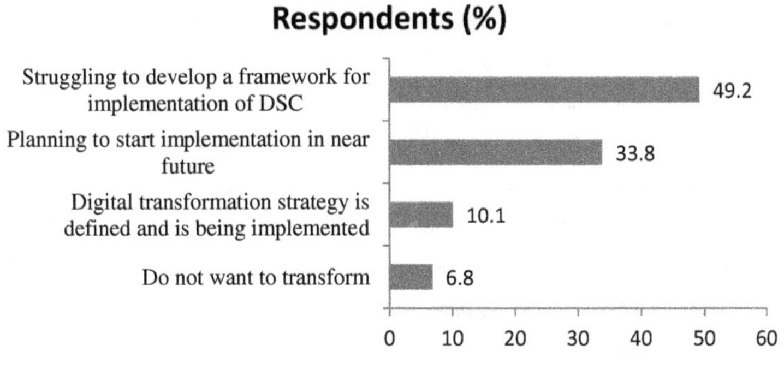

Respondents (%)

Figure 4. Progress done by organizations in implementation of DSC.

recognize the criticality of DSC for their business but are struggling to develop an implementation framework.

Enablers of DSC

A number of innovative technologies facilitating DSC are mentioned in the literature (Ardito *et al.*, 2019; Queiroz *et al.*, 2019; Attaran, 2020; Zekhnini *et al.*, 2021). Therefore, it becomes imperative to investigate the crucial and relevant technologies with respect to DSC. Figure 5 shows the rankings given by respondents to various emerging technologies enabling the digital transformation of the SC. It can be seen from Figure 9 that BDA, IoT, blockchain technology, and AI are indicated as the most crucial technologies (all having a mean of 4 and above) from the DSC perspective. The other important technologies include cloud computing, social media platforms, AR, wearable devices, 3D printing, advanced robotics, and drones or self-guided vehicles. The findings lead to the conclusion that BDA, IoT, blockchain, and AI are the most dominating technologies for the digital transformation of businesses. The broad utilization of IoT exceedingly promotes the generation of Big Data, and the effective analysis and visualization of Big Data enable data-driven decision-making that will significantly improve the adequacy of SCM (Rathore *et al.*, 2018). Therefore, for digital transformation, organizations must improve their overall data analytics capabilities, develop IoT platforms, and employ

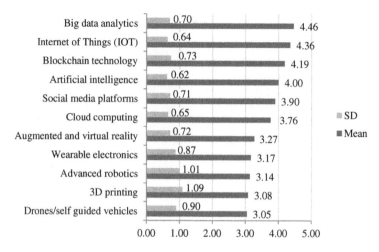

Figure 5.   Enablers of digital supply chain.

blockchain technology to enhance traceability, transparency, and communication between machines and people.

Critical Success Factors for the Digital Transformation of SC

The questionnaire then inquired about the critical success factors for the digital transformation of the SC. Critical success factors are key areas or activities that must be well implemented for the success of a project (Zhou *et al.*, 2011). Figure 6 shows respondents' rankings on different success factors for digital transformation. It can be observed from the figure that top management commitment, creating a culture of being "open to change" and adaptation, obtaining the right skills and resources, securing necessary platforms, technologies, and devices, and having an implementation framework are indicated as the most critical factors for the transformation to DSC. The other important factors include aligning initiatives with execution plans, closer collaboration with partners and suppliers, and ensuring employees understand the capabilities, urgency, and importance of DSC. The findings illustrate that multiple factors need to be considered for the successful digital transformation of the SC. The top management commitment is responsible for articulating a clear vision regarding the transformation. It exhibits the largest role in transformation in every sphere, whether

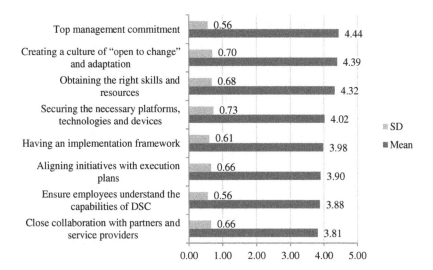

Figure 6. Critical success factors for the digital transformation of SC.

it is technological developments, infrastructure, partner selection, human resources, or capital allocation (Eder & Koch, 2018). Therefore, management must be committed to continuous improvement, as it is the most influential factor. It should formulate a clear and detailed transformation strategy, considering every factor and trade-off for optimal benefits.

Implementing the digital SC requires a paradigm shift in organizational culture. None of the changes would be realized without an accompanying "open to change" culture within the organization. The digitalization of SC requires new workforce skills and capabilities to understand all the aspects of DSC. The success of the digital transformation of SC depends on the companies' workforce, as digitization is dependent on new technologies, and new technologies require a new set of skills and capabilities within the workforce (Schlegel & Kraus, 2021). DSC requires much deeper digital knowledge and an open attitude toward emerging technologies. Organizations have to install the necessary platforms and technologies in place, as emerging technologies, such as IOT, BDA, CC, AI, blockchain, and AR, facilitate the digitalization of the SC. An implementation framework is needed for any transformation program, which provides the necessary guidelines for the realization of digital transformation. Hence, it can be concluded that focusing on these factors will help organizations successfully transform their SC to DSC.

Barriers to the Digitalization of Supply Chain

To identify the major barriers responsible for hindering the digital transformation of the SC, the respondents were asked to rate the parameters as
listed in Figure 7. It has been reported that "no sense of urgency" is the
most prominent barrier among all, which is quite obvious because of
human nature, which performs only those actions that are extremely
urgent or essential. Bonnet and Nandan (2011) advocated that it is people,
not technology, who are hindering the digitalization of the SC. People
should be aware of the criticality of digital SC and its importance in the
present scenario. So, creating a sense of urgency within people is the very
first step of any digital transformation program. "Lack of industry specific
guidelines for implementation" is another significant barrier to digital
transformation of the SC, which is quite logical as industries from different sectors (for e.g., automobile, FMCG, e-commerce, etc.) have different

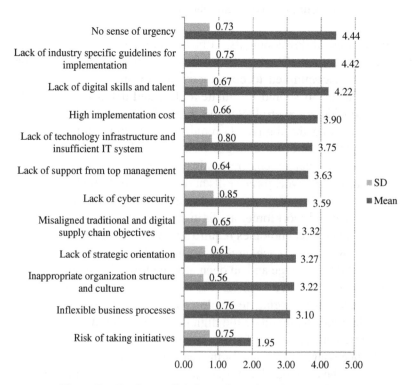

Figure 7.   Barriers to digital transformation of supply chain.

technological landscapes, different manpower requirements, and different customers. So, it is necessary to have an implementation framework specifically for industrial sectors. The available literature on DSC also concluded that there is no widely accepted framework for the adoption of DSC (Büyüközkan & Göçer, 2018; Zekhnini *et al.*, 2021). "Lack of digital skills and talent in the present workforce" is another important barrier to DSC. The literature (Bughin *et al.*, 2015; Kohnke, 2017) acknowledged a lack of digital skills and talent within the current workforce of organizations. Therefore, organizations need to develop new skills in their employees so that they become familiar with the new technologies. For example, they would require data experts with skills to refine, process, integrate, and analyze data. High implementation costs are another significant barrier to DSC, which is quite obvious because transformation to DSC would require the development of new platforms and a technological landscape that involves high implementation costs.

Recent innovations in technology enable the digital transformation of the SC. Thus, the lack of technology infrastructure is considered one of the major reasons for the limited adoption and slow growth of DSC among Indian organizations. The next considerable barriers reported by respondents include a lack of top management support and a lack of cyber security. Transformation to DSC will not be possible without the commitment of top management, and a lack of cyber security is one of the prominent barriers to DSC specified in the available literature. Pereira *et al.* (2017) mentioned that information security and the threat of losing classified data are significant hurdles while adopting advanced technologies in organizations. DSC includes more technology, more users, more transactions, and more data, which itself increases the potential for cyber security risks. Therefore, it will be imperative for organizations to have suitable strategies in place to preemptively address cyber security risks, along with the value chain, and protect data from external attacks to minimize the negative impact on operations and brand. Other considerable barriers with relatively fewer ratings reported by respondents are misaligned traditional and digital SC objectives, a lack of strategic orientation, inappropriate organizational structure and culture, and inflexible business processes. The risk of taking initiative is reported as the least important barrier by respondents. Thus, these findings have highlighted the significant barriers to the digital transformation of SC that an organization should consider while approaching the digitalization of SC.

Benefits of DSC

The potential benefits of the digital transformation of the SC have been broadly classified into two categories: product enhancement and process enhancement. Numerous benefits of DSC are mentioned in the available literature. So, the respondents were asked to rate various benefits of the digital SC under these two categories. Their responses are given in Figures 8 and 9. Higher automation has been given the highest rating. The main focus of DSC is on delivering unprecedented services and experiences to customers throughout their purchases to let them feel the difference brought about by DSCM. A higher level of automation essentially helps in achieving this objective. DSC will increase the level of

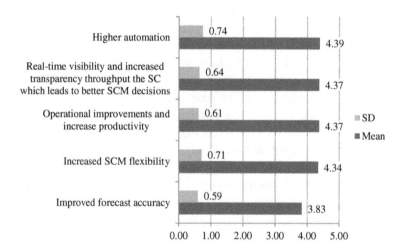

Figure 8.   Expected benefits of DSC in process enhancement.

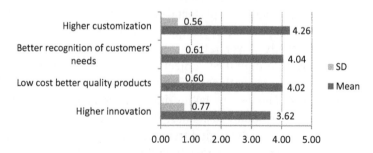

Figure 9.   Expected benefits of DSC in products enhancement.

automation by automating everything that can be automated (Choudhury *et al.*, 2021). Real-time visibility and increased transparency throughout the SC will further improve the organization's performance. DSC will drive seamless transparency, traceability, and integration within the SC. Enhanced operational efficiency and productivity, increased flexibility, low-cost better quality products, and higher customization are other highly rated benefits of DSC with a mean of 4 and above. The other benefits include an increase in market share, greater after-sales services, decentralized inventories to meet delivery time requirements, improved forecast accuracy, better recognition of customers' needs, and higher innovation. These improvements will lead to an increase in customer satisfaction, which will further result in increasing market share, profit margins, and revenue.

Hypotheses Development

The hypotheses proposed in this study are grounded on the findings of the survey. Emerging digital technologies have the potential to enhance SC processes through several transformations in the SC, such as product optimization, design process optimization, logistics optimization, and operational efficiency. The digital transformation of the SC will enhance the processes of maintenance, sales, and logistics by introducing the concepts of descriptive, predictive, and prescriptive analysis, information sharing, smart manufacturing, etc., which will ultimately lead to improved SC profitability and customer experience. Therefore, hypotheses have been developed for the following two premises: the first premise is related to process enhancement, and the second is related to product enhancement. Figure 10 presents the research model and associated hypotheses.

Process Enhancement through DSCM

Several studies (Attaran, 2020; Balakrishnan & Ramanathan, 2021; Yang *et al.*, 2021) have concluded that new digital technologies, such as IOT, BDA, CC, AI, and 3DP, are seen as promising means to improve SC processes by driving higher flexibility, transparency, traceability, automation, productivity, and reducing waste, lead times, costs, and inefficiencies. Figure 8 also depicts that higher flexibility and automation, real-time

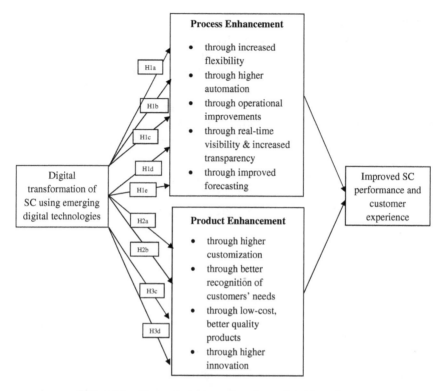

Figure 10. Research framework and associated hypotheses.

visibility, and operational improvements will lead to SC process enhancement. Thus, the following hypotheses have been developed:

H1: The digital transformation of SC facilitates process enhancement:

H1a: through increased flexibility.

H1b: through higher automation.

H1c: through operational improvements.

H1d: through real-time visibility and increased transparency.

Product Enhancement Through DSCM

Ceipek *et al.* (2020) reported that emerging digital technologies are changing products and processes along with value chains and business models. Providing innovative and customized products to fulfill every individual's differentiated and unique needs is a suitable strategy for organizations to differentiate themselves in terms of products from competitors. New technologies, such as 3D printing, enable companies to offer customized products to individual customers at reasonable rates. Social media platforms provide a channel that enables customers to interact directly with companies, where they can share their reviews of any product or service. In this way, companies get direct feedback and complaints from clients regarding their products and services, which facilitate better recognition of customers' preferences and innovation priorities (Devi & Ganguly, 2021). Moreover, DSC is always open to changes and looks to bring new innovations into processes and products to remain competitive and ensure excellence. Overall, employing new digital technologies in various SC functions can enhance the products. Figure 9 also depicts that recognition of customers' preferences, higher customization, and innovation will lead to product enhancement. Thus, the following hypotheses have been developed:

H2: The digital transformation of SC facilitates product enhancement:

H2a: Through better recognition of customers' needs and preferences.

H2b: Through higher customization.

H2c: Through innovative products.

H2d: Through low-cost, better quality products.

Hypotheses Testing

To test the assumed hypotheses, the chi-square test (χ^2 test) has been employed, as illustrated by Haddud and Khare (2020). The chi-square test has been broadly used to investigate the survey data for differences, associations, and relationships to be able to accept or reject the assumed hypotheses. It compares the response frequencies (RN) with the corresponding expected frequencies (EN) under each of the considered Likert-scale levels of agreement. The expected frequency can be determined by dividing the total number of responses (122 in this study) by the number of Likert-scale levels of agreement options used (5 in this study). On dividing 122 by 5, the result is 24.4, denoted as EN, which is used to calculate the residual values for the constructs used in the expected benefits of DSC (Figures 8 and 9). For example, the construct in Figure 8, "higher automation," has actual responses, RN, as follows: Strongly Disagree (SD = 0), Disagree (D = 1), Neutral (N = 13), Agree (A = 42), and Strongly Agree (SA = 66). Subtracting EN = 24.4 from these response frequencies gives the residual values of −24.4, −23.4, −11.4, 17.6, and 41.6, respectively. It can be observed that the highest residual value belongs to the "Strongly Agree" option. The highest residual value will be the decisive factor when selecting under which of the five categories is the majority of responses. Any examined impact under the constructs that have the highest residual value under SA, D, or N will be considered insignificant, and the item will then be considered "Not supported."

The mean values of the constructs used in the development of the hypotheses are given in Figures 8 and 9. The respondents perceived the impact of the digital transformation of SC on the examined constructs as high. Tables 3 and 4 represent the results of the chi-square test (the

Table 3. Frequencies residual values of constructs of expected benefits of DSC for process enhancement.

Constructs	Mean (N = 59)	Factor loading	χ^2 test (frequencies residual values)					Item is supported
			SD(1)	D(2)	N(3)	A(4)	SA(5)	
Higher automation	4.39	0.756	−24.4	−23.4	−11.4	17.6	41.6	Yes
Operational improvements	4.37	0.824	−24.4	−24.4	−13.4	41.6	20.6	Yes
Real-time visibility and increased transparency	4.37	0.802	−24.4	−24.4	−6.4	27.6	27.6	Yes
Increase SCM flexibility	4.34	0.847	−24.4	−23.4	−4.4	24.6	27.6	Yes
Improved forecast accuracy	3.83	0.721	−24.4	−23.4	−0.4	27.6	20.6	Yes

Table 4. Frequencies residual values of constructs of expected benefits of DSC for product enhancement.

| Constructs | Mean (N = 59) | Factor loading | χ^2 test (frequencies residual values) | | | | | Item is supported |
			SD(1)	D(2)	N(3)	A(4)	SA(5)	
Low cost better quality products/ services	4.02	0.800	−24.4	−23.4	−10.4	45.6	12.6	Yes
Higher customization	4.00	0.837	−24.4	−23.4	−16.4	37.6	26.6	Yes
Better recognition of customers' needs	3.80	0.600	−24.4	−22.4	0.6	44.6	1.6	Yes
Higher innovation	3.62	0.708	−24.4	−21.4	8.6	37.6	−0.4	Yes

frequency of residual values of the examined constructs). It can be observed from the above tables that the highest residual values for all the examined constructs come under the "Agree" or "Strongly Agree" options. Therefore, all the assumed hypotheses are accepted.

Discussion and Conclusions

The concept of SCM has witnessed many transformations (such as ERP and e-procurement) since its inception (MacCarthy *et al.*, 2016). The digital transformation of the SC is seen as the next revolution in SCM and has become a hot topic these days. Factors such as rapid technological innovations, increasing customer demand, and higher penetration of the Internet in our day-to-day lives are compelling organizations to implement DSC. Therefore, a large number of organizations are approaching toward the digital transformation of SC owing to the many benefits and competitive edge that DSC offers. However, digital transformation is a risky endeavor because it requires huge financial investments, time, and structural changes. So, before starting the implementation of DSC, organizations should be well versed with its enablers, barriers, success factors, and other parameters related to the DSC. This chapter presented the findings of a questionnaire survey, which featured the issues related to digital SC practices as followed in the cross-section of Indian industries. Many organizations have understood that new digital technologies have diffused into the market;

consequently, they have to transform accordingly to stay competitive and relevant. As of now, it seems that it is mainly the large-scale organizations facing the heat of global competition which are taking part in the digital transformation of the SC with the objective of delivering an unprecedented customer experience by offering innovative processes, products, and services. The survey has highlighted the most promising enablers, drivers, critical success factors, and barriers to DSC. The survey has also enumerated various benefits associated with the digital SC, which can motivate more organizations to transform their SCs. Also, this study empirically verified the effect of emerging technologies on SC processes and products. The testing of hypotheses shows that the digital transformation of SC will positively impact various factors and strategic aspects, such as SCM flexibility, real-time visibility, automation, operational efficiency, customization, innovation, product quality and price, recognition of customers' demands, decentralized inventories, and new product development. These will facilitate product enhancement and process enhancement, which ultimately leads to improved SC profitability and customer experience.

In a country like India with a huge population, opportunities for business are immense. Companies need to understand the needs and preferences of customers, which can be effectively done by deploying innovative digital solutions in various SC operations. Organizations that can grab the opportunities offered by the digital transformation of the SC as quickly as possible will acquire the much-needed competitive edge required to last long in the market.

References

Agrawal, P. & Narain, R. (2023). Analysis of enablers for the digitalization of supply chain using an interpretive structural modelling approach. *International Journal of Productivity and Performance Management*, ahead-of-print.

Agrawal, P. & Narain, R. (2018). Digital supply chain management: An overview. *IOP Conference Series: Materials Science and Engineering*, 455(1), 012074.

Agrawal, P., Narain, R., & Ullah, I. (2019). Analysis of barriers in implementation of digital transformation of supply chain using interpretive structural modelling approach. *Journal of Modelling in Management*, 15(1), 297–317.

Ardito, L., Petruzzelli, A. M., Panniello, U., & Garavelli, A. C. (2019). Towards Industry 4.0: Mapping digital technologies for supply chain management-marketing integration. *Business Process Management Journal*, 25(2), 323–346.

Attaran, M. (2020). Digital technology enablers and their implications for supply chain management. *Supply Chain Forum: An International Journal*, 21(3), 158–172.

Balakrishnan, A. S. & Ramanathan, U. (2021). The role of digital technologies in supply chain resilience for emerging markets' automotive sector. *Supply Chain Management: An International Journal*, 26(6), 654–671.

Bonnet, D. & Nandan, P. (2011). Transform to the Power of Digital. Capgemini Consulting, 2-5. https://www.capgemini.com/wp-content/uploads/2017/07/Transform_to_the_Power_of_Digital.pdf (Accessed October 24, 2018).

Bughin, J., Holley, A., & Mellbye, A. (2015). Cracking the digital code; mcKinsey global survey results. https://www.mckinsey.com/business-functions/mckinsey-digital/our-insights/cracking-the-digital-code (Accessed June 10, 2018).

Büyüközkan, G. & Göçer, F. (2018). Digital supply chain: Literature review and a proposed framework for future research. *Computers in Industry*, 97, 157–177.

Calatayud, A., Mangan, J., & Christopher, M. (2019). The self-thinking supply chain. *Supply Chain Management: An International Journal*, 24(1), 22–38.

Ceipek, R., Hautz, J., Petruzzelli, A. M., De Massis, A., & Matzler, K. (2020). A motivation and ability perspective on engagement in emerging digital technologies: The case of Internet of Things solutions. *Long Range Planning*, 54(5), 101991.

Chiou, J. S., Wu, L. Y., & Hsu, J. C. (2002). The adoption of form postponement strategy in a global logistics system: The case of Taiwanese information technology industry. *Journal of Business Logistics*, 23(1), 107–124.

Choudhury, A., Behl, A., Sheorey, P. A., & Pal, A. (2021). Digital supply chain to unlock new agility: A TISM approach. *Benchmarking: An International Journal*, 28(6), 2075–2109.

da Silva, V. L., Kovaleski, J. L., & Pagani, R. N. (2019). Technology transfer in the supply chain oriented to industry 4.0: A literature review. *Technology Analysis & Strategic Management*, 31(5), 546–562.

Devi, Y. & Ganguly, K. (2021). Social media in operations and supply chain management: A systematic literature review to explore the future. *Operations and Supply Chain Management: An International Journal*, 14(2), 232–248.

Dolgui, A. & Ivanov, D. (2022). 5G in digital supply chain and operations management: Fostering flexibility, end-to-end connectivity and real-time visibility through internet-of-everything. *International Journal of Production Research*, 60(2), 442–451.

Dougados, M. & Felgendreher, B. (2016). The current and future state of digital supply chain transformation: A cross-industry study with 337 executives in over 20 countries reveals expectations on digital transformation. https://www.supplychainquarterly.com/ext/resources/files/pdfs/whitepapers/gtexus_digital_transformation.pdf?1589233644 (Accessed June 10, 2018).

Eder, F. & Koch, S. (2018). Critical success factors for the implementation of business intelligence systems, *International Journal of Business Intelligence Research*, 9(2), 27–46.

Ellis, S., Knickle, K., Veronesi, L., & Brown, V. (2017). Digital transformation drives supply chain restructuring imperative. *International Data Corporation.* https://www.opentext.*com*/file_source/OpenText/en_US/PDF/opentext-idc-digital-transformation-supply-chain.pdf (Accessed March 2, 2018).

Farahani, P., Meier, C., & Wilke, J. (2017). Digital supply chain management agenda for the automotive supplier industry. In: Oswald, G., Kleinemeier, M. (Eds.), *Shaping the Digital Enterprise* (pp. 157–172). Cham: Springer.

Fatorachian, H. and Kazemi, H. (2021). Impact of Industry 4.0 on supply chain performance. *Production Planning & Control*, 32(1), 63–81.

Garay-Rondero, C. L., Martinez-Flores, J. L., Smith, N. R., Morales, S. O. C., & Aldrette-Malacara, A. (2019). Digital supply chain model in Industry 4.0. *Journal of Manufacturing Technology Management*, 31(5), 887–933.

Ghadge, A., Kara, M. E., Moradlou, H., & Goswami, M. (2020). The impact of Industry 4.0 implementation on supply chains. *Journal of Manufacturing Technology Management*, 31(4), 669–686.

Haddud, A. & Khare, A. (2020). Digitalizing supply chains potential benefits and impact on lean operations. *International Journal of Lean Six Sigma*, 11(4), 731–765.

Horváth, D. & Szabó, R. Z. (2019). Driving forces and barriers of Industry 4.0: Do multinational and small and medium-sized companies have equal opportunities? *Technological Forecasting and Social Change*, 146, 119–132.

Jones, M. D., Hutcheson, S., & Camba, J. D. (2021). Past, present, and future barriers to digital transformation in manufacturing: A review. *Journal of Manufacturing Systems*, 60, 936–948.

Kayikci, Y. (2018). Sustainability impact of digitization in logistics. *Procedia Manufacturing*, 21, 782–789.

Kinnett, J. (2015). Creating a digital supply chain: Monsanto's Journey. In *Washington: 7th Annual BCTIM Industry Conference.* https://www.slide share.net/BCTIM/creating-a-digital-supply-chain-monsantos-journey (Accessed November 30, 2020).

Koh, L., Orzes, G., & Jia, F. J. (2019). The fourth industrial revolution (Industry 4.0): Technologies disruption on operations and supply chain management. *International Journal of Operations & Production Management*, 39(6/7/8), 817–828.

Kohnke, O. (2017). It's not just about technology: The people side of digitization. In: Oswald, G., Kleinemeier, M. (Eds.), *Shaping the Digital Enterprise* (pp. 69–91). Cham: Springer.

Leech, N. L., Barrett, K. C., & Morgan, G. A. (2005). *SPSS for Intermediate and Statistics: Use and Interpretation* (2nd edn.). New Jersey: Lawrence Erlbaum Associates, Inc. Publishers.

MacCarthy, B. L., Blome, C., Olhager, J., Srai, J. S., & Zhao, X. (2016). Supply chain evolution — Theory, concepts and science, *International Journal of Operations & Production Management*, 36(12), 1696–1718.

Moeuf, A., Lamouri, S., Pellerin, R., Tamayo-Giraldo, S., Tobon-Valencia, E., & Eburdy, R. (2020). Identification of critical success factors, risks and opportunities of Industry 4.0 in SMEs. *International Journal of Production Research*, 58(5), 1384–1400.

Nasiri, M., Ukko, J., Saunila, M., & Rantala, T. (2020). Managing the digital supply chain the role of smart technologies. *Technovation*, 96, 102121.

Panda, S. & Rath, S.K. (2021). How information technology capability influences organizational agility: Empirical evidences from Indian banking industry. *Journal of Indian Business Research*, 13(4), 564–585.

Penthin, S. & Dillman, R. (2015). Digital supply chain management, Germany, https://www.bearingpoint.com/files/BearingPoint-Digital-Supply-Chain-Management.pdf&download=0 (Accessed October 24, 2018).

Pereira, T., Barreto, L., & Amaral, A. (2017). Network and information security challenges within Industry 4.0 paradigm, *Procedia Manufacturing*, 13, 1253–1260.

Pozzi, R., Rossi, T., & Secchi, R. (2021). Industry 4.0 technologies: Critical success factors for implementation and improvements in manufacturing companies, *Production Planning & Control*, 34(2), 1–21.

Queiroz, M. M., Pereira, S. C. F., Telles, R., & Machado, M. C. (2019). Industry 4.0 and digital supply chain capabilities: A framework for understanding digitalisation challenges and opportunities. *Benchmarking: An International Journal*, 28(5), 1761–1782.

Raab, M. & Griffin-Cryan, B. (2011). *Digital Transformation of Supply Chains: Creating Value–when Digital Meets Physical*. Capgemini Consulting. https://www.capgemini.com/wp-content/uploads/2017/07/Digital_Transformation_of_Supply_Chains.pdf (Accessed October 24, 2018).

Raj, A., Dwivedi, G., Sharma, A., de Sousa Jabbour, A. B. L., & Rajak, S. (2020). Barriers to the adoption of industry 4.0 technologies in the manufacturing sector: An inter-country comparative perspective. *International Journal of Production Economics*, 224, 107546.

Rathore, M. M., Paul, A., Hong, W. H., Seo, H., Awan, I., & Saeed, S. (2018). Exploiting IoT and big data analytics: Defining smart digital city using real-time urban data. *Sustainable cities and Society*, 40, 600–610.

Schlegel, D. & Kraus, P. (2021). Skills and competencies for digital transformation — A critical analysis in the context of robotic process automation. *International Journal of Organizational Analysis*, ahead-of-print.

Schrauf, S. & Berttram, P. (2016). Industry 4.0: How digitization makes the supply chain more efficient, agile, and customer-focused. *Strategy and Pwc*. https://www.strategyand.pwc.com/media/file/Industry4.0.pdf (Accessed November 30, 2018).

Singh, A., Narain, R., & Yadav, R. C. (2006). A survey on relationships and cultural issues in supply chain management practices in Indian organisations. *International Journal of Services and Operations Management*, 2(3), 256–278.

Sony, M. & Naik, S. (2019). Key ingredients for evaluating Industry 4.0 readiness for organizations: A literature review. *Benchmarking: An International Journal*, 27(7), 2213–2232.

Tiwari, S. (2020). Supply chain integration and Industry 4.0: A systematic literature review. *Benchmarking: An International Journal*, 28(3), 990–1030.

Tjahjono, B., Esplugues, C., Ares, E., & Pelaez, G. (2017). What does industry 4.0 mean to supply chain? *Procedia Manufacturing*, 13, 1175–1182.

Yang, M., Fu, M., & Zhang, Z. (2021). The adoption of digital technologies in supply chains: Drivers, process and impact, *Technological Forecasting and Social Change*, 169, 120795.

Zekhnini, K., Cherrafi, A., Bouhaddou, I., Benghabrit, Y., & Garza-Reyes, J. A. (2021). Supply chain management 4.0: A literature review and research framework. *Benchmarking: An International Journal*, 28(2), 465–501.

Zhou, Q., Huang, W., & Zhang, Y. (2011). Identifying critical success factors in emergency management using a fuzzy DEMATEL method. *Safety Science*, 49(2), 243–252.

Chapter 4

Paths to Digital Transformation in Services Marketing

Sasmita Kant Maurya

Modulyst Learning
Pune, Maharashtra, India

sasmita.maurya@gmail.com

Abstract

Technological innovations and interventions are guiding today's business environment. Disruptions in existing business models have enabled newer forms of production and consumption trends. Applications of new-age technology like artificial intelligence and blockchain in the services sector are vastly visible. However, the path to digital transformation of different services marketing environments is unclear.

This chapter uses multiple case studies (from data available in the public domain) of four service companies from India to help understand the digital transformation strategies of service companies in general. It examines the digital transformation of marketing of services given their unique characteristics of heterogeneity (service offered by other staff will be perceived differently by customers), intangibility (service cannot be owned or seen, it is only experienced), inseparability (service is produced and consumed at the same time), perishability (service experience cannot be stored), demand fluctuation and service quality measurement.

Finally, it draws on the Indian ethos and wisdom to suggest a comprehensive framework to pull together a digital transformation program for services marketing with organizational and technological implications.

Keywords: Digital disruption, customer-centricity, Indian ethos, artificial intelligence, case studies.

Introduction

Marketing of Services and Services Sector

Services marketing as a discipline focuses on service delivery and promotion. The concept of services as a separate entity gained widespread recognition in the 20th century as the old businesses and traders recognized the importance of offering customer-centric services. Founded in 1852, Marshall Field's in Chicago was one of the first and most service-oriented department stores in the United States. Harry Gordon Selfridge, a retailer from Wisconsin was a popular figure at the store, who coined this phrase: *"The customer is always right"* (bbc.com). In 1909, he founded his own department store called Selfridges in London with the aim to set new standards in the business world by being creative as well as unconventional to offer extraordinary customer experiences. His vision was to create not just a shop but also a social space where everyone was welcome.

Similarly, Choice Hotels, the first hotel chain that opened in 1939, established specific service standards to meet customer needs and expectations. In subsequent years, this chain became the first in the hotel industry to offer 24-hour desk service, guaranteed reservations, toll-free reservation system, and many other services for the guests or customers. By this time, other service businesses such as restaurants and transportation companies had also realized the importance of promoting and marketing their services to attract and retain customers.

The services sector is a significant part of most modern economies and includes a wide range of industries, such as real estate, healthcare, education, finance, tourism, hospitality, and retail. Many countries have been witnessing significant growth in this sector. According to a 2019 report of the World Trade Organization, the share of services in the global trade has seen a rise of almost 50% in just two decades: from 9% in 1970, it went up to 20% in 2018.

Three major factors have been contributing to the growth of the services sector. These are listed as follows:

(a) The increasing importance of knowledge-based industries, such as finance, technology, and consulting has led to growth in these business services.
(b) The digital revolution has made it easier for services companies to scale up their operations more efficiently and with better productivity. This has also led to the growth of digital marketing services along with Internet-based companies, such as Uber, Amazon, and Airbnb.
(c) A shift toward a service-based economy is another factor for the growth of the services sector. The production and exchange of goods are deemed less important than the provision of services. This shift is due to an increasing demand for personalized and high-quality services.

Overall, the growth of the services sector has had a significant impact on the global economy and will likely continue to do so in the future. Meanwhile, the concept of services marketing has evolved. In the 1950s and 1960s, the idea of focusing on intangible services in marketing took shape. Services marketing framework started building on the pillars of customer relationship management, service quality management, and service design and delivery. This shift happened because we realized that apart from intangibility, services have their own characteristics: these cannot be stored and are offered in real time, by real people, hence one experiences heterogeneity in service delivery.

Gronroos (2007) has identified three basic characteristics of services:

(a) Services are processes that consist of a series of activities.
(b) Services are mostly produced and consumed simultaneously.
(c) The customer is a co-producer of the service to some extent.

The characteristics listed above imply that marketing of services should engage customers at all levels, starting from understanding their needs and expectations. The companies have been strategizing accordingly, and today, services marketing is a well-established discipline that is used by businesses of all sizes and in a wide range of industries. It involves a variety of strategies and tactics, including advertising, promotion, pricing, and customer service. It has been designed to attract and retain customers by building brand loyalty.

Digital Transformation in Business Operations

More recently, the year 2020 began with radical shifts in how businesses operate. With the COVID-19 pandemic, most nations imposed lockdowns, and we embraced technology by adopting work-from-home, online classes, video streaming, and social media feeds and chats. Technology has transformed how people consume services and businesses engage with their customers. So, how do we understand digital transformation?

When an organization initiates data and technology-driven foundational change in delivering value to its customers, it is said to be undergoing a digital transformation.

According to George Westerman, author of *Leading Digital: Turning Technology into Business Transformation*, digital transformation implies radical rethinking in businesses' use of technology, processes, and human resources. The use of technology leads to a fundamental change in business performance (Boulton, 2019). It is vital to embark on this journey to reap maximum business benefits.

Let us understand the relevance of transformation in businesses by turning the pages of business history. In the 1970s, when Swiss watch companies were slow in responding to challenges from Japanese watch companies and did not redesign/reengineer quickly enough, from manufacturing mechanical watches to digital watches, they lost a large chunk of their world market share (Glasmeier, 1991). In contrast, IBM introduced IBM 5150, a personal computer (PC), in 1981, which was not only much smaller in size but also much cheaper and faster than its mainframe computers, for which it was known. This transformation story is inspiring because IBM was a large, successful, legacy company. Nevertheless, it could explore beyond its "business-as-usual" approach to roll out a top-quality product in just one year. Thus, the history of digital transformation is entwined with the philosophy of innovation-driven business.

Joseph Schumpeter, an Austrian economist, suggested an innovation-driven business cycle where a business needs to innovate while moving along a route of "new combinations of explicit knowledge" and that "route" has the following critical "stops" (Figure 1).

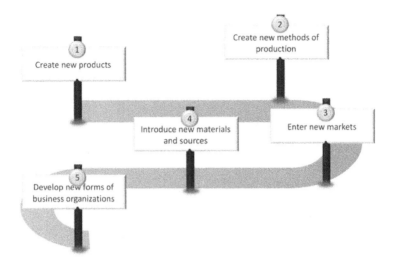

Figure 1.   The route of innovation.

Source: Adapted from Dekkers *et al.* (2014).

The "Route of Innovation" ends with developing new forms of business organizations. The reality is not different as one can easily spot or experience changes in how businesses operate. Think of how you booked a cab, watched television, or shopped for groceries a decade ago. Most of the old ways of conducting business have experienced disruption.

Disruption and Disruptive Technologies

Over the years, many leading companies lost their status as industry leaders when the market or technologies changed. Most of the time, the loss in leader status happened because the incumbent legacy companies failed to invest in new technology exploration. Bower and Christensen (1995) suggest a fundamental reason for this failure as a paradox: Successful companies stay close to their customers and rarely commercialize new technologies that do not immediately meet the needs of their existing customers. These new technologies that are accepted and valued only in new markets or in novel applications are known as disruptive technologies.

One can assess any disruptive technology by tracking its performance over some time. If its progress is faster than the existing market's demand for performance improvement, then the said technology, even if unable to

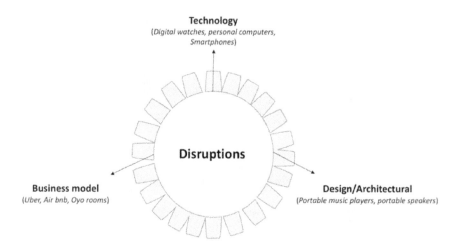

Technology
(*Digital watches, personal computers, Smartphones*)

Disruptions

Business model
(*Uber, Air bnb, Oyo rooms*)

Design/Architectural
(*Portable music players, portable speakers*)

Figure 2.   Forms of disruptions.

address the needs of existing customers today, may be able to do so tomorrow, making it a strategically critical investment. The use of new technology leads to disruption, whereby a business with fewer resources successfully challenges established incumbent organizations (Christensen *et al.*, 2015). A report by Boston Consulting Group (BCG) (July 2019) states that only two of the top 10 global companies by market capitalization have been able to maintain their positions in the last decade (Reeves & Whittaker, 2019).

Thus, disruption has been referred to as a natural product of market economics. Any disruptive strategy is often associated with unexpectedness, where any change in the larger environment of technology, infrastructure, or consumer preference propositions a profitable new business model (Hagel *et al.*, 2015) (Figure 2). Reeves and Whittaker (2019) report that incumbents are conscious of the mounting impact of technological disruptions, hence they are adopting digital transformation as a strategic tool to manage any threats arising due to disruptions.

A World Economic Forum (WEF) study surveyed 2000 companies in 26 countries. One of the findings was that 72% of these companies would have digitization at advanced levels by 2020 (Botha & Theron, 2016). Klaus Schwab of WEF has referred to businesses in the digital age as Industry 4.0 or the Fourth Industrial Revolution because an array of new technologies can now bring together our biological, physical, and digital worlds. Evidence of dramatic shifts is visible in intelligent robots,

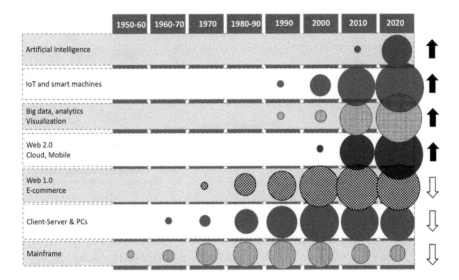

Figure 3. Cumulative capability of technologies.

Source: Adapted from Accenture's report on Digital Transformation in Industry, January 2016.

self-driving cars, genetic editing, on-demand additive manufacturing, and real-time visibility of invoices and payments to all stakeholders. Billions of people are connected through digital networks, and organizations are experiencing incremental as well as radical improvements in their efficiencies with the rise of the next generation of digital technologies, such as Big Data, Artificial Intelligence, Machine Learning, and Blockchain.

After almost 40 years of exponential increase in computing and processing power, there is astonishing progress in technological capabilities, and their cost is also decreasing. With improved and faster computing power and plummeting cost, the cumulative capacity of a combination of technologies (Figure 3) is meeting world demand with further sophistication leading to an acceleration in the pace of change (Accenture report, 2016). Figure 3 also indicates the declining impact of early technologies like mainframe and client-server.

Digital Transformation in Industries

As broader access to technology for the masses gains traction, organizations across industries have been making strategic changes in their

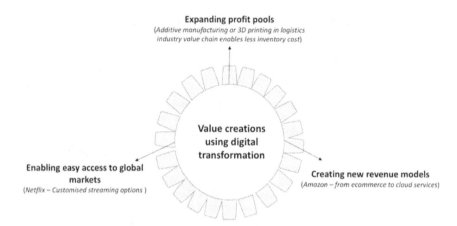

Figure 4.   A general approach to value creation through digital transformation.

Source: Adapted from Accenture's report on Digital Transformation in Industry, January 2016.

business models and long-term goals and objectives. A general approach to value creation by businesses has been expanding their profit pools,[1] creating new revenue models, and enabling easy access to global markets (Accenture Report, 2016) (Figure 4).

The digital initiatives of businesses have been focusing either on improving growth, efficiency, or both. Figure 5 summarizes the findings of a study by Accenture, which lists the nature of a few such initiatives.

Thus, digital transformation entails a collaborative ecosystem involving different teams and functions and external stakeholders of an organization. Wald *et al.* (2019) of BCG have suggested five rules of digital strategy (Figure 6) which provide a broad understanding and roadmap for incumbents looking at digital transformation.

In the edited book, *Strategic Digital Transformation: A Results-Driven Approach* (edited by Fenton *et al.*, 2019), Griggs *et al.* (2019) have explained the HINGE model based on the collective experience from their digital transformation projects (Figure 7). This model enables businesses to break up their mega problems into multiple HINGE cycles for faster results. In a recent podcast, *Digital Transformation: One Discovery at a Time*, hosted by *Harvard Business Review*, Rita McGrath, a strategy

---

[1]Gadiesh and Gilbert (1998) define a profit pool as the total profits earned in an industry at all points along its value chain.

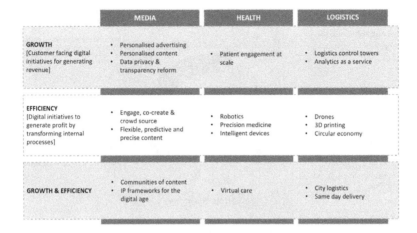

Figure 5. Focus of digital initiatives in three industries of the services sector.

Source: Adapted from Accenture's report on Digital Transformation in Industry, January 2016.

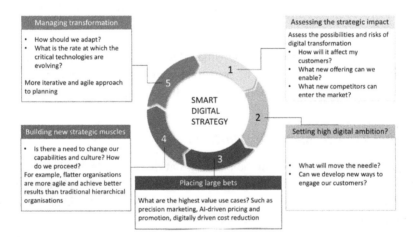

Figure 6. Smart digital strategy (Wald *et al.*, 2019).

Source: Adapted from BCG Analysis and The Five Rules of Digital Strategy.

expert, has given a similar suggestion. The COVID-19 pandemic has seen a colossal shift in employee and consumer behavior, and many non-digital-economy natives are forced to adopt digital business models. McGrath suggests the incremental building of their digital capabilities in a step-by-step manner, allowing the businesses to absorb more minor changes along the path.

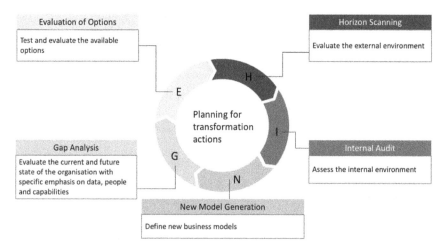

Figure 7. HINGE Digital Transformation Model (Heinze *et al.*, 2018 cited by Griggs *et al.*, 2019).

Source: Adapted from Strategic Digital Transformation: A Results-Driven Approach, 2019.

The HINGE model, like the Smart Digital Strategy, emphasizes an analysis of the current state of organizational capabilities and resources for creative definitions of new business (digital) models.

Digital Transformation in Marketing

Experts have acknowledged the bearing that disruptive technologies have had/will have on the marketing function. Erevelles *et al.* (2016) have proposed a conceptual framework to explain the impact of Big Data on marketing, while Pagani and Pardo (2017) examined the adoption of digital technologies in the B2B marketing space. Peter Gloor's work in Competitive Advantage through Collaborative Innovation Networks (COINS) has provided evidence of how creative collaboration, knowledge sharing, and social networking can be leveraged to grow better customer relations and achieve other successes (Gloor, 2006).

Digitally mature companies apply the right mix of all available digital technologies in the social, mobile, analytics and cloud space to reach out to their customers in their journey of digital consumer decision-making. Vassileva (2017) has given three stages of digital transformation in marketing: Activate, Adapt, and Anticipate. Based on these stages, the

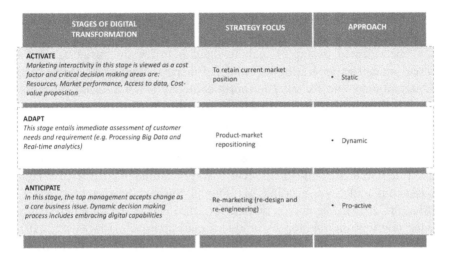

STAGES OF DIGITAL TRANSFORMATION	STRATEGY FOCUS	APPROACH
ACTIVATE *Marketing interactivity in this stage is viewed as a cost factor and critical decision making areas are: Resources, Market performance, Access to data, Cost-value proposition*	To retain current market position	• Static
ADAPT *This stage entails immediate assessment of customer needs and requirement (e.g. Processing Big Data and Real-time analytics)*	Product-market repositioning	• Dynamic
ANTICIPATE *In this stage, the top management accepts change as a core business issue. Dynamic decision making process includes embracing digital capabilities*	Re-marketing (re-design and re-engineering)	• Pro-active

Figure 8. Marketing 4.0 (Stages in digital transformation).

Source: Adapted from Marketing 4.0: How technologies transform marketing organization (Vassileva, 2017).

transformation approach of incumbents could be static, dynamic, and proactive, respectively (Figure 8).

Digitization has enabled the designing of novel practices to provide added value to customers and new opportunities to generate revenue (Skylar *et al.*, 2019). Businesses need to foster service-centricity to reap the most benefits of digitization.

Digital Transformation in Services Marketing

To investigate the digital transformation in the marketing of services, let us look at four examples of services marketing from India for a better understanding of complex social units with multiple variables. India not only has a billion consumers with a multicultural and multilingual base but also has a long business history with evidence of trade and commerce dating back to ancient civilizations. Throughout its history, India has been a major player in the global economy, and its businesses have played a significant role in shaping the country's economic development. In recent decades, India's economy has undergone significant transformation, with the country becoming a major player in the global economy. The services sector has become the largest contributor to India's gross domestic product (GDP).

The selected examples include incumbent legacy businesses from three industries operating in India: Financial Services, Media and Entertainment, and Retail. The fourth company is not a legacy business, but it is from the health sector, which, according to IDC research (Reinsel *et al.*, 2018), is expected to grow at the rate of 36% (2018–2025 CAGR), and it had featured in dataquest.com (Sharma, 2015).

Three of the selected businesses (from the Financial Services, Media and Entertainment, and Health sectors) were featured in an article on data-quest.com under the heading "11 Digital Success Stories from India" (Sharma, 2015). The choice of case for retail was based on a newspaper interview that highlighted its unique digital approach (Malwiya, 2019). The cases are compared using the Marketing 4.0 framework, focusing on the "Anticipate" stage of digital transformation, where the approach is proactive (Figure 8).

Case 1: Kotak Mahindra Bank

Kotak Mahindra Bank was established in 2003 when the parent company, Kotak Mahindra Finance Ltd., got the banking license from the Reserve Bank of India.

One of the key drivers of Kotak Mahindra Bank's digital transformation has been the need to stay competitive in a rapidly evolving financial services market. The bank has quickly embraced new technologies, such as mobile banking and digital payments, to provide customers with the latest and most convenient banking services. This has helped the bank differentiate itself from its competitors, providing customers with a more seamless and efficient banking experience.

In 2014, Kotak Mahindra Bank launched KayPay, a money transfer service (KayPay). The service was available to users through social media platforms, and the payee did not need to have an existing account with the bank. This service was launched to enable people to easily make utility payments, recharges, money transfers, or donations. This was stated to be a first-of-its-kind real-time funds transfer platform.

The bank had earlier launched a digital product called Jifi for better customer engagement, which is no longer available. Currently, it offers e-commerce and m-commerce shopping experiences to its customers, as more than 90% of savings account customer transactions have moved

Exhibit 1.   Keya, the virtual assistant for smart banking at Kotak Mahindra Bank.
Source: Adapted from Website of Kotak.

online through net banking or mobile banking. Mobile banking being more common, it has been offering simplified payment options without compromising on security through services like mail money and message money. Its Artificial Intelligence (AI) powered virtual assistant Keya answers banking queries round the clock.

Finally, Kotak Mahindra Bank's digital transformation has focused on customer engagement and experience. The bank has sought to understand its customers' needs and preferences, and to use this information to develop new and innovative services that meet their needs. This has included the use of data analytics and machine learning, as well as regular customer surveys, in order to gather insights and feedback on its digital services.

Case 2: Yash Raj Films

Yash Raj Films (YRF) is one of India's largest and most successful film production and distribution companies. Founded in 1970, YRF has produced hundreds of successful films and is widely regarded as one of the most innovative and dynamic film companies in India. A 50-year-old legacy business in film production, it is the only privately held, vertically integrated studio in India with around 80 films in its portfolio. It controls almost every aspect of the film value chain from production to post-production (domestic and international distribution, music and home entertainment, marketing, designing, licensing, merchandising, talent management, brand partnerships, music studios, film studios, and digital).

In recent years, YRF has embraced digital transformation to stay ahead of the curve in a rapidly changing media landscape. This case study explores YRF's digital transformation journey and the key strategies and technologies that have helped the company succeed.

One of the key drivers of YRF's digital transformation has been the need to stay competitive in a rapidly evolving media landscape. With the rise of digital platforms and the increasing importance of online distribution channels, YRF has quickly embraced new technologies to reach and engage audiences in new and innovative ways. This has included the development of its own digital platforms as well as partnerships with leading digital media companies.

It activated its digital-first strategy by digitizing the film release campaigns and using catalog content promotion methods where it reaches out to audiences at all digital touchpoints, such as social media, video streaming services, and its website. It releases movie assets online, shifting from

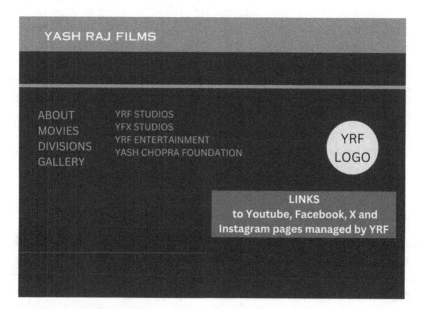

Exhibit 2.   Yash Raj Film's presence on social media platforms, YouTube, Facebook, X (previously Twitter) and Instagram.

Source: Adapted from YRF Website.

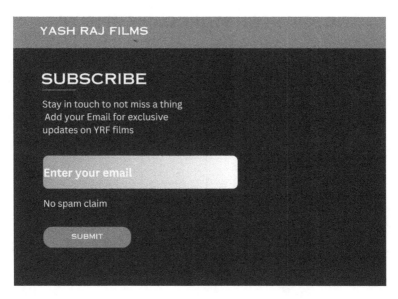

Exhibit 3.   Yash Raj Films' attempt to engage the website visitors.

Source: Adapted from YRF Website.

hosting grand launches and allowing for real-time analytics based on views or comments on any asset, such as a movie trailer or song. It uses the data generated thus to tweak the marketing strategies and strategize marketing approaches for business decision-making. It has been using the digital ecosystem to open newer avenues and reach new geographies. Its social media channels/pages on YouTube, Facebook, X (previously Twitter), and Instagram have millions of subscribers.

Case 3: Decathlon

Decathlon is a sporting goods retailer from France with 1500 stores in 49 countries. With more than 75 stores in India, it is the second largest single-brand retailer after Xiaomi, and it opened its first store in the country in 2009 (Pahuja, 2020). Decathlon used digital technology to launch the concept of Phygital[2] to provide a hassle-free shopping experience (Kaila, 2018).

One of the key benefits of Decathlon's phygital stores in India is the ability to offer customers a much wider range of products than traditional

---

[2]Read more about Phygital at https://awabot.com/en/in-a-phygital-world/.

DECATHLON STORE DAILY UPDATE

KARNATAKA

STORE NAME	QTY	STATUS	TIMINGS	DRIVE THROUGH

Exhibit 4. The facility to check or locate a physical Decathlon store.

Source: Adapted from Website of Decathlon India.

brick-and-mortar stores. With the help of digital kiosks, customers can access a vast virtual store and view products unavailable in the physical store. In many stores abroad, customers can also use interactive displays to learn more about products and how to use them, which can be especially helpful for those new to a particular sport or activity. Whether this service is available in India is not clear at present.

The Phygital stores have self-checkout counters where customers can scan and pay directly from the Decathlon app, thus providing a hassle-free shopping experience. The retail store chain has combined physical with digital to design *Phygital* to provide a seamless customer experience. The retail chain plans to use multiple cloud platforms and the Internet of Things (IoT) inside the store, where customers can find the right products easily.

Case 4: Nightingales Home Health Services

Established in 1996, Nightingales offers a range of more than 28 services, such as doctor's consultation at home, physiotherapy, caregivers, ICU care at home, and speech and language therapy. It has services in three cities in India (Bengaluru, Hyderabad, and Mumbai) at present and has serviced more than five lakh patients/customers with its team of 1,100 plus medical and paramedical experts.

Delivering Smiles Everyday

Exhibit 5. The interactive website of Nightingales Home Health Services.

Source: Adapted from www.nightingales.in.

Exhibit 6. The LIVE session on a social media group, by an expert.

Source: Adapted from https://www.facebook.com/NightingalesTheHomeHealthSpecialist/.

It has used digital technology for promotions and to enable process improvement where caregivers do not make any manual entries, eliminating any chances of human error. The website and social media campaigns on LinkedIn, Facebook, YouTube, and X (previously Twitter) focus on images of health camps, health issues, and educative videos on health tips and diseases.

The highlight of their digital strategy is that they have integrated the vital signs measurement in smart devices from third-party vendors into their app, and the vitals are available on the patients' app too for records. The app optimizes the routes of caregivers (through mobile devices) to enable more patient visits.

Another key aspect of Nightingale Health Services' approach is its focus on patient-centered care. The company has sought to understand the needs and preferences of its patients and to use this information to design and deliver medical services that meet their needs. This has included the development of patient-centered care plans and the use of patient feedback and regular surveys to continuously improve its services.

Learnings on Services Marketing Strategies

We can summarize the learnings on the services marketing strategies of the four examples discussed as follows:

- In the case of Kotak Mahindra Bank, they have proactively launched digital services like KayPay and Keya to provide a hassle-free customer journey. Its digital transformation journey is a great example of how a large and established financial institution can successfully embrace digital transformation to remain competitive and relevant in a rapidly changing financial services market. By focusing on innovation, security, and customer engagement, Kotak Mahindra Bank has been able to stay ahead of the curve and provide customers with a range of digital services that meet their needs and expectations.
- YRF have digitized their films and are using their social media pages/ channels to promote new releases and monetize (via advertising revenue) the old films by sharing their clippings. This approach to digital transformation has ensured that the production company stays relevant and immune to newer forms of competition, such as Netflix, Amazon Prime Video, and other OTT platforms.
- Decathlon has designed its service, the Phygital store, with customer focus at its core. Its phygital stores in India are also helping the company reduce costs and increase efficiency. By leveraging technology and data, Decathlon can track sales and customer behavior in real time,

which can help the company to make more informed decisions about inventory and staffing. Additionally, using digital kiosks and other technologies can help streamline the shopping experience, reducing wait times and increasing customer satisfaction.

- Similarly, Nightingales' app-based approach to service delivery not only helps in efficient operations but also creates convenience for its users to keep track of their vitals — a customer-focused approach. One of the biggest challenges facing Nightingales Health Services would be the need to provide high-quality care in a cost-effective and sustainable way. In order to address this challenge, the company has to be proactive in identifying new and innovative solutions that meet the needs of its patients while also being cost-effective. It has been using digital technologies, such as social media platforms and data analytics, to reduce costs and improve customer base.

All the four companies have websites that encourage interactivity and share sufficient information for the customers or prospects. The path of digital transformation of these four companies is paved with social selling (using social media and website to locate and address existing customers and fresh prospects), data analysis, customer engagement at all digital touchpoints, and providing proactive customer service with the help of FAQs, forums, instructional videos, etc.

It won't be incorrect to assume that the traditional sources of competitive advantage do not hold much value in the present business ecosystem. What has changed?

Earlier, technology teams offering support services would work in silos. But today's marketing team has to work along with its technological counterpart to form strategies based on real-time analysis of data.

The Path of Digital Transformation for Services Marketing

Marketing is one of the most dynamic managerial functions that have to continuously capture the changing trends in customer needs and the market landscape. The models and views discussed before in this chapter have emphasized customer-facing digital initiatives and digital remodeling of internal processes to offer better value to customers, engage them further and, in the end, build a sustainable demand for products and services. This is in a manner similar to the ancient Indian wisdom of conducting business. The Indian ethos of doing business has been shaped by a number of cultural, social, and economic factors. Some of the key characteristics of Indian ethos include the following:

- **Relationship building:** Building and maintaining strong relationships with customers, clients, and partners is highly valued in the Indian business ethos. In 2005, a tourism initiative campaign, *"Atithi Devo Bhavah,"* was launched by the Government of India to promote responsible and hospitable behavior toward tourists in India. The campaign encourages people to treat tourists as honored guests and to provide them with a warm and welcoming experience. The goal of the campaign is to make India a more attractive destination for tourists by improving the country's hospitality industry and showcasing its rich cultural heritage. *"Atithi Devo Bhavah"* is a Sanskrit phrase that means "a guest is equivalent to God." It is a traditional Indian belief that guests should be treated with the highest level of respect and hospitality.
- **Focus on morality and teamwork:** Teamwork and collaboration for the moral conduct of an enterprise are highly valued in the Indian business ethos, and group harmony is often prioritized over individual achievement. *"Niti"* is the ancient concept of moral conduct and decision-making. It involves considering the long-term consequences of one's actions and choosing the option that is most likely to lead to the greatest good for the greatest number of people.
- **Emphasis on personal connections:** Personal connections and networks often play a significant role in business in India, and building and maintaining these connections is considered important. *"Dharma"* is the moral principle that guides the conduct of an individual and is considered more important than wealth or pleasure.
- **Importance of trust:** Building and maintaining trust with the stakeholders is an important element of ancient Indian wisdom. The *"Law of Karma"* states that every action has consequences, and this principle can be applied to business. According to this law, if a business is conducted ethically and with integrity, it will ultimately lead to success.

Figure 9 attempts to sum up an understanding of the digital transformation of services marketing with the help of the services triangle.

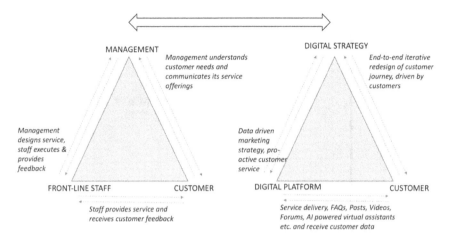

Figure 9. Services marketing triangle and digital transformation.

It draws on the Indian business ethos mentioned before and suggests how services marketing companies can manage their existing business model while simultaneously developing disruptive new products/services using digital technology.

Today's hyper-connected society is seeking hassle-free, seamless, and convenient buying experiences. Thus, businesses have to be user-centric, and any strong marketing strategy is based on understanding consumer expectations. In services marketing, the challenges stem from the intangibility, heterogeneity, inseparability, and perishability of the services. The service delivery blueprint needs to be resilient enough to absorb some level of unpredictability in the business ecosystem. So, when organizations opt for digital transformation, they have to design a framework with malleability (of business strategies) and unpredictability (of the business environment) as key strategy drivers for the marketing function. Verhoef *et al.* (2019) suggest that the digital transformation of organizations is multidisciplinary in nature, and for managerial guidance on the same, one must understand the following:

- How can a firm identify and build on resources to gain a competitive advantage that is sustainable?
- What are the winning strategies?
- What are the changes needed in the firm's internal structure to support the above strategies?

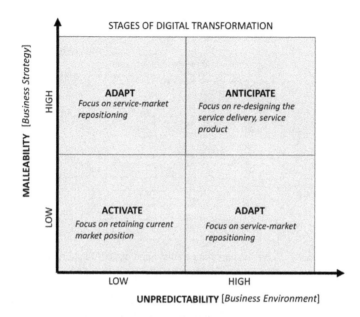

Figure 10.   Strategy framework for the digital transformation of services marketing.

Based on Verhoef's suggestions and the marketing 4.0 framework of Vassileva, Figure 10 suggests a framework to guide how organizations can focus on different stages of digital transformation of their marketing based on the malleability of their business strategy and unpredictability of the business environment.

This framework will work only if an organization keeps track of the following key points:

- The organization should disrupt itself before others, which can be achieved only if it manages to develop a culture of innovation and experimental mindset, and implement massive change in how it thinks and functions.
- The organization should manage its legacy business while simultaneously developing its digital strategies; data analytics should be embedded in daily business operations.
- The organization should be prepared for dynamic resource allocation depending on the business environment and market demands.
- The organization should be ready to work in an integrated and collaborative ecosystem with cross-functional teams and partners.

- The organization should be vigilant enough to protect data and should not ever think of itself as an owner of data. Any entitlement over data may lead to misuse, and customers or the legal system has no tolerance for such misuse.

Data centers dominate the digital ecosystem, and the cloud provides centralized storage, archive data, enables service delivery and analytics, and complies with regulations and policies. Services companies can effectively use these technology and data analytics solutions to manage the intangibility, heterogeneity, inseparability, and perishability of their products/services by customizing the offerings and delivery. The immense scope lies in further research on the industry-specific marketing transformation strategy and identification of new elements in the services marketing mix.

In India, the mindsets are changing (Ghosh, 2019), and penetration of digital services is expected to rival electricity as telecommunication services reach far and wide, and become more affordable. Thus, there is no question whether the marketing function will experience digital transformation. It is a matter of how to tread that path.

The digital transformation of marketing of services (Figure 11) starts from digitizing the company's core, which is first to understand the customer's point of view. Following this, it has to find a balance between its

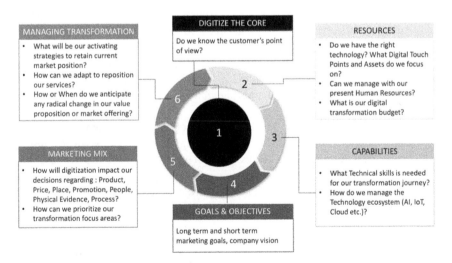

Figure 11. Suggested path to digital transformation of services marketing.

resources, capabilities, goals and objectives, and marketing mix before activating, adapting, and anticipating its digital strategy. Digital transformation is not merely using digital tools to advertise or manage communication. Its prime focus should be to generate meaningful consumer data that can be analyzed for strategic decision-making.

References

Accenture Report (2016). Digital transformation of industries: Demystifying digital and securing $100 trillion for society and industry by 2025. https://www.accenture.com/t00010101t000000z__w__/ru-ru/_acnmedia/accenture/conversion-assets/dotcom/documents/local/ru-ru/pdf/accenture-digital-transformation.pdf.

Botha, T. & Theron, P. (2016). How are companies around the world really embracing digital? https://www.weforum.org/agenda/2016/05/industry-4-0/.

Boulton, C. (2019). What is digital transformation? A necessary disruption. https://www.cio.com/article/3211428/what-is-digital-transformation-a-necessary-disruption.html.

Bower, J. L. & Christensen, C. M. (1995). Disruptive technologies: Catching the wave. *Harvard Business Review* (January–February). https://hbr.org/1995/01/disruptive-technologies-catching-the-wave.

Christensen, C. M., Raynos, M. E., & McDonald, R. (2015). What is disruptive innovation? *Harvard Business Review* (December). https://hbr.org/2015/12/what-is-disruptive-innovation.

Dekkers, R., Talbot, S., Thomson, J., & Whittam, G. (2014). Does Schumpeter still rule? Reflections on the current epoch. *Journal of Innovation Economics & Management*, 13(1), 7–36. doi:10.3917/jie.013.0007. https://www.cairn.info/revue-journal-of-innovation-economics-2014-1-page-7.htm#.

Erevelles, S., Fukawa, N., & Swayne, L. (2016). Big Data consumer analytics and the transformation of marketing. *Journal of Business Research*, 69(2), 897–904.

Fahrni, S., Jansen, C., John, M., Kasah, T., Koerber, B., & Mohr, N. (2020). Coronavirus: Industrial IoT in challenging times. https://www.mckinsey.com/industries/advanced-electronics/our-insights/coronavirus-industrial-iot-in-challenging-times.

Gadiesh, O. & Gilbert, J. L. (1998). Profit pools: A fresh look at strategy. *Harvard Business Review* (May–June). https://hbr.org/1998/05/profit-pools-a-fresh-look-at-strategy.

Ghosh, D. (2019). When it comes to digital transformation India is building a powerful edge. *The Hindu Business Line*. https://www.thehindubusinessline.com/info-tech/when-it-comes-to-digital-transformation-india-is-building-a-powerful-edge/article28252527.ece#.

Glasmeier, A. (1991). Technological discontinuities and flexible production networks: The case of Switzerland and the world watch industry. *Research Policy.* https://dusp.mit.edu/sites/dusp.mit.edu/files/attachments/publications/ Technological%20discontinutities%20and%20flexible%20production%20 networks%20-The%20case%20of%20Switzerland%20and%20the%20 world%20watch%20industry.pdf.

Gloor, P. (2006). COINs and communications technology. In *Swarm Creativity: Competitive Advantage through Collaborative Innovation Networks.* New York: Oxford University Press. https://www.oxfordscholarship.com/view/10.1093/ acprof:oso/9780195304121.001.0001/acprof-9780195304121-chapter-7.

Hagel, J., Wooll, M., Brown, J., & deMaar, A. (2015). Patterns of disruption. *Deloitte Insights.* https://www2.deloitte.com/us/en/insights/focus/disruptive-strategy-patterns-case-studies/anticipating-disruptive-strategy-of-market-entrants.html.

IBM's OC debut. https://www.ibm.com/ibm/history/exhibits/pc25/pc25_intro.html.

Kaila, R. (2018). Transforming retail through phygital. *BWCIO World.* http://bwcio. businessworld.in/article/Transforming-retail-through-Phygital-/04-09-2018-159233/.

KayPay: A social media banking platform. https://www.bankbazaar.com/ifsc/ kaypay.html.

Kohli, J. (2015). Media and entertainment at digital inflection point. https://www. dqindia.com/media-and-entertainment-at-digitial-inflection-point/.

Kotak Mahindra Bank website. https://www.kotak.com/en/digital-banking.html.

Lee, F. (2020). Be a data custodian–Not a data owner. *Harvard Business Review.* https://hbr.org/2020/05/be-a-data-custodian-not-a-data-owner?utm_medium= email&utm_source=newsletter_daily&utm_campaign=dailyalert_not_active subs&referral=00563&deliveryName=DM79438.

Malviya, S. (2019). Decathlon overtakes Adidas, Nike in sports gear retailing. *The Economic Times.* https://economictimes.indiatimes.com/industry/services/ retail/decathlon-overtakes-adidas-nike-in-sports-gear-retailing/articleshow/ 68804024.cms?from=mdr.

McGrath, R. (2020). Digital transformation, one discovery at a time. *HBR Ideacast, Episode 738.* https://hbr.org/podcast/2020/04/digital-transformation-one-discovery-at-a-time?utm_medium=email&utm_source=newsletter_ daily&utm_campaign=dailyalert_not_activesubs&referral=00563&delivery Name=DM78142.

Nightingales Health Services Website. https://www.nightingales.in/.

Pagani, M. & Pardo, C. (2017). The impact of digital technology on relationships in a business network. *Industrial Marketing Management*, 67, 185–192.

Pahuja, R. (2020). Here's how decathlon provides hassle free shopping experience with phygital. *ET CIO.* https://cio.economictimes.indiatimes.com/ news/strategy-and-management/heres-how-decathlon-provides-hassle-free-shopping-experience-with-phygital/73997120.

Reeves, M. & Whittaker, K. (2019). Disruptions, delusions, and defenses in digital transformation. https://www.bcg.com/publications/2019/disruptions-delusions-defenses-in-digital-transformation.aspx.

Reinsel, D., Gantz, J., & Rydning, J. (2018). The digitization of the world: From edge to core. https://www.seagate.com/files/www-content/our-story/trends/files/idc-seagate-dataage-whitepaper.pdf.

Schwab, K. *The Fourth Industrial Revolution by Klaus Schwab*. New York, Crown Business, 2017, https://www.weforum.org/about/the-fourth-industrial-revolution-by-klaus-schwab.

Sharma, P. (2015). 11 Digital success stories from India. *Dataquest*. https://www.dqindia.com/11-digital-success-stories-from-india/.

Skylar, A., Kowalkowski, C., Tronvoll, B., & Sorhammar, D. (2019). Organizing for digital servitization: A service ecosystem perspective. *Journal of Business Research*. 104, pp. 450–460, https://doi.org/10.1016/j.jbusres.2019.02.012.

Vassileva, B. (2017). Marketing 4.0: How technologies transform marketing organization. Óbuda *University e-Bulletin*, 7, 47–56.

Verhoef, P. C., Broekhuizen, T., Bart, Y., Bhattacharya, A., Fabian, N., & Haemlein, M. (2019). Digital transformation: A multidisciplinary reflection and research agenda. *Journal of Business Research*. 122, pp. 889–901, https://doi.org/10.1016/j.jbusres.2019.09.022.

YRF Website. https://www.yashrajfilms.com/about-us/yrf-milestones.

Part III

Responsibility Approach

Chapter 5

Social Responsibility in Indian Organizations: Developments Since Independence

Syed Mohammad Akrama Ali Rizvi[*,§]**, Chayan Poddar**[†,¶]**, and Iqra Fatima**[‡,∥]

Indian Institute of Technology Guwahati, Guwahati, India

†*International Management Institute New Delhi, New Delhi, India*

‡*Jamia Millia Islamia, New Delhi, India*

§*syedakrama786@gmail.com*

¶*chayan.iit.imi@gmail.com*

∥*iqra.fatimah.IF@gmail.com*

Abstract

This chapter explores the social responsibility measures undertaken by Indian organizations since independence and, in the process, identifies existing policies, practices, and patterns of development leading to the introduction of the Social Responsibility in Companies Act, 2013. The chapter highlights the notable social contributions of Indian organizations over the years and draws a *vis-à-vis* parallel between economic development and social responsibility undertaken by organizations in India.

Moreover, this chapter focuses on emerging trends and challenges facing Indian organizations with respect to their stakeholder responsibilities and analyzes the 10-year period after the Social Responsibility Act was legislated in 2013. The chapter concludes by identifying critical areas of focus for Indian organizations in discharging their social responsibility duties in the near future.

Keywords: Social responsibility, corporate social responsibility, Companies Act, India.

Introduction

Businesses and organizations are on the verge of serious changes in terms of their impact on the overall well-being of humans and the planet. Gone are the days of profit accumulation at the cost of rampant exploitation of resources, with the shareholders deciding the fate and course of running business as usual. The most important change the world has faced in the last 4 years was the novel coronavirus (COVID-19), which dented the engines of economic growth. Coupled with it are the growing impacts of climate change, which has started showing its effects on the business interests of organizations. We are also witnessing sweeping changes in society and across generations of consumers, as tastes and preferences of customers shift, along with the democratizing nature of information available at fingertips through the internet at very low costs. As organizations invest in creating and maintaining their brands over time, their actions and responsibilities toward different stakeholders, as well as their inaction in some cases, face the risk of name-calling and brand-shaming by concerned parties, affecting brands and businesses. The overall situation calls for an increased focus by organizations on their social responsibilities, which posits the recognition of the needs of different stakeholders and taking appropriate actions to address concerns in tandem with sustainably creating profits.

The Indian business scenario is unique as far as this situation is concerned. India pioneered as the first country across the globe in legislating corporate social responsibility of organizations. This was done by ratifying the Companies Act in 2013, by virtue of which organizations above a certain threshold of their net worth, annual turnover, or net profit in a financial year were obligated to spend a certain percentage of profits to fulfill their social responsibilities. Started on a pilot basis to be followed by public sector organizations, the act later encompassed public and private sector organizations alike. On a broad level, these initiatives included reducing their waste and pollution footprint or running welfare schemes, such as contributions toward education, hygiene, and social programs, impacting the lives of concerned stakeholders positively in places where these organizations conducted their businesses. In turn, this would contribute toward improving the social welfare conditions of people in terms of their overall well-being. At the same time, environmental concerns arising out of resource usage by the organizations could also be addressed. As the Companies Act of 2013 completes a decade of implementation, this chapter explores the social responsibility initiatives undertaken by organizations in India.

The purpose is well served if we consider the entire gamut of factors that contemporary India faces — addressing and mitigating them would simply be impossible without organizations committing to their social responsibility objectives. India aspires to be a five trillion dollar economy as well as the third largest economy in nominal gross domestic product terms by the end of this decade. India is blessed with the largest young working-age population in the world and needs their active participation from all sectors to reap the demographic dividend. At the same time, India has committed to becoming a net-zero emitter by 2070, addressing its environmental concerns as it remains one of the most vulnerable nations to the impacts of climate change — both environmentally and economically. Combining all these factors with the aspiration of the new-age Indian worker armed with knowledge at the behest of some of the cheapest internet prices in the world, it is high time for Indian organizations to double down on their social responsibility objectives to ensure organizational sustainability as well as effectively contributing to nation building and the aspirations of more than a billion Indians.

The chapter has been divided into the following sections: understanding what constitutes social responsibility of organizations; exploring the context of social responsibility practices of Indian organizations by providing the third largest economy in nominal gross domestic product terms by the end of this decade as well as developments after independence; and identifying government policies and legislations concerning the social responsibility of organizations. In the following section, we look at the Social Responsibility in Companies Act, 2013, and review the implementation and developments around the act in the 10-year period from 2013 to

2022, after it came under legislation. Finally, we delve into the current and critical areas that Indian organizations need to focus on in terms of their social responsibility objectives and being prepared for emerging challenges in contemporary times.

Social Responsibilities of an Organization

As we explore the social responsibility of organizations in India, we need to focus on having a clear idea about what constitutes the social responsibility of an organization in the first place. Social responsibility entails the need to address the concerns of all stakeholders related to the business of an organization. Different stakeholders include the employees, the shareholders, the customers, the production and supply chains, and the ecology and natural environment of where the organization sets up its office or factory. Thus, for an organization to address its social responsibilities, it needs to take care of its employees and invest in maintaining their physical and mental health to retain critical talent, generate profits for shareholders, provide quality products to customers, maintain appropriate relations with the supply chain for raw materials, and minimize its overall impact on the environment.

Corporate social responsibility, on the other hand, especially with respect to Section 135 of the Companies Act, 2013, is a government mandate toward the board members of an organization in creating a social responsibility committee that creates established policies, by virtue of which the organization contributes toward meeting its social responsibility objectives. So, while social responsibility encompasses the entire spectrum of stakeholders, corporate social responsibility funds, especially in the Indian context, need to be spent on a specific list of areas, which will be elaborated upon later in this chapter.

Thus, the social responsibility of organizations is about inherently creating social values in their course of activities. The central idea is to solve the problems and challenges that stakeholders, or people, and the planet face while continuing to generate profits. How can organizations achieve this? Apart from the onus of a top-down approach, in which senior management decides to focus on a particular policy of mitigating responsibilities, another possible way is to leverage the skillset of engaged and motivated employees in creating processes and systems that contribute toward social value creation. This, in turn, would lead to addressing the needs of all stakeholders by enhancing several aspects of well-being — physical, psychological, social, and economic. The idea is to percolate benefits over local contexts that impact local people but improve the conditions of society as a whole, including taking the health of the local environment into consideration.

Indian Organizations and Social Responsibilities

There is a dedicated history of Indian organizations engaging in their social responsibilities, particularly those which stem from the philanthropic ideas of rich business houses and families of the past. The Gandhian mode of trusteeship has also had its fair share in how businesses fulfilled their contributions toward society since the days of British rule (Verma *et al.*, 2015). Ancient Indian commerce, dating back to 1500–600 BC, has been explored in literature with respect to fulfilling their social responsibilities (Sundar, 2000). So, while philanthropy has remained the dominant contributor before and after independence, eventually development and initiatives led by the government took over in this aspect (Mohan, 2001). An increase in the number of initiatives toward investing in social work by Indian business communities can also be attributed to over the years. Overall, a noticeable change in the phenomenon of addressing social responsibilities seriously began in the 1990s, when corporate organizations as well as public policymakers started taking an active interest in fulfilling these objectives (Sarkar & Sarkar, 2015). This culminated in the Companies Act of 2013 being passed in India, the first of its kind in the world. It is noteworthy that spending on social responsibility across the world has remained mainly voluntary in nature.

Previously, social responsibility measures on behalf of organizations were considered to be voluntary (Sarkar & Sarkar, 2015). The passing of the Companies Act in 2013 attempted to institutionalize it, with the aim of bringing homogeneity across practices followed by corporates (Sarkar & Sarkar, 2015). Indian traditions have played a fundamental role for a long time in which wealthy individuals and business houses have engaged in charity and contributed to benefiting the poorer sections of society (Kulkarni, 2014). When considered in their previous voluntary form, social responsibility measures, in the form of charity, were driven by guidelines and traditions in society and culture (Chatterjee & Mitra, 2017).

The literature establishes that most of these initiatives were undertaken by senior management, and the principal format was donating old equipment such as computers, providing scholarships, constructing infrastructure, and supporting institutions without stakeholders actually participating (Kulkarni, 2014). These were one-time initiatives and lacked a long-term vision (Sharma, 2011). So, as far as corporates were concerned, the process of spending for social responsibilities lacked transparency, whether it be budgets, implementation, planning and design, or even conducting audits and assessments of partnering firms that were supposed to carry out the tasks (Sharma, 2011).

In such a state, when the act was passed in 2013, the act mandated not only a certain amount to be spent for eligible organizations but also constituting a committee for overlooking CSR initiatives, having clear CSR policies, and developing a culture of CSR within the organizations themselves (Bhatia & Dhawan, 2021). The sectors chosen for intervention were primarily health and education, and organizations could either intervene in projects themselves or partner with verified non-governmental organizations (NGOs) and trusts. The idea behind passing the act reflected fulfilling social responsibilities on the part of organizations on the same pedestal as their core business initiatives (Bhatia & Dhawan, 2021). Studies conducted in the aftermath of passing the act saw increases across budgets and compliances for CSR, with around 44% of corporate organizations spending more than their prescribed budget (Kapoor & Dhamija, 2017). However, the lack of focus on communities, or a distance between where organizations would like to spend their CSR budgets and benefits actually reaching the last mile, has been widely reported (Jayaraman et al., 2018; Singh et al., 2018). This is the focus area of this chapter: to identify critical areas of focus for Indian organizations in discharging their social responsibility duties so that these initiatives remain parallel to economic development.

The Need for Organizations to fulfill their Social Responsibilities

India's economic development since the 1990s owes its origins to the liberalization policies through which organizations profited at the cost of using natural resources rampantly, leading to a rise in inequality across communities and negatively impacting the environment (Bergman et al.,

2019). An external pressure was created by NGOs, who, acting as watchdogs, wanted to remind organizations to behave responsibly (Visser, 2009). These pressures catapulted to institutionalizing CSR on a broader level, where organizations themselves were identified as causing problems (Almunawar & Low, 2014). The principal understanding behind legislating the CSR Act stemmed from the idea that organizations and their actions were an inherent part of society, and they did not function in isolation. So, fulfilling social responsibilities becomes integral to the functioning of organizations (Jackson *et al.*, 2020).

There is a significant difference between how CSR activities are carried out in developing countries and developed countries. In developing countries, such as India, the focus of intervention is on communities through philanthropy and social development measures. This is owing partly to the existence of socioeconomic problems for the masses on a widespread level, as well as traditional value systems which believe in "giving back to the society" (Almunawar & Low, 2014, p. 182) and have been carried out in countries such as China and India. On the other hand, CSR policies in developed countries focus on conducting ethical business and reducing carbon footprints (Sarkar & Sarkar, 2015).

Addressing social responsibilities for Indian organizations holds a different meaning. If understood through the lens of longstanding traditions and the adoption of a grounded approach through culture, the motivation of wealthy individuals or business houses dealing with charitable and philanthropic activities can be attributed to "dharma," or carrying out one's conduct righteously. Across the broad spectrum of religions, we can refer to "Dharmada," promoted by Hinduism, and similar concepts of "Zaakat" in Islam or "Dasvandh" in Sikhism, which focus on carrying out charitable activities and donations. Thus, the need for organizations to fulfill their social responsibilities is associated with the welfare of society. CSR in the contemporary Indian context is a blend of the traditional ethos of contemporary transitions through homogeneity in practices and institutionalization.

CSR Vignettes across Different Types of Organizations

Even though the aim of mandating CSR was to bring homogeneity to practices regarding how organizations would spend their CSR budgets, there have been widespread differences. Spending on CSR has been associated with the image and brand of an organization, so the identification of areas and projects in which a particular organization would spend its budget depends on the approval of its top bosses. Moreover, there exist differences in terms of resources and workforce capabilities that an organization is able to afford in its CSR, the capabilities of the partnering NGOs, or pledges and contributions toward certain programs and funds set up by the government. Most of the time, organizations are dependent on the design and implementation of CSR projects by the partnering NGOs (Jayaraman *et al.*, 2018), and the inherent focus remains on producing measure-worthy outputs rather than exploring the impact of those projects at the ground level. Often times, this overarching focus on outcomes, coupled with inadequate understanding by organizational representatives of communities, leads to poor monitoring and assessment of these projects (Singh *et al.*, 2018).

CSR has been studied in the literature from the perspective of rural development (Pradhan & Ranjan, 2011) and whether rural people are considered stakeholders by organizations. CSR initiatives for the socioeconomic development of rural communities involve initiatives developing livelihood, infrastructure, education, healthcare, and even agricultural practices. Recommendations include the involvement of rural people in the planning and implementing phases, leading to better outcomes, with the government acting as a facilitator and appropriate audits being carried out by external agencies. Some of the challenges for implementing CSR initiatives involved the lack of capacity-building programs in NGOs and rural society, with the local community not participating effectively.

There is a significant difference in expectations as to how organizations fulfill their social responsibilities, depending on their size. Large organizations or conglomerates, such as the Tata Group, the Mahindra Group, or the Indian Oil Corporation, have well-documented and detailed CSR programs (Deodhar, 2015). The contributions toward fulfilling social responsibilities have been attributed to "a long tradition of being engaged in social activities that have gone beyond meeting a corporation's immediate financial objectives" (Sarkar & Sarkar, 2015, p. 1). Thus, large corporations are entrusted with huge expectations, such that they are expected to serve as corollaries of the government to finance, set up, and manage social programs (Matten & Moon, 2008). The social development goals of the government are expected to be assisted by large organizations by promoting inclusive growth (Hussain, 2015) and ensuring that wealth is distributed with the aim of improving the well-being of communities (Singh & Verma, 2014). Thus, well-established CSR programs of large organizations address challenges plaguing the environmental and socio-economic conditions — to improve the lives of underprivileged people, reduce poverty and levels of inequality in society, and ensure accessibility to healthcare programs, education, clean water, and sanitation facilities, even to the extent of developing infrastructures in both rural and urban livelihoods (Hussain, 2015). The onus of responsibility that large corporations have toward developing Indian society has been captured by Singh and Verma (2014, p. 455): "It is recognized the world over that integrating social, environmental and ethical responsibilities into the governance of businesses ensures their long term success, competitiveness and sustainability. This approach also reaffirms the view that businesses are an integral part of society, and have a critical and active role to play in the sustenance and improvement of healthy ecosystems, in fostering social inclusiveness and equity, and in upholding the essentials of ethical practices and good governance."

As for the banking sector in the country, they have been heavily involved in carrying out financial inclusion programs and providing literacy to people in semi-urban and rural places so as to fulfill their responsibilities toward society (Pratihari & Uzma, 2020). Activities of CSR by the banking sector include carrying out education programs, such as providing scholarship; promotion of the girl child; plantation drives and organizing beach cleaning initiatives; opening zero-balance accounts, loans for agriculture, micro-finance initiatives, and financial literacy drives; organizing health camps for blood donation, eye and health check-ups, and donating ambulances; raising awareness toward social issues, including child labor, road safety, and diseases, such as AIDS; relief programs during calamities; sponsoring education and school stationery for kids; providing doorstep banking services for senior citizens; and organization of sporting tournaments and providing vocational and skill development trainings. Banks contribute to the overall impact of programs for delivering welfare to society.

Mandating the spending of CSR budgets entails the question of whether organizations really care about their social responsibilities. There is no question that India needs social development rapidly, and that too on a large scale, and the development of business–society partnerships could definitely help the process. However, there arises the question of whether mandating CSR leads to a forced form of philanthropy and whether organizations, in order to avoid compliance procedures, care only to "check the box," or perhaps even engage in corruption or tokenism (Carroll & Brown, 2018). Research on the CSR initiatives of some of the top state-owned enterprises found that these organizations were forced to spend CSR budgets on activities that had less impact, primarily owing to challenges in implementation and from politics (Jain *et al.*, 2022). Overall, despite mandatory regulations, CSR projects in India have suffered from weak implementation practices (Jain *et al.*, 2021). Research pertaining to the relationship of CSR with organizational outcome variables has had mixed outcomes; for example, Garg *et al.* (2021) found that mandatory spending on CSR had a negligible impact on the firms' stock. However, CSR has been found to positively impact firm value after regulation (Jadiyappa *et al.*, 2021).

The discussion on CSR activities in India would be incomplete without mentioning the contribution of family firms and family-run businesses because large private organizations in India have mostly been family-owned, with fewer occurrences of non-family organizations managed professionally. The uniqueness of India's CSR programs centers around management practices by family-led organizations, such that CSR is not essentially a part of overall corporate objectives, nor is it related to how the organization is governed or their attitude toward customers. Management, in this way, depends on inheritance from one generation to the next, with the family keeping control over the businesses. Some of the CSR activities carried out by such type of organizations include establishing educational institutions and places of worship and taking part in providing relief and support when calamities and tragedies strike. It is interesting to note that Indian philanthropic activities are comfortably ahead of other countries with similar levels of prosperity (Sheth *et al.*, 2015).

Contemporary CSR Implementation and the Way Forward

Despite becoming the first country to mandate CSR spending, there are certain factors which plague the implementation of CSR initiatives, preventing benefits from reaching the last mile for the people they are actually meant for. Observing regulations is generally poor due to a lack of proper structures related to monitoring and reporting (Preito-Carron *et al.*, 2006). There is an inherent recognition and rising pressure to recognize the parity between the growing economic prowess of India and its social progress. Institutionalizing CSR practices has been the first step in a series of developments, but practices such as finding and verifying NGOs before partnering, providing support for research in academic institutions, and conducting proper audits and assessments of CSR projects will go a long way in improving the implementation woes plaguing the social responsibility initiatives of organizations in India.

References

Almunawar, M. N. & Low, K. C. P. (2014). Corporate social responsibility and sustainable development: Trends in Asia. In K. C. P. Low, S. O. Idowu, and S. L. Ang (Eds.), *Corporate Social Responsibility in Asia: Practice and Experience* (pp. 173–196). Cham: Springer International Publishing. doi: 10.1007/978-3-319-01532-3_10.

Bergman, M. M., Bergman, Z., Teschemacher, Y., Arora, B., Jyoti, D., & Sengupta, R. (2019). Corporate responsibility in India: Academic perspectives on the Companies Act 2013. *Sustainability*, 11(21), 5939.

Bhatia, A. & Dhawan, A. (2023). A paradigm shift in corporate social responsibility: India's transition from mandatory regime to the COVID-19 era. *Social Responsibility Journal*, 19(1), 166–183.

Carroll, A. B. & Brown, J. A. (2018). Corporate social responsibility: A review of current concepts, research, and issues. *Corporate Social Responsibility Business and Society*, 360(2), 39–69.

Chatterjee, B. & Mitra, N. (2017). CSR should contribute to the national agenda in emerging economies-the 'Chatterjee Model'. *International Journal of Corporate Social Responsibility*, 2, 1–11.

Deodhar, S. Y. (2015). *India's Mandatory CSR, Process of Compliance and Channels of Spending*. Ahmedabad: Indian Institute of Management.

Garg, A., Gupta, P. K., & Bhullar, P. S. (2021). Is CSR expenditure relevant to the firms in India? *Organizations and Markets in Emerging Economies*, 12(1), 178–197.

Hussain, A. (2015). Corporate social responsibility under Companies Act 2013: A welcome step to bridge the welfare gap in India. *International Research Journal of Commerce and Law*, 2, 48–56.

Jackson, G., Bartosch, J., Avetisyan, E., Kinderman, D., & Knudsen, J. S. (2020). Mandatory non-financial disclosure and its influence on CSR: An international comparison. *Journal of Business Ethics*, 162, 323–342.

Jadiyappa, N., Iyer, S. R., & Jyothi, P. (2021). Does social responsibility improve firm value? Evidence from mandatory corporate social responsibility regulations in India. *International Review of Finance*, 21(2), 653–660.

Jain, A., Kansal, M., & Joshi, M. (2021). New development: Corporate philanthropy to mandatory corporate social responsibility (CSR) — A new law for India. *Public Money & Management*, 41(3), 276–278.

Jain, A., Kansal, M., Joshi, M., & Taneja, P. (2022). Is the Indian corporate social responsibility law working for the public sector? *Public Money & Management*, 42(8), 648–657.

Jayaraman, A., D'souza, V., & Ghoshal, T. (2018). NGO–business collaboration following the Indian CSR Bill 2013: Trust-building collaborative social sector partnerships. *Development in Practice*, 28(6), 831–841.

Kapoor, G. K. & Dhamija, S. (2017). Mandatory CSR spending — Indian experience. *Emerging Economy Studies*, 3(1), 98–112.

Kulkarni, A. (2014). Corporate social responsibility in Indian banking sector: A critical analysis. In Ray, S., Siva Raju, S. (Eds.) *Implementing Corporate Social Responsibility: Indian Perspectives* (pp. 111–127). New Delhi: Springer, India.

Matten, D. & Moon, J. (2008). "Implicit" and "explicit" CSR: A conceptual framework for a comparative understanding of corporate social responsibility. *Academy of management Review*, 33(2), 404–424.

Mohan, A. (2001). Corporate citizenship: Perspectives from India. *Journal of Corporate Citizenship*, 2, 107–117.

Pradhan, S. & Ranjan, A. (2011). Corporate social responsibility in rural development sector: Evidences from India. *School of Doctoral Studies (European Union) Journal*, 2, 139–147.

Pratihari, S. K. & Uzma, S. H. (2020). A survey on bankers' perception of corporate social responsibility in India. *Social Responsibility Journal*, 16(2), 225–253.

Sarkar, J. & Sarkar, S. (2015). Corporate social responsibility in India — An effort to bridge the welfare gap. *Review of Market Integration*, 7(1), 1–36. https://doi.org/10.1177/0974929215593876.

Sharma, S. (2011). Corporate social responsibility in India. *Indian Journal of Industrial Relation*, 46(4), 637–649.

Sheth, A., Ayilavarapu, D., & Bhagwati, A. (2015). Indian philanthropy report, Bain and Company (India). www.bain.com/publications/articles/india-philanthropy-report-2015.aspx.

Singh, A. & Verma, P. (2014). CSR@ 2%: A new model of corporate social responsibility in India. *International Journal of Academic Research in Business and Social Sciences*, 4(10), 455–464.

Singh, S., Holvoet, N., & Pandey, V. (2018). Bridging sustainability and corporate social responsibility: Culture of monitoring and evaluation of CSR initiatives in India. *Sustainability*, 10(7), 2353.

Sundar, P. (2000). *Beyond Business: From Merchant Charity to Corporate Citizenship: Indian Business Philanthropy through the Ages.* New Delhi: Tata McGraw-Hill Publishing Company.

Verma, H., Selvalakshmi, M., & Jaine, N. (2015). CSR stipulations of companies act 2013 and actual CSR expenditure by top Indian companies prior to its implementations: a comparative study. *International Journal of Science Technology and Management,* 4(2), 113–121.

Visser, W. (2009). Corporate social responsibility in developing countries. In A. Crane, D. Matten, A. McWilliams, J. Moon, & D. S. Siegel (Eds.), *The Oxford Handbook of Corporate Social Responsibility.* (pp. 473–499). UK: Oxford University Press.

https://doi.org/10.1142/9789811296444_0006

Chapter 6

Social Responsibility in Indian Organizations: The Way Forward for Sustainable Development

Nivedeeta Thombare*‡ and Moitrayee Das†,§

*Department of Management and Labor Studies,
Tata Institute of Social Sciences, Mumbai, India*

†*Department of Psychology, FLAME University, Pune, India*

‡*nivedeeta.thombare@gmail.com*

§*moitrayee.das@flame.edu.in*

Abstract

The post-liberalization phase has seen a significant change in the stakeholder participation-based model of corporate social responsibility (CSR) in India. Although CSR is optional for Small and Medium Enterprises (SMEs), there are apparent benefits if concrete mechanisms are in place. Since CSR and corporate governance are complementary and interconnected, including CSR provisions within the framework of corporate governance will create capabilities for Indian Micro, Small and Medium Enterprises (MSMEs). For SMEs, the formal structures of CSR and corporate governance hardly prevail in ways typical of big organizations in India.

This chapter highlights the role of CSR and corporate governance within SMEs, the challenges they face, and the benefits they receive from CSR and corporate governance. The chapter also draws attention to the fact that CSR and corporate governance are crucial for sustainable development.

Keywords: CSR, corporate governance, SMEs, sustainable development, challenges of CG, benefits of CG, role of CSR and CG.

Introduction

The concept of corporate social responsibility (CSR) was initially based on charity or philanthropy. On the other hand, the phase of post-liberalization has seen a major change in the stakeholder participation-based model of CSR (Verma & Kumar, 2012). Moreover, CSR is progressively fusing with practices of corporate governance. Both of these streams focus on ethical practices within the organization and the awareness of the organization to its stakeholders and surroundings where they operate.

Corporate governance is a collection of rules, regulations, and procedures to manage, direct, and control mechanisms. It also maintains relationships with the stakeholders and the goals that the organization upholds. Moreover, a company's reputation and long-term profitability may be impacted by business ethics and social and environmental concerns (Organization for Economic Co-operation and Development (OECD), 2004).

The role of corporate governance is indispensable; every business needs a governing body that ensures that the enterprise is running in the right direction and running well. The importance of corporate governance dramatically increased at the beginning of the 21st century after a series of corporate fraud, managerial misconduct, and negligence cases that caused a massive loss of shareholder wealth (Krechovska & Prochazkova, 2014). These failures happened as a result of a lack of sincerity and reliability that emanated from individuals and groups. Corporate governance finds solutions to address these deficiencies and assists in setting up an effective monitoring system to assure the organization's functions toward protecting the well-being of its stakeholders.

Nowadays, societies expect industries to have high ethical and corporate governance behavior regarding stakeholders' needs (Aras &

Crowther, 2010). For SMEs, the formal structures of CSR and corporate governance hardly prevail. In this chapter, we examine the role of CSR and corporate governance within SMEs, the challenges they face, and the benefits they will get from CSR and corporate governance. The chapter also highlights that CSR and corporate governance are crucial for sustainable development.

Corporate Governance in SMEs

The framework of "corporate governance" relies on the institutional and legal atmosphere. It explains the organization's functioning, control, and direction. It is about holding and supervising the accounts of people who direct and control management. For SMEs, it is related to the particular shareholder's roles as managers and owners, including the directors and other members. It is about setting procedures and regulations for the functioning of organizations. It is also about setting checks and balances in place to avoid abuses of authority and make sure the reliability of monetary results.

Abor and Adjasi (2007) argue that SMEs follow a bottom-up method where unions' views, specifically representing the labor, are laid out at board meetings. In this situation, there will be a clear set of rules that are articulated to the governing board.

Certainly, similar techniques may be used to channel the well-being of customers, communities, and related stakeholders.

CSR directly links to the idea of sustainable development by requiring businesses to act in accordance with society's broader aims (Schönherr *et al.*, 2017). The existing and future stakeholders, who have particular expectations for appropriate corporate behavior and results, are the intended audience for CSR implementation (Ebner, 2007). Businesses can benefit from corporate governance in both concrete and abstract ways. Performance is also dependent on the corporate governance framework being implemented with a high level of stability and discipline (Singh & Pillai, 2022).

An established framework of corporate governance is a challenge for SMEs, where managers may often be their owners or the organization's ownership is shared across family members (Dube *et al.*, 2011).

There are several challenges to encouraging improved corporate governance within SMEs. The schematic representation of the challenges of Corporate Governance (CG) faced by SMEs is drawn in Figure 1.

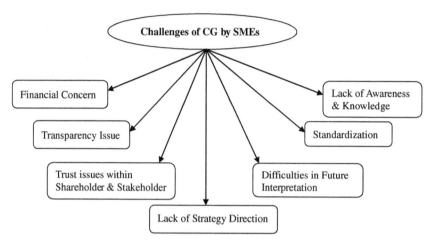

Figure 1.   Challenges of CG to SMEs.

Source: Developed by author through analysis.

In general, corporate governance focuses on developing the effectiveness of the business and operations and reducing the monitoring of management actions for SMEs. The schematic representation regarding the benefits of CG to SMEs is drawn in Figure 2.

Corporate Governance & CSR

Through the direct supply chain, legislation development, certification, international standardization, and relationships, CSR has an impact on SMEs in developing countries. CSR denotes a shift to a profit-making environment that aligns with society. There will be a decline in welfare if CSR introduces environmental and social clauses, placing an unreasonable bureaucratic monitoring burden on small businesses. On the other hand, CSR suggests ways to cut costs; increase efficiency, innovation, and productivity; provide better access to markets; and provide significant social advantages, including community and educational advancement (Raynard & Forstater, 2002).

Corporate governance has traditionally been linked with big organizations. This is primarily because of the separation between control and ownership. However, SMEs are unlikely to have structures like corporate governance because agency problems are less likely to exist (Abor & Biekpe, 2007). SMEs often consist of just the owner, the manager, and

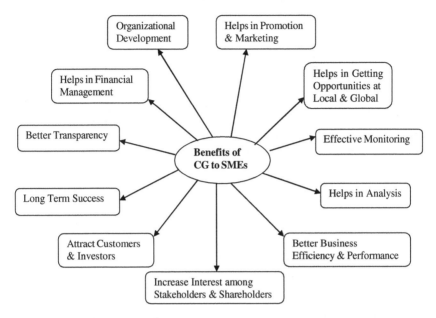

Figure 2. Benefits of CG to SMEs.

Source: Developed by author through analysis.

the sole proprietor (Hart, 1995, as cited by Abor & Biekpe, 2007). Compared to big organizations, SMEs have separate management and ownership.

There are concerns about the functioning of corporate governance for SMEs globally. It is frequently argued that SMEs should be subjected to similar regulations as big organizations are (Abor & Biekpe, 2007).

Role of CSR & CG in SMEs

CSR strengthens the convergence between governance, accountability, and mission. Therefore, the direction toward CSR is reflected in SME governance. Along with SMEs, the direction toward CSR starts with the entrepreneur. It is a manifestation of the standards linked to individual goals and the values attached to social and cultural dimensions.

CSR inspires the organization to act by contributing economically, environmentally, and socially through engaging in activities. The discussion on the role of CSR and CG in SMEs is schematically represented in Figure 3.

Figure 3.   Role of CSR & CG in SMEs.

Source: Developed by author through analysis.

The Indian Scenario

The concept of CSR is not new in India. It emerged from the Vedic period, when history was not recorded in India. In that period, kings had an obligation toward society and merchants and displayed their own business responsibility by building places of worship, education, inns, and wells (Sengupta, 2012).

Indian society is witnessing a market in rapid transition, characterized by a growing degree of liberalization, privatization, and globalization. The acceptance of social responsibility is redirecting Indians to their cherished values and teachings of their ancestors and their religious scriptures in the field of business (Sengupta, 2012). The requirements for how corporations communicate their CSR activities are, however, considerable. CSR communication is gaining importance, and there is an increasing awareness and interest in the challenges and practices of communicating CSR (Sengupta, 2012).

Today, the concept of CSR has undergone a radical change. It has integrated social and environmental issues into their missions and decisions. Companies take keen interest in informing about their CSR activities to their stakeholders as well. Across the globe, business enterprises have undertaken CSR initiatives in the areas of water conservation, healthcare, rural welfare, environment protection, poverty alleviation, education, community investment projects, culture and heritage, biodiversity, disaster management and relief, culture and heritage, green environment, product responsibility, governance, waste management, and gender equality.

Compared to other countries, India has one of the richest traditions of CSR, which is reflected in the idea of "Paropkar," or charity, that we have been practicing since ancient times (Government of Maharashtra, 2013–2014). Indian corporates have been flag bearers of practicing CSR and also make their contributions toward the development of the society. Corporate bodies have been taking up numerous initiatives in the areas that have helped make a positive effect on the lives of those affected by them.

Some of the initiatives on social responsibilities taken by organization situated in different regions of India are presented in the following.

Reliance Industries, Swachhata Hi Seva Campaign

The following extract about the campaign on *"Swachhata Hi Seva"* by Reliance Industries is taken from the 2017–2018 Annual Report on Corporate Social Responsibility:

> Reliance Foundation launched a massive awareness and cleanliness campaign titled Swachhata Hi Seva across the country. The week-long campaign organized during September–October, 2017 aimed at supporting the Government of India's Swachh Bharat Mission. The campaign mobilized communities and enabled them to actively participate in the Swachh Bharat Mission by "shramdaan," that is, donating labor. The campaign covered 15 States and Union Territories and engaged around 1,00,000 people.

The Infosys Foundation, Karnataka: (Information given on website as dated on March 27, 2023).

Since its inception in 1996, the Infosys Foundation has constructed hospital wards, built dharma-shalas (rest houses), and provided medical equipment to various hospitals across India. The Foundation has also donated medicines in addition to organizing health camps in rural India. Their campaign has included a vision for a blind-free India, caring and comforting the ill, and personalized treatment for psychiatric and neurological problems.

TVS's Srinivasan Service Trust (SST), Tamil Nadu: (Information given on website as dated on March 27, 2023).

The aim of the SST campaign has been primarily to partner in the transformation of rural India by enabling people and communities to achieve sustainable development. Their mission is to take their model of empowerment and transformational change to over 20,000 villages in India, so they become sustainable and self-reliant. They plan to reach their goal by partnering with the government and other organizations working together to create a prosperous rural community. Their impact is seen in multiple avenues ranging from the social sector, economic development, education, health, environment, and infrastructure. Their work has been able to impact about 2,500 villages. They have formed 25,000+ women self-help groups, 16 lakh people served, around 100+ crores income generated, 830+ schools renovated, 130+ health centers renovated, and 980+ *anganwadis* renovated among countless other contributions.

Mannapuram Foundation, Kerala: (Information given on website as dated on March 26, 2023).

Manappuram Foundation, the CSR body of Manappuram Finance Ltd., one of India's leading gold loan Non-Banking Financial Corporations (NBFCs), commenced its operations well before CSR became a law of the land. Through its flagship project: "Janaraksha Manappuram Free Health Insurance Scheme," which was rolled out in the year 2010, it provided free health insurance for around 20,000 Below Poverty Line (BPL) families in the coastal belt of Thrissur district. During the seven years that the scheme has run, an amount of nearly Rs. 11 crore was reimbursed to the beneficiaries. The foundation now manages two schools, various coaching centers for varied skills, yoga centers, fitness and wellness centers, and a sports complex with badminton and basketball courts and an aquatic complex with state-of-the-art swimming pools. The counseling & psychotherapy centers offer counseling and psychotherapy services. It also has a fleet of 7 ambulances equipped with the latest advanced medical support systems and the services of experienced paramedics. All the services in these institutions are offered to the BPL community at subsidized rates.

The foundation also has a professional team to cater to the various needs of society and make meaningful interventions in the community for its well-being. Homes for the homeless, medical aid for the sick, education assistance for the needy, need-based services for the differently abled, and a plethora of community services are executed regularly by this team.

Their major CSR contributions have been in the areas of quality education (public schools, an institute of automotive skill, and an institute of skill development), health (ambulance services, aquatic complex, fitness centers, counseling and psychotherapy, and diagnostic center), and community development (elderly day care and organic farming).

Hero MotoCorp, New Delhi: (Information given on website as dated on March 26, 2023).

The CSR team focuses on redefining mobility through the creation of a mobility roadmap. The CSR vision is to have a greener, safer, and equitable world. Their campaigns include:

  (i) **Ride Safe India:** A 360° initiative on making Indian roads safer to drastically reduce fatalities. This initiative is supported by the Ministry of Road Transport & Highways, Government of India.
 (ii) **Hamari Pari:** This campaign's effort is directed to specifically empower the women of tomorrow — a concentrated initiative targeted toward girls aged 6+ from the underprivileged sections of society to help and support them in their holistic development.
(iii) **Happy Earth:** This campaign aims at bringing change to our environment to literally make our world a happy place to live in. Happy Earth is focused on addressing environmental degradation, climate change or global warming, which is the greatest threat we have ever faced.
(iv) **Educate to Empower:** This campaign aims to support education, knowledge sharing, and skills development at all levels.

ITC Project, West Bengal: (Information given on website as dated on March 26, 2023).

ITC's avowed mission to create larger societal value has driven the company's CSR policy and practices for over two decades. Through its social investment program, Mission Sunehra Kal, ITC engages with multiple stakeholders — rural communities across India where ITC has agribusiness operations or those residing close to ITC's production units, as well as government bodies, program implementation partners and technical institutions — to develop and implement sustainable, replicable, and scalable models for the conservation of natural resources and ensuring societal welfare and inclusive development across its catchments in 27 states. The core purpose of ITC's Mission Sunehra Kal program is to secure the livelihoods of these marginalized communities for the future. The program encompasses interventions in water stewardship, social forestry, animal husbandry, sustainable agriculture, education, skilling, sanitation and solid waste management, and women empowerment. ITC's CSR interventions are spread across 235 districts of 27 states.

Satluj Jal Vidyut Nigam, Himachal Pradesh: (Information given on website as dated on March 27, 2023).

Satluj Jal Vidyut Nigam Ltd. (SJVN) implements its CSR activities with the belief that a business cannot succeed unless the society around it also develops alongside it. Government guidelines, millennium development goals, human rights, and the national agenda are the principles which guide the organization's CSR orientation. Their CSR activities have ranged from managing various disaster management and relief activities (2020–2021) to ensuring environmental sustainability (2020–2021), measures for the benefit of armed forces veterans, war widows, and their dependents (2020–2021), providing financial assistance for the promotion of sports (2020–2021), undertaking activities related to the protection of national heritage, arts, and culture (2020–2021), and activities related to gender equality (2020–2021), among many others.

Finolex Industries Limited (FIL): (Information given on website as dated on April 4, 2023).

FIL, which is primarily a agri-manufacturing company, has its units in the states of Maharashtra and Gujarat. FIL CSR implements its activities in the districts of Pune, Ratnagiri, Satara, and Vadodara. The CSR initiatives under FIL focus on: healthcare, education, social and community welfare, sanitation, and water conservation. FIL CSR, with the help of MukulMadhav Foundation, claimed the plantation of 18,864 trees over the last 5 years, 226 medical equipment's donated during the first and second waves of COVID-19, 745 pediatric surgeries since 2014, 24 water projects, 450 individual toilets in Wada and Jawahar blocks in Palghar district, 660 students provided with quality education, 312 widowed women farmers supported since 2019, and 29,990 ration kits donated under the "Give with Dignity" campaign.

TATA Steel: The Maternal and Newborn Survival Initiative (MANSI) program of Tata Steel Limited is a preventive healthcare initiative for pregnant women and newborns in the tribal villages of Jharkhand and Odisha.

With the well-trained "Sahiyya Women," a network of 2,400 Accredited Social Health Activist (ASHA) workers across villages in Jharkhand and Odisha, the MANSI program strengthens the rural healthcare system of these two Indian states. A Sahiyya undergoes classroom training, field training, learns the ways of home-based care and consultation, provision of basic medicine, and medical facilities, and equips herself to handle situations independently both during crises and otherwise. Through "Operation Sunshine," a mobile-based application used as a real-time tracker, the program detects high-risk cases among registered newborns or mothers. The 41 member staff of MANSI monitors all cases through Operation Sunshine and remains in constant touch with the 2,400 strong Sahiyya network.

"Masti Ki Pathshala" is an initiative to address the dark spot of the city of Jamshedpur to eradicate the worst forms of child labor from the city through education. The mission of rags to books is very challenging as the children have already picked up ways for earning and spending and got used to having financial freedom. Substance abuse is an added challenge, where there is addiction and an attitude of carefree existence. The intervention has to address all of this by genuinely creating an alternative environment which attracts the attention of these children, motivates them enough to return to the system, and creates an alternative way of life.

A separate unit for Dalit and tribal communities was created in 1984: "Adivasi & Harijan Welfare Cell" by Tata Steel, which was transformed thereafter into an independent entity presently known as the "Tribal Cultural Society" (TCS). TCS has been the company's efforts toward sustainable development in a manner which respects the traditional wisdom, knowledge, skills, and diversity that are vested in these communities where the company has its projects. The purpose of TCS includes the preservation and promotion of ethnic identity of the tribal communities, promoting education, especially among the youth to create an empowered society, promoting employability of the economically weaker sections through skill development, and improving health and hygiene among marginalized families. Apart from language preservation, conserving music and culture, promoting education, encouraging indigenous sports, and creating employability are the other wings of the initiative.

Jindal Steel and Power Limited: (information given on website as dated on April 4, 2023) Jindal Steel and Power Limited (JSPL) carries out its CSR activities in India through the JSPL Foundation. The JSPL Foundation was founded on the basis of doing good for the society and taking care of all its stakeholders. The triple bottom line (TBL) is a framework or theory that recommends that companies focus on social and environmental concerns along with profits. The TBL proposes that instead of one bottom line, there should be three: profit, people, and the planet. JSPL collaborated with HP in creating a telemedicine center to provide advanced health and medical services to the community to reduce mortality and morbidity. The telemedicine centers are linked to the Fortis OP Jindal Hospital at Raigarh, Chhattisgarh. In 2018–2019, more than 20,000 people visited these telemedicine facilities across the 7 centers and received advance medical care. JSPL operates majorly in Chhattisgarh, Odisha, and Jharkhand. These regions have a number of difficult geographical pockets, where medical resources and help are scarce. These camps not only provide curative services but also help raise health awareness, thereby sensitizing the communities in improving their healthcare-seeking behavior. In 2018–2019, more than 46,000 people were provided help or assistance with healthcare-related requirements through these healthcare dispensaries. Swachh Bharat Abhiyan, Kishori Express, and Vatsalya Programme are the other initiatives taken by JSPL.

Indian Oil: (information given on website as dated on April 4, 2023).

In the last 28 years, Indian Oil has contributed INR 3,347 crore toward various community development and CSR projects, improving the quality of lives of societies/communities primarily residing in the vicinity of the company's units/installations. Indian Oil's CSR thrust areas include "Safe drinking water and protection of water resources," "Healthcare and sanitation," "Education and employment-enhancing vocational skills," "Rural development," "Environment sustainability," and "Empowerment of women and socially/economically backward groups." Indian Oil undertakes CSR activities across the country, from Leh in J&K in the north to the north-eastern states, to Gujarat in the west and Tamil Nadu and Kerala in the south. The key CSR initiatives of Indian oil include: intercontinental rehabilitation of cheetah, Intensified Tuberculosis (TB) Elimination Project in Uttar Pradesh and Chhattisgarh, comprehensive cancer care, Indian Oil Vidushi, Skill Development Institute in Bhubaneswar, Odisha, Institute of Chemical Technology, Mumbai-Indian Oil Odisha Campus (ICTM-IOC) in Bhubaneswar, Odisha, and Assam Oil School of Nursing in Digboi, Assam, among many others.

Bandhan Bank: (information given on website as dated on April 4, 2023). Bandhan Bank's motto is committed to inclusive growth for all. The bank runs its CSR programs through various CSR implementing agencies, including Bandhan-Konnagar. Each program of Bandhan-Konnagar has been devised to bring about far-reaching effects in the fields of education, health, livelihood development, climate action, financial literacy, skill development, and employment generation. Each of these programs are designed to help the individuals who are most vulnerable and require the benefits of the programs the most. Bandhan Bank is targeting the hard-core poor program, which is a unique program designed for the poorest of the poor. Grants (in the form of free assets, not cash) are offered to destitute women. They start generating income out of this asset and are subsequently able to support themselves by independently making a living. It is seen that within 18–24 months of this grant intervention, these extremely poor beneficiaries start to graduate to a basic income-earning capability, uplifting themselves from extreme poverty and connecting with mainstream society. This program follows a 360° approach. Besides providing free assets, consistent counseling and mentoring support are also extended. A weekly subsistence allowance is also given to these women to help them meet their daily basic expenses until the assets begin to yield returns. Financial literacy is imparted so that they can make informed financial decisions. Education on socially relevant issues is also offered to increase their awareness and help them live better lives. A critical component of this program is the Ati Daridra Sahayak Committee, which brings together influencers in villages to serve as guardians of these beneficiaries even beyond the program period of 24 months. Overall confidence-building is done so that they do not fall into the poverty trap again. Over the years, it has been seen that there has been a positive impact of this intervention in the lives of many. There are certain beneficiaries who have been able to move away from a stage in life where they were even contemplating suicide for want of money to a stage where they earn thousands of rupees as monthly income, have a healthy life, and meet all the basic needs of their families.

Through these social initiatives, big or multinational (MNCs) organizations are trying their best to do sustainable activities for the development of Indian society and economy. The schematic representation of these initiatives is given in Figure 4. These MNCs are situated at particular places in India, and SMEs are situated in every part of India. To reach

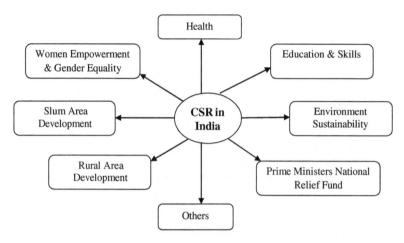

Figure 4.   CSR initiatives by organizations in India.

Source: Developed by author through analysis.

local and remote places, SMEs are the best resources for MNCs to implement these social activities sustainably. Through this, MNCs are able to create value addition to SMEs as well as to society.

Discussion

In developing nations such as India, CSR is viewed as a form of corporate philanthropy in which businesses support governmental programs by supporting social development. The idea of a trusteeship supporting socio-economic growth was first proposed by Mahatma Gandhi at the beginning of the 20th century. India has to modernize its CSR framework and put a stronger emphasis on shared responsibility for everyone's benefit in order to achieve sustainable development.

The most effective CSR plans ensure that, while organizations comply with legislation, their investments also respect the growth and development of marginalized communities and the environment. Involving initiatives that an organization can maintain without having an adverse effect on their business objectives, CSR should also be sustainable. Indian businesses have been fairly wise in embracing CSR activities and incorporating them into their operational procedures. It has gradually gained importance in the Indian corporate environment as organizations have realized how crucial it is to develop relationships with society at large in addition to expanding their enterprises.

Nowadays, organizations have separate departments and teams that create specific goals, plans, and budgets for their CSR initiatives. These programs are frequently built on clearly defined social views or are carefully matched to organizational goals.

Under Section 135 of the Companies Act of 2013 (Nikhil & Bhavani, 2020), India became the first nation to enact legislation mandating companies to engage in CSR activities and report CSR initiatives. As part of any CSR compliance, companies are permitted to put their earnings toward causes including hunger, gender equality, women empowerment, poverty, health, skill development, and education. However, some of the present CSR frameworks have certain issues, including a lack of transparency, poor community engagement in CSR initiatives, and insufficient time for audits.

Through legislation and regulation, governments have attempted to enforce social and environmental goals in business. Voluntary and non-regulatory efforts are being investigated as a result of decreasing government resources and skepticism about rules.

There is lack of clear guidelines and direction about CSR in India, and because of this, the level of CSR is based on the size of the organizations. Consequently, a larger organization has a bigger role in CSR activities than a smaller one, even though these SMEs want to contribute to the CSR activities.

There is a lack of local stakeholder engagement within CSR projects. This lack of engagement frequently results in similar CSR activities by the organizations within their areas of involvement, due to which there will prevail a more competitive environment between local stakeholders rather than building collaborative approaches to finding solutions to local problems through CSR activities.

Organizations should gather regular feedback on their CSR activities and adopt a more professional approach to measuring the impact of their CSR activities. They should also set clear objectives and align their stakeholders with them. Simultaneously, it is equally significant to let their stakeholders know of their business needs. Governments should also address the issues of stakeholders and increase awareness about the importance of CSR within society.

The time has come to link CSR and the Sustainable Development Goals (SDGs) because India has prioritized and achieved the SDGs by making them a mainstream part of the national agenda. India would be able to advance toward sustainable and green growth while increasing CSR responsibilities. End-of-life conceptions for products should be replaced by technologies and rules that make recycling and reusing easier as part of CSR. By doing this, waste can be kept to a minimum and pollution can be decreased while also extending the life cycle of products. India can make the shift to a circular economy in due course. This may be an effort to bring about the society we envision — one that is just, compassionate, and equitable — where every action, no matter how small, is motivated by this broader, sustainable vision.

Conclusion

The concept of CSR in India was based on charity or philanthropy, but that has changed now. CSR activities have been done by MNCs or large organizations, but now this has extended to SMEs as well. However, there are various difficulties in understanding the responsibility with which corporate governance is able to participate in supporting SMEs. New research needs to comprehend the effects of "corporate governance" on SMEs. Different hurdles come within the mode of the more excellent execution of efficient corporate governance.

It can be challenging to persuade SME owners to spend the time necessary to learn about "corporate governance," and it might be advantageous to strengthen the organization. Moreover, it is essential to consider the basic terms. The word "corporate" may cause family-owned or not-incorporated SMEs to believe that the framework of corporate governance does not apply to them.

Theories and approaches to corporate governance were often created for big organizations. This may also prevent SMEs from implementing them. Flexible use of a framework is required, considering SMEs' heterogeneous nature. However, large organizations may impact SMEs by supporting research, developing standards, understanding the challenges, and promoting better governance standards.

CSR is optional for SMEs, but if practical processes are in place, there are obvious benefits. Since CSR and corporate governance go hand in hand and are connected, incorporating CSR provisions within the corporate governance framework will provide Indian MSMEs with new skills. These ideas within SMEs have yet to become important elements of sustainable development. CSR and corporate governance are therefore essential for sustainable growth in SMEs.

References

Abor, J. & Adjasi, C. K. D. (2007). Corporate governance and the small and medium enterprises sector: Theory and implications. *Corporate Governance*, 7(2), 111–122. https://doi.org/10.1108/14720700710739769.

Abor, J. & Biekpe, N. (2007). Corporate governance, ownership structure and performance of SMEs in Ghana: Implications for financing opportunities. *Corporate Governance: The International Journal of Business in Society*, 7(3), 288–300.

ABOUT US. (n.d.). Manappuram Foundation. https://manappuramfoundation. org/about-us/ (Accessed March 26, 2023).

Aras, G. & Crowther, D. (2010). *A Handbook of Corporate Governance and Social Responsibility*. Gower Publishing Limited, London.

Assessment of corporate social responsibility by addressing sustainable development goals.

Corporate Governance: The International Journal of Business in Society, 22(1), 23–41.

Corporate Social Responsibility — Hero MotoCorp Ltd. (n.d.). Hero MotoCorp Ltd. https://www.heromotocorp.com/en-in/csr.php (Accessed March 26, 2023).

Corporate Social Responsibility and Environmental Management, 28(2), 686–703.

Corporate Social Responsibility: The India Drive — Outlookindia. (n.d.). Outlookindia. https://www.outlookindia.com/csr_2019_02/itc.php (Accessed March 26, 2023).

Dube, I., Dube, D., & Mishra, P. (2011). Corporate governance norm for SME. *Journal of Public Administration and Governance*, 77–123.

Ebner, D. (2007). Assessing corporate social responsibility: CSR-SCAN. https:// crrconference.org/Previous_conferences/downloads/crrc2007ebner2.pdf.

Elkington, J. (2018). 25 years ago I coined the phrase "triple bottom line." Here's why it's time to rethink it. *Harvard Business Review*, 25, 2–5. https://hbr. org/2018/06/25-years-ago-i-coined-the-phrase-triple-bottom-line-heres-why-im- giving-up-on-it (Accessed August 19, 2021).

Hart, O. (1995). Corporate governance: Some theory and implications. *The Economic Journal*, 105(430), 678–689.

Infosys Foundation — Supporting Underprivileged Sections of Society Create Opportunities and Strive Towards a More Equitable Society. (n.d.). Infosys. https://www.infosys.com/infosys-foundation.html (Accessed March 27, 2023).

Krechovská, M. & Procházková, P. T. (2014). Sustainability and its integration into corporate governance focusing on corporate performance management and reporting. *Procedia Engineering*, 69, 1144–1151.

OECD, O. (2004). The OECD principles of corporate governance. *Contaduría y Administración*, (216).

Raynard, P. & Forstater, M. (2002). Corporate social responsibility: Implications for small and medium enterprises in developing countries.

Schönherr, N., Findler, F., & Martinuzzi, A. (2017). Exploring the interface of CSR and the sustainable development goals. *Transnational Corporations*, 24(3), 33–47.

Singh, K. & Pillai, D. (2022). Corporate governance in small and medium enterprises: A review. *SJVN Limited — Himachal Pradesh — Company CSR Profile.* (n.d.). CSRBOX. https://csrbox.org/India_Company_SJVN-Limited--Himachal- Pradesh_5383 (Accessed March 27, 2023).

Srinivasan Services Trust. (n.d.). https://www.tvssst.org/vision-mission/ (Accessed March 27, 2023).

Verma, D. P. & Kumar, R. (2012). Relationship between corporate social responsibility and corporate governance. *Journal of Business and Management*, 3, 24–26.

Websites

- https://iocl.com/pages/csr-overview (INDIAL OIL).
- https://www.finolexpipes.com/csr/ (FINOLEX).
- https://bandhanbank.com/beyond-banking (BANDHAN BANK).
- https://thecsrjournal.in/jspl-jindal-csr-report-2020/ (JINDAL).
- https://www.infosys.com/infosys-foundation.html (Infosys Foundation).
- https://www.tvssst.org/vision-mission/ (Srinivasan Service Trust).
- https://csrbox.org/India_Company_SJVN-Limited--Himachal- Pradesh_5383 (SJVN Ltd.).
- https://www.heromotocorp.com/en-in/csr.php (Hero MotoCorp Ltd.).
- https://manappuramfoundation.org/about-us/ (Manappuram Foundation).

https://doi.org/10.1142/9789811296444_0007

Chapter 7

Green Organizations and Strategies toward Sustainability

Seema Garg* and Namrata Pancholi†

Amity University, Noida, UP, India

*sgarg3@amity.edu

†namratapancholi@gmail.com

Abstract

In recent years, there has been a growing awareness of the urgent need to address environmental challenges and embrace sustainable practices. Green organizations, also known as environmental or eco-friendly organizations, play a pivotal role in driving positive change toward a more sustainable future. India has experienced significant growth in recent years in terms of its green organizations and initiatives. This is because an organization's sustainability has a big impact on the environment. Organizational environmental sustainability is a significant concern as the world concentrates on achieving the Sustainable Development Goals (SDG) (UNDP, 2021) and corporate social responsibility. The United Nations advises that eco-friendly practices and knowledge reach all stakeholders in the present globalized market, not just one particular organization (UNDP, 2021). The country's growing awareness about environmental issues, climate change, and sustainable development has led to the emergence of numerous organizations and initiatives dedicated to promoting eco-friendly practices, conservation, and environmental protection. This chapter explores the significance of green organizations, their various forms and functions, and the key initiatives they undertake to promote environmental conservation and protection.

Keywords: Environmental challenges, sustainable practices, climate change, waste management, global collaboration, circular economy.

Introduction

Green organizations, also known as environmental organizations, eco-friendly organizations, or environmental non-governmental organizations (NGOs), are entities established with the primary objective of promoting environmental conservation, sustainability, and protection. These organizations are dedicated to addressing various environmental issues, such as climate change, biodiversity loss, pollution, deforestation, and resource depletion. Their activities encompass a wide range of areas, including advocacy, education, research, community engagement, and on-the-ground conservation efforts. The scope of green organizations extends beyond individual actions, aiming to foster systemic change at regional, national, and global levels. These organizations play a crucial role in shaping public opinion, influencing policies, and advocating for environmentally responsible practices across sectors. Eco-friendly businesses, also known as sustainable businesses or green businesses, are enterprises that prioritize environmental responsibility and integrate sustainability into their core operations. These businesses aim to minimize their negative impact on the environment while striving for economic success. Understanding how these businesses incorporate sustainability practices is crucial to fostering a more sustainable and environmentally conscious economy. In the era of the knowledge economy, organizations have paid attention to maintaining the suitability of products and services (Yu *et al.*, 2022).

Role of Green Organizations

High expectations are placed on businesses to engage in behaviors for ecological maintenance as a result of the rise in environmental challenges, such as global climate change and the endangerment of animal species. Scholars, managers, and decision-makers have all paid close attention to how corporate management contributes to sustainable development. Hence, environmental conservation and protection are the main objectives. Green organizations work to safeguard ecosystems, wildlife, and natural resources to ensure their sustainable use for present and future generations. Green organizations actively address climate change by advocating for policies and initiatives aimed at reducing greenhouse gas emissions, promoting renewable energy adoption, and building resilience to climate impacts. Rosenbaum and Wong (2015) investigated a guest's subjective appraisal of a hotel's green marketing program, or green equity, and they found that green equity plays a significant role in customers' overall assessment of a hotel's marketing programs. These organizations are committed to preserving biodiversity by protecting endangered species and habitats and promoting sustainable land-use practices that maintain ecological balance. They engage in lobbying and advocacy efforts to influence governments, policymakers, and international organizations to adopt environmentally friendly policies and regulations. It is essential to raise public awareness about environmental issues, their consequences, and the importance of sustainable practices. By educating the public, they encourage behavioral changes that contribute to a more eco-friendly lifestyle. Also, green organizations support sustainable development practices that balance economic growth with environmental protection and social well-being. They advocate for responsible consumption, waste reduction, and green technologies. According to organizational theory, firms need more external relationships to produce Geographical Indicator's (GIs) (Messeni Petruzzelli *et al.*, 2011). Through the sharing of fresh perspectives and cutting-edge techniques, the development and management of external relationships with stakeholders promote environmentally friendly activities (Zhou *et al.*, 2019).

Role in Influencing Policies and Societal Behaviors

Green organizations use their expertise and research to advocate for policy changes and legal measures that address environmental challenges effectively. They engage in discussions with policymakers, participate in international climate conferences, and collaborate with governments to shape environmental regulations. Through public awareness campaigns, green organizations aim to inform and mobilize individuals and communities to take action on environmental issues and education. These campaigns may involve media outreach, educational programs, and public events to influence societal behaviors. They often form alliances with other environmental and social groups, businesses, and academia to strengthen their impact. Collaborative efforts allow them to pool resources and expertise and reach broader audiences. They also conduct scientific research and collect data to support their advocacy efforts and demonstrate the urgency and importance of environmental conservation and an ecologically balanced world.

Environmental NGOs are independent organizations that operate without government affiliation and play a crucial role in environmental advocacy and conservation efforts. These NGOs are driven by a mission to address environmental challenges, protect natural resources, and promote sustainable practices. Their key roles and contributions are concerned with environmental advocacy, in which they actively lobby and campaign for environmental issues, aiming to influence policymakers, governments, and international organizations to adopt environmentally friendly policies and regulations. By voicing concerns and providing scientific evidence, these organizations seek to bring attention to pressing environmental problems and push for effective solutions. Environmental NGOs work on policy development, suggesting innovative solutions to environmental challenges and collaborating with policymakers to implement them. They provide expert advice, research findings, and data to shape environmental policies at local, national, and global levels. They advocate for climate action, promote renewable energy, and encourage sustainable land-use practices to mitigate the impacts of climate change. Additionally, they work toward building resilience in communities vulnerable to climate-related events. They play a vital role in raising public awareness about environmental issues. Through educational programs, workshops, public events, and media campaigns, they inform and engage the public, inspiring individuals to adopt more environmentally friendly behaviors. For global engagement, they engage in international environmental negotiations and agreements. They participate in conferences and summits, advocating for strong commitments to address global environmental issues such as climate change and biodiversity loss. Hence, these green organizations contribute significantly to preserving the planet's natural resources and promoting a more sustainable future.

Green Organization and Sustainability

Green management is all about ensuring corporate sustainability without compromising future requirements. The relationship between sustainability and corporate strategy suggests a chance for businesses to offer long-term solutions, including the requirement to improve the standard of the workplace and surrounding environment. Corporate sustainability, sustainable development, and corporate social responsibility (CSR) are some of the names for sustainability in management. According to the World Commission on Environmental Development (WCED), sustainability refers to development that fulfills present needs without jeopardizing the ability of future generations to meet their own needs. It focuses on three areas: environmental protection, economic growth, and social equity. Corporate sustainability focuses on the three Ps of people, planet, and profit and looks for ways to strike a balance between them.

Improved environmental performance may result from the implementation of an integrated organizational approach. Therefore, in order to implement green initiatives, top management commitment and staff desire to adopt ecological practices are required (Tang *et al.*, 2018). As a result, a company can increase organizational effectiveness and gain a competitive edge in a variety of product development domains (Ortiz-de-Mandojana & Aguilera-Caracuel, 2013). Reduced use of energy and natural resources, fewer waste and pollution emissions, greater financial performance, and enhanced environmental performance are all potential organizational benefits of green practices (Lin & Ho, 2011).

Green Community

Green community groups, also known as environmental or sustainability community groups, are grassroots organizations that operate at the local level with a primary focus on promoting sustainable practices within communities. These groups are driven by a shared commitment to environmental stewardship and work collectively to address environmental challenges and create positive change in their neighborhoods and regions. Their localized approach allows them to connect intimately with community members and address specific environmental issues in meaningful and impactful ways. By fostering local engagement, promoting sustainable living, and advocating for change, these groups play a significant role in building environmentally conscious and resilient communities.

Green community groups engage with residents and stakeholders at the local level, empowering them to take action for the environment. These groups often begin with passionate individuals coming together with a common concern for their community's well-being and natural surroundings. A key initiative of green community groups is to raise awareness and educate community members about sustainable living practices. They organize workshops, seminars, and events to provide information on topics such as energy conservation, waste reduction, recycling, and eco-friendly lifestyle choices. They undertake various environmental projects tailored to the specific needs of their community. These projects may include tree planting initiatives, community gardens, urban greening, litter clean-ups, and habitat restoration efforts. Also, while primarily focused on local initiatives, green community groups often engage in advocacy efforts to influence local policies and decision-making processes. They collaborate with local government officials and other stakeholders to promote sustainability-minded policies and practices.

They work to reduce waste in their neighborhoods and encourage recycling. They may organize recycling drives, support composting initiatives, and promote the use of reusable products. They advocate for the adoption of solar, wind, or other renewable energy sources. They also emphasize energy efficiency measures in homes, businesses, and public spaces. They are often involved in protecting and preserving natural areas and green spaces within their communities. Green strategies not only help in creating a sustainable environment but also make the earth more clean and green (Rathee & Rajain, 2013). They may collaborate with local conservation organizations to safeguard parks, wetlands, and wildlife habitats.

India's Growth in Green Organizations

There has been a notable increase in the number of NGOs and non-profit groups focusing on environmental issues across the country. These organizations work at both grassroots and national levels, addressing various aspects of environmental conservation. Also, the Indian government has taken various steps to encourage and support green initiatives. Initiatives like Swachh Bharat Abhiyan (Clean India Mission) have promoted waste management and cleanliness. Additionally, the government has emphasized renewable energy projects and sustainable development through schemes such as the National Action Plan on Climate Change. India, like other United Nations member states, has adopted the 17 Sustainable Development Goals (SDGs), which include objectives related to environmental conservation, clean energy, and climate action. This has led to increased attention and investment in green initiatives. Many companies in India have started incorporating sustainability practices into their operations. CSR initiatives in India by different green organizations often include environmental conservation projects, renewable energy adoption, and waste management efforts. Some climate activism and awareness programs, including the rise of global climate movements such as Fridays for Future, have also influenced India's environmental landscape. Young activists and concerned citizens have been pushing for stronger environmental policies and actions from both the government and the private sector.

The growth of green organizations in India has been accompanied by advancements in green technology and innovation. These include renewable energy projects (solar, wind, and biomass), water conservation methods, and eco-friendly agricultural practices. Indian green organizations have also collaborated with international bodies, NGOs, and environmental experts to exchange knowledge and resources for tackling global environmental challenges. While India still faces significant environmental challenges, such as air and water pollution, deforestation, and waste management, the growth of green organizations indicates a positive shift toward greater environmental consciousness and sustainability. With continued efforts from the government, civil society, and private entities, India's environmental landscape is expected to witness further progress in the coming years.

Several organizations in India have taken significant steps toward sustainability and environmental responsibility. A few examples of such green organizations and their strategies are mentioned as follows:

Infosys: Infosys, a prominent Information Technology (IT) services company, has implemented various sustainability initiatives. They have set ambitious goals to become carbon neutral and achieve zero waste in landfills. Infosys has invested in renewable energy sources, such as solar and wind power, to reduce its carbon footprint. They also focus on water conservation, energy efficiency, and sustainable building designs on their campuses.

Tata Motors: Tata Motors, a leading automobile manufacturer, is known for its commitment to sustainable practices. They have developed electric and hybrid vehicles to reduce emissions and dependence on fossil fuels. Tata Motors also works on waste reduction and recycling initiatives in their manufacturing processes.

Godrej Group: The Godrej Group, a conglomerate with interests in consumer goods, real estate, and industrial products, has integrated sustainability into its business operations. They have adopted eco-friendly manufacturing processes, energy-efficient technologies, and sustainable packaging practices. The company also focuses on community development and education programs related to environmental issues.

Wipro: Wipro, another major IT services company, has implemented a range of sustainability initiatives. They have achieved carbon neutrality and reduced water consumption through efficient practices. Wipro's campuses are designed to be energy-efficient, and they have invested in renewable energy projects to power their operations.

Adani Green Energy: Adani Green Energy is one of the largest renewable energy companies in India. They focus on developing solar and wind power projects to contribute to India's renewable energy goals. The company's strategy revolves around expanding their renewable energy capacity and reducing the country's reliance on fossil fuels.

Indian Tobacco Company (ITC) Limited: ITC Limited, a diversified conglomerate, has undertaken several sustainability initiatives. They have integrated environmental considerations into their product development processes, leading to sustainable and eco-friendly products. ITC has also worked on forestation and water conservation projects to enhance environmental stewardship.

Mahindra Group: The Mahindra Group, with interests in various sectors, emphasizes sustainability through their "Rise for Good" philosophy. They have developed electric vehicles, promoted rural sustainability through various initiatives, and focused on sustainable agriculture practices.

Suzlon Energy: Suzlon Energy is a renewable energy company that specializes in wind power. They have played a significant role in expanding India's wind energy capacity and promoting clean energy sources.

Hero MotoCorp: Hero MotoCorp, a leading motorcycle manufacturer, has been working on developing fuel-efficient and electric two-wheelers. They aim to reduce emissions and promote sustainable mobility solutions.

Coca-Cola India: Coca-Cola India has invested in water replenishment projects to balance the water usage in their operations. They focus on efficient water management, recycling, and community engagement to address water scarcity issues.

These examples showcase how various organizations in India are adopting diverse strategies to promote sustainability, reduce environmental impacts, and contribute to a greener future.

Future of Green Organizations Toward Sustainability

The future of green organizations and their strategies toward sustainability holds great promise and potential for even more significant positive impacts on the environment and society. As the world continues to grapple with environmental challenges, these organizations' commitment to sustainability is likely to evolve and adapt so as to remain at the forefront of responsible business practices. They could invest further in research and development to identify and adopt cutting-edge technologies that enhance sustainability efforts. These might involve advancements in renewable energy, resource-efficient production processes, waste reduction methods, and smart systems for monitoring and managing environmental impacts. Embracing a circular economy approach could become a central focus. The organizations could develop strategies to minimize waste by designing products for durability, repairability, and recyclability. This approach would involve collaborating with suppliers and partners to create closed-loop systems that extend product lifecycles.

From the perspective of global expansion and global collaboration, they could extend their influence globally by partnering with international entities, governments, and organizations. Collaborative initiatives on a larger scale could lead to a broader adoption of sustainable practices and policies across industries and regions. Educating and involving stakeholders in sustainability initiatives can build a stronger sense of ownership and commitment to the organization's goals.

In conclusion, green organizations' journey toward sustainability is likely to be a dynamic and evolving process. By embracing innovation, collaboration, and a holistic approach to environmental responsibility, these organizations have the potential to shape a more sustainable and resilient future for themselves and the broader community.

Conclusion

The green organizations' dedication to sustainability and their strategic initiatives represent an important step toward a future that is more environmentally conscious. These organizations have employed a variety of techniques to attain sustainability goals along the way, demonstrating a thorough knowledge of the urgent need to address environmental concerns. The green organizations have decreased their ecological impact and set a good example for others to follow by adopting sustainable practices. They have demonstrated their commitment to reducing adverse environmental effects by using eco-friendly technologies, effective resource management, waste reduction programs, and the use of renewable energy sources. Furthermore, a sense of shared responsibility for sustainability has been cultivated thanks to these organizations' emphasis on stakeholder participation, collaboration, and openness. They have built a wider network of support for their sustainability goals by incorporating their staff, clients, suppliers, and neighborhood groups into their activities.

Finally, the green organizations' sustainability strategies demonstrate their dedication to a greener, more sustainable future. Their proactive attempts to strike a balance between economic development and environmental protection illustrate the possibility for firms to be both successful and socially responsible. The organizations are in a position to not only achieve their own sustainability goals but also to motivate others to take significant actions toward a more sustainable world as they continue to hone and broaden their methods.

References

Lin, C. Y. & Ho, Y. H. (2011). Determinants of green practice adoption for logistics companies in China. *Journal of Business Ethics*, 98, 67–83.

Messeni Petruzzelli, A., Maria Dangelico, R., Rotolo, D., & Albino, V. (2011). Organizational factors and technological features in the development of green innovations: Evidence from patent analysis. *Innovation*, 13(3), 291–310.

Ortiz-de-Mandojana, N. & Aguilera-Caracuel, J. (2013). Green innovation and financial performance: An institutional approach. *Organization & Environment*, 26(4), 365–385.

Rathee, R. & Rajain, P. (2013). Green marketing: Consumer perception and competitive strategies. In *International Conference on Reinventing Thinking beyond Boundaries to Excel*, pp. 76–82. April 6, 2013. Faridabad, India.

Rosenbaum, M. S. & Wong, I. A. (2015). Green marketing programs as strategic initiatives in hospitality. *Journal of Services Marketing*, 29(2), 81–92. http://doi.org/10.1108/JSM-07-2013-0167.

Tang, M., Walsh, G., Lerner, D., Fitza, M. A., & Li, Q. (2018). Green innovation, managerial concern and firm performance: An empirical study. *Business strategy and the Environment*, 27(1), 39–51.

UNDP. (2021). Sustainable development goals. United Nations Development Programme. https://unstats.un.org/sdgs/report/2021/The-Sustainable-Development-Goals-Report-2021.pdf.

Yu, S., Abbas, J., Alvarez-Otero, S., & Cherian, J. (2022). Green knowledge management: Scale development and validation. *Journal of Innovation & Knowledge*, 7(4), 1–9.

Zhou, Y., Shu, C., Jiang, W., & Gao, S. (2019). Green management, firm innovations, and environmental turbulence. *Business Strategy and the Environment*, 28(4), 567–581.

Part IV

Ecosystem Approach

Chapter 8

Start-Ups in Smaller Cities of India: Ecosystem Challenges and Unique Opportunities

**Kumar Mukul[*,‡], Monoo John[*,§], Amit N. Angadi[†,||],
S. Jayadatta[†,**], and M. Preethi[*,††]**

[*]*CMS Business School, Faculty of Management Studies,
Jain Deemed-To-Be University, Bengaluru, India*

[†]*KLE 'Society's Institute of Management Studies and
Research (IMSR), Hubli, India*

[‡]*dr.kumar_mukul@cms.ac.in*

[§]*dr.monoojohn@cms.ac.in*

[||]*amit.angadi@kleimsrhubli.org*

[**]*jayadattas@kleimsrhubli.org*

[††]*preethi_manishekar@cms.ac.in*

Abstract

In recent times, India has observed significant entrepreneurial activity. These activities are spearheaded by new-age start-ups driven by break-through ideas, innovations, and technology adoption, on the one hand, and awareness of their context and ecosystem, on the other. Entrepreneurship is well accepted as a socioeconomic phenomenon, and start-up activities are best explained considering their embeddedness in the ecosystem where they operate. Though India is among the leading countries in terms of overall start-up activities and ecosystem, the growth is not uniformly distributed when it comes to participation by all parts of the country. Although a few pockets have traditionally led the entrepreneurship movement, there is a noticeable increase in the participation of start-ups from the smaller cities and towns in the country's interior parts. Apart from the regular start-up-related resource constraints, they also have to overcome ecosystem-related challenges in their entrepreneurial journey. The current chapter explores the impact of context, its effect on the growth of start-ups, and the impact of the start-up ecosystem in smaller cities. The purpose of the study is to identify unique strategies adopted by start-ups in facing these challenges.

Keywords: Start-ups, entrepreneurship, ecosystem challenges and opportunities.

Introduction

India is in a very favorable demographic state with the largest pool of young population, which may propel economic and entrepreneurial activities and help the country leap ahead of its emerging economy counterparts. With over 600 million youth in the age group of 18–34, there is unparalleled potential available to be leveraged for developmental activities. Around 65% of India's population is below 35 years of age (Deo, 2023). However, due to a lack of skills and opportunities, most of this workforce are "job seekers" and "unemployable." So, there is a lurking danger of "demographic disaster," which may happen if things are not put on track. The youth of India are high on aspirations, and with growing educational and awareness levels, there must be corresponding industrial growth and job creation. Unfortunately, this is not happening as expected, resulting in high unemployment among the young population. Despite an impressive growth of Gross Domestic Product (GDP) in the range of 6–8% over the last two and a half decades, the unemployment rate has been lurking at high levels of 8–9%. The International Labour Organization (ILO) stated that the unemployment rate has increased from 4.9% in 2018 to an astounding 7.5% in 2020, with the COVID-19 pandemic aggravating the situation (Deo, 2023). The only possible solution to this seems to be to give the highest priority to job creation through self-employment initiated by entrepreneurial endeavors.

Entrepreneurship seems to be the apt response, and the current government, realizing this fact, is giving utmost importance to encouraging the start-up culture and creating a supportive environment to nurture entrepreneurial ventures in the country. Despite the abundance of resources and opportunities for entrepreneurial activities, the lack of a supportive ecosystem undermines the cause of entrepreneurship. Regarding entrepreneurial performance, India ranks very low (78th out of 137 nations ranked in the Global Entrepreneurship and Development Index, 2019). Another problem is the disparities seen within the different states and regions of the country. It is estimated that five Indian states account for more than 60% of all start-ups in India, according to the Ministry of Commerce and Industry (Choudhary *et al.*, 2022). Bengaluru, Delhi-National Capital Region (NCR), and Mumbai, with 95% of overall investment value across 443 deals in H1 of 2021, continue to dominate the Indian start-up ecosystem (Choudhary *et al.*, 2022). Recent successful initiatives of the Indian government, such as "Start-up India" and "Make in India," are positive steps toward creating an all-inclusive technology-driven support system in the country.

Keeping this context in mind, the study's main objective is to explore the major facilitating and hindering factors in the present ecosystem of entrepreneurship in the interior regions of India, with a focus on smaller towns, and to understand how these factors are affecting the growth of start-ups. While some regions, especially the metros such as Bengaluru, Pune, Hyderabad, Gurugram, New Delhi, and NCR regions, have always been at the forefront of the start-up movement, the smaller cities and interior regions are somehow lagging. Only 20% of the 50,000 start-ups in India operate out of the Tier 2 and Tier 3 cities, and they have only raised a small proportion of the overall investment (Choudhary *et al.*, 2022). There are still plenty of improvements to be achieved, especially in the country's smaller cities, towns, and interior regions. What are the constraints that start-ups face in these regions which deter their growth? The chapter explores these issues.

Start-ups and Their Unique Challenges

A start-up is a business enterprise in the initial stages of its operations (Bhatt *et al.*, 2022). Start-ups and entrepreneurial businesses are vulnerable due to their "newness and smallness" (Stinchcombe, 1965; El Hanchi & Kerzazi, 2020). Gage (2012) states that three out of four start-ups fail. Entrepreneurial firms are vulnerable due to a lack of resources and their inability to attract resources in their early stages. In various studies, it has been established that the entrepreneurial ecosystem and supporting institutions play a prominent role in start-ups' survival and growth (Chortareas *et al.*, 2013; Korreck, 2019). The environment in which entrepreneurs strive to start up, operationalizing their innovative ideas into sustainable ventures, is no less important than the entrepreneurial traits and business ideas conceptualized by an entrepreneur.

Start-up Ecosystems

The success of an entrepreneur's business ideas and the growth of their ventures are profoundly impacted by the ecosystem in which their start-ups essentially operate. The ecosystem is essential to the initial development of the firm, the later stages of the firm's evolution, and the overall growth of the regional business environment. Furthermore, it ensures innovative products and services, sustainable solutions to perennial problems, and employment opportunities within a country (Krajcik & Formanek, 2015). "Entrepreneurial ecosystem" is a term that refers to a complex network of interconnected actors in the entrepreneurial realm.

A rich, nurturing, and fertile start-up ecosystem requires the adequate presence and support of key constituents such as government bodies, available market, human capital, business associations, funding agencies, professional bodies, educational institutions, incubators, infrastructure, and support systems. The smaller towns generally lack the depth of abundant availability and easy access to these ecosystem elements (Mukul & Saini, 2021). Entrepreneurs possess the skillset to conduct environmental scans, identify and evaluate opportunities, and subsequently convert them into viable business propositions. This process involves the establishment of significant economic entities, which in turn facilitates the redirection of resources from less productive to more productive uses, ultimately resulting in the creation of wealth. By optimizing the utilization of natural and national resources, they serve as drivers of economic progress and catalysts for social change and transformation (Jayadatta, 2017).

Start-ups and COVID-19

The Indian start-up ecosystem has consistently been seen as "thriving," "booming," and "progressive" until the onset of the COVID-19 pandemic (Kumar & Rai, 2023). India has experienced significant growth in the range of opportunities for start-up growth during the past 20 years, from having no experience at all with start-ups to now being the third-largest country globally.

The global pandemic of 2020 was predicted to be the "black swan" of the century, with the International Monetary Fund (IMF) declaring the recession worse than the one in 2009 (Makridakis *et al.*, 2009). India was one of the nations whose economies saw the full effects of the global epidemic and was subjected to one of the strictest lockdowns worldwide. Around 40% of start-ups were adversely affected by the pandemic, with almost 15% shutting shop (*Economic Times*, October 14, 2020).

The smaller town start-ups underwent harsh times with fatal consequences, though the resilient ones leaped ahead by grabbing opportunities. The lockdown measures resulted in a cessation of demand, which had a severe impact on the revenues of start-ups in smaller towns. Consequently, numerous businesses were compelled to either cease operations or modify their business strategies to endure the crisis. There was a significant decrease in investors engaged in start-up fundraising until 2020. Many industries have undergone transformations because of the COVID-19 pandemic, from their methods of operation to their modes of operation. Early-stage and mid-stage start-ups are the most impacted, and the pandemic prompted numerous SMEs to close their doors, significantly impacting the economy.

Although the pandemic had a brutal bearing on start-ups, it also paved the way for growth in terms of reimagining, refocusing, and reengineering. There was a surge in creative thinking and problem-solving abilities, with start-ups becoming more solution-oriented, cost-effective, radically innovative, and committed to sustainability. Some evident examples of this can be extracted from healthcare and biotech start-ups, such as Nocca, MyLab, and Bione (COVID-19 testing kits and diagnostic solutions). Start-ups have demonstrated their resilient character, becoming unicorns during the pandemic, including Nykaa, Unacademy, Razorpay, and Postman.

According to a survey done by Nasscom during the second wave of COVID-19, the technology firms of India (Multinational Companies (MNCs), start-ups) have shown a sensible and rapid response to the pandemic-posed challenges (National Association of Software and Service Companies (NASSCOM), 2020). As per the survey, the Indian tech start-ups not only survived but also grew during the pandemic, mostly in cases where founders have leveraged the opportunities of remote work as a capability, focused on growth at an affordable cost, and developed a mind-set of "think global, act local" to keep growing, despite all the odds of the pandemic.

According to another report (NASSCOM, 2021), the five verticals of Indian start-ups — fintech, health tech, retail tech, edtech, and enterprise tech — did not see an adverse impact during COVID-19 from a funding perspective. In addition, as per the recent Global Entrepreneurship Monitor (GEM) Report, despite the pandemic, less than one in 10 adult entrepreneurs have exited the business in most economies (GEM, 2021). This is a positive sign in the growth cycle of the start-ups, and the resilience that the founders illustrated during the crisis times has added to their future possibilities.

Growing Start-up Activities in Smaller Cities of India

The emergence of Tier 2 and Tier 3 cities in India has created new opportunities for businesses due to the comparatively lower cost of doing business. Furthermore, the government has selected many of these cities for transformation into smart cities, thereby enhancing their potential for future growth. Moreover, a considerable number of these urban centers are evolving into pivotal locations for the storage and transportation of goods. The availability of quality housing at affordable rates, cheap labor, seamless connectivity, and unexplored markets make these attractive destinations for businesses, working-class people, and start-ups. The government plans to improve infrastructure, such as additional airports and health and education facilities, in smaller cities to add to the prospects. The peaceful and less-polluted environment also provides opportunities for quality of life and professional growth. The untapped potential of Tier 2 and Tier 3 cities in India remains to be fully realized. The COVID-19 pandemic has presented novel opportunities for smaller cities amidst the crisis.

The start-up activity in India's smaller cities and towns has witnessed a steep rise since the onset of COVID-19. According to a report by the Department for Promotion of Industry and Internal Trade (DPIIT), in

2022, a total of 72,993 start-ups have been recognized in India. Notably, over 38,250 of these start-ups were found to be operational in cities classified as Tier 2 and Tier 3. The cities of Mumbai, Delhi, Chennai, Kolkata, Bengaluru, Hyderabad, Ahmedabad, and Pune are classified as Tier 1 cities, while the remaining cities are classified as belonging to either Tier 2 or Tier 3. Therefore, over 50% of the recognized start-ups belong to non-metropolitan cities (*The Economic Times*, 2022; Choudhary *et al.*, 2022; Khan & Magd, 2022). The technological advancements observed in Tier 2 and Tier 3 cities are contributing to the economic growth of the nation and facilitating socioeconomic transformation at a global level (Ojha, 2023). The acceleration of start-up growth in small cities can be attributed to various factors, such as enhanced infrastructural support, faster Internet connectivity, favorable working conditions, improved transport communication, and accessibility to a vast pool of talented individuals.

According to the Economic Survey 2020–2021, nearly half of the recognized start-ups were from smaller cities in India. The reasons are many, and they are solving local problems in various areas, such as healthcare, education, agriculture, and services. Developing localized, decentralized, and grass-roots-level start-up ecosystems in smaller cities will subsequently improve the quality of life there and generate jobs and wealth sustainably (Surana *et al.*, 2020).

The traditional perception of interior towns and cities as being averse to business and entrepreneurship is fast changing. According to Jain *et al.* (2022a), a recent survey has indicated that half of the online urban shoppers in 2021 were residents of Tier 2 or Tier 3 cities. The study further projects that this percentage is expected to increase to almost 60% by the year 2030. The emergence of a start-up ecosystem is dependent on the conducive business environment in these locations. However, in the long run, their success will only boost the local economy by creating jobs, increasing consumption power, and attracting investment and development in these cities.

A skilled and hardworking labor pool, a lower cost of living, a creative environment, and support systems create an excellent nurturing ground for innovation and entrepreneurship. Start-ups focusing on e-commerce, edutech, fintech, and digital technologies are working toward creating sustainable solutions and clean energy, aligned with the triple bottom line goals. Start-ups in agritech, fisheries, dairying, forestry, tradition-based healthcare (such as Ayurveda-based), and rural tech have vast potential in the agrarian context of these interior locations.

One promising aspect of start-ups in smaller cities is their engagement in solving local problems traditionally ignored by government bodies or larger companies. They are familiar with the structural deficiencies in the local ecosystems and the roots of the problems. They can create social value like none other and with a long-lasting impact. The changes may prove to be transformational rather than incremental or *ad hoc*. An example of an innovative start-up is Goods Finished Forecast (GFF) Innovations, which was incubated by Chandigarh University. This company has developed a machine named "Moksh," which is capable of collecting crop stubble and converting it into biofuel. Husk Power Systems, located in Patna, utilizes agricultural waste, specifically rice husks that are commonly discarded, to produce gas that is utilized to power a readily available turbine, thereby generating electricity.

To add thrust and energy to these positive developments, there is an increasing engagement of start-ups on social media platforms and an inclination to leverage e-commerce and the latest technological advancements, including Artificial Intelligence (AI), robotics, and machine learning, even in the Tier 2 and Tier 3 cities' markets. Tech-based start-ups in the domains of edtech, agritech, healthcare, drone technology, rural logistics, and social tech are also making a mark in the smaller towns. These trends are creating space for a huge consumer base for start-ups to leverage. Edtech start-ups are increasingly focusing on Tier 2 and Tier 3 cities due to the significant number of students in these areas who lack access to adequate educational resources, which could otherwise improve their career opportunities. As per a report published by Boston Consulting Group, it is projected that by 2030, more than half (54%) of the online shoppers in India will originate from rural regions, and their online retail expenditure will constitute 24% of the total online retail spending.

What Do the Smaller Cities Lack In?

According to Wiesenberg *et al.* (2020), the success of start-ups is contingent upon the presence of an ecosystem that comprehends the unique requirements of entrepreneurs and offers a supportive environment for their growth. Start-ups have limited resources at their disposal, and the resource scarcity problems are even more defining and profound in smaller cities and towns (Mukul & Saini, 2021). In developing countries like India, the severity of these problems worsens. Indian start-ups face several difficulties, including a lack of awareness, a lack of trust and credibility, poor physical infrastructure, an underdeveloped Research and Development (R&D) environment, inadequate institutional support, limited access to professional expertise, and a lack of institutional support. For start-ups to succeed in their early stages, they need a robust ecosystem that provides them with the resources to overcome the above challenges, as well as mentoring, management advice, consulting, and an all-around encouraging environment.

Challenges Faced by Start-ups in Smaller Cities in India

More than one billion Indians reside outside of metropolitan areas. The demographic landscape in question, constituting 70% of the overall market scope within the nation, primarily resides in cities categorized as Tier 2, Tier 3, and beyond. Facilitating the growth of entrepreneurs in these regions (a large segment of these regions are underdeveloped) is imperative for India to attain the status of an economic powerhouse and for the equitable distribution of employment opportunities and wealth. Currently, despite the high demand in said regions, entrepreneurs originating from Tier 2 and Tier 3 cities and especially villages and smaller towns tend to gravitate toward metropolitan areas where a favorable start-up ecosystem and requisite resources are readily accessible. Entrepreneurs who firmly endeavor to establish their businesses in non-metropolitan areas and expand their operations encounter numerous obstacles.

Major start-up challenges in smaller towns and cities of India

The lack of knowledge and guidance on the process of developing an idea into a workable company endeavor is one of the main problems that many entrepreneurs experience. Despite the advancements made and the supportive actions taken by governing bodies, the process of starting a new business is still burdened by a significant number of bureaucratic procedures and complications associated with incorporation. Inadequate access to information about start-up activities and opportunities is one prime concern faced by start-ups. In the current era of digitalization, entrepreneurs who live outside of major cities face a significant and unexpected issue. Despite the start of the 5G rollout in metropolitan regions, a sizeable chunk of rural India continues to struggle to acquire reliable and sufficient 4G data coverage. Also, start-ups in Tier 2 and Tier 3 cities face significant logistical difficulties. The manufacturing sector has a number of challenges, such as high costs, a lack of modern storage and transit services, erratic power supplies, and restricted access to multimodal transportation. Many smaller towns, such as Davangere, Hosur, Bellari, and Honnavar, which possess great entrepreneurial potential, are unable to offer local entrepreneurs the same chances as those found in Bengaluru.

Funding difficulties are one prime concern for start-ups in the interior of India. Financial considerations are frequently at the root of entrepreneurial dreams, and during the early phases of a start-up, it is vital to spend resources until the company's growth trajectory gathers speed. Despite the presence of many ground-breaking ideas and technologies, start-ups located in Tier 2 and Tier 3 cities have difficulties when trying to launch their operations due to the lack of venture capital firms. Despite the great potential for success in these businesses, it can be difficult for entrepreneurs to secure capital for start-ups in smaller towns for a variety of reasons. Before closing their USD 2.5 million seed investment round with India Quotient and Dholakia Ventures, Vishal and Rahul of Dhiwise were turned down by 40 venture investors.

Advantages of smaller towns

Recently, the start-up ecosystem in the Indian context has undergone a unique change. Highly educated and experienced start-up founders are moving their start-ups from metros to Tier 2 and Tier 3 cities (Bakshi, 2021). There are many advantages to smaller towns for start-ups. In smaller towns, the availability of resources, such as office space and workforce, is at economical rates. This is a significant factor for pulling start-ups toward Tier 2 and Tier 3 cities, especially in the initial phases when start-ups are bootstrapped. For start-ups, an added advantage to the readily available skilled workforce at a lesser cost is a higher retention rate in smaller cities (Bakshi, 2021). Smaller cities have low human resources costs, cheaper real estate, and more affordable amenities. Also, smaller cities consist of close knit start-up communities, which helps start-up entrepreneurs find their customers easily (Sushma UN, 2017).

Start-ups in smaller cities and their social capital

Social capital represents the various benefits that one can attract through their networks. Researchers define social capital as benefits that actors obtain through their social ties (Coleman, 1990b; Portes, 1998). Social capital refers to friends, colleagues, and more general contacts through whom you receive opportunities to use other forms of capital (Burt, 1992, p. 9). Burt (2000) proclaimed appropriately that "social capital is a metaphor for advantage." Social capital has been found to be quite an essential factor for start-up survival and growth in the case of resource scarcity scenarios (Batjargal, 2003).

In the case of smaller cities and towns, people are familiar with many of their network connections, and the chances of building meaningful and fruitful networks with inherent professional benefits are higher. The understanding of local community norms, mindsets, ways of operating, and expectations helps entrepreneurs mobilize resources on a regular basis. Family businesses in these areas have deeply rooted connections with many stakeholders, be they suppliers, creditors, customers, distributors, and so on. In recent studies (Mukul & Saini, 2021; Mukul *et al.*, 2022) based in Tier 2 cities of Hubli-Dharwad in the north Karnataka region of India, it was found that start-ups get social capital benefits through their networks rooted in these locations, resulting in business support, such as talent acquisition, customer acquisition, marketing and sales benefits, and higher credibility. The presence of social capital in the case of start-ups was found to help build reputation, trust levels, word-of-mouth publicity, and repeat business, which can be of great help, especially in times of crisis situations like the COVID-19 pandemic.

Professional Networks and Association Enriching the Ecosystem of Smaller Towns

The pace of change in the entrepreneurial landscape is accelerating, with incubation firms and angel networks increasingly collaborating with start-ups located in small towns to provide guidance during the nascent stages of their development and facilitate access to funding opportunities. Professional bodies and associations of entrepreneurs, such as National Entrepreneurship Network (NEN), The IndUS Entrepreneurs (TiE), and Jain International Trade Organisation (JITO), offer a range of services to entrepreneurs, including mentorship, access to resources, IT infrastructure support, and legal and tax advisory services. Additionally, they facilitate connections between founders and suitable investors. Networks like TiE have built their credibility by providing platforms for resource mobilization and information sharing among members. It provides mentorship and networking opportunities in many smaller cities. Similarly, Desh Deshpande's social venture, "Deshpande Foundation," through its incubators (e.g. Sandbox, based in Hubli, Karnataka), helped many start-ups overcome their resource constraints and initial barriers through investment and mentoring support.

There are many instances of venture capitalists and angel investors extending a supportive hand to start-ups from smaller cities across the country. Chennai-based payment aggregator IppoPay has invested around INR 3 crore in 24 start-ups in the last 1 year, including start-ups in smaller places, such as the Trichy-based Frigate. Bhubaneswar-based Milk Mantra has raised around USD 32.7 million from 35 investors.

These changes are a result of improved infrastructural support, quicker Internet, favorable working conditions for start-ups, better transport facilities, and accessibility to an immense pool of talent (Ojha, 2023).

Entrepreneurial Activities in Rural Parts of India

Rural India has long been experiencing a consistent digital revolution, entrepreneurial activities, funded developmental activities, and necessity-driven innovation on a small scale. Since demonetization, coupled with a constant thrust on digital transactions, things have picked up, and people in remote places can quickly obtain benefits, including Internet access and financial independence, for improved lifestyles and general growth. They are more involved in mainstream activities. According to the Innovation, Incubation and Invention (ICUBE) 2021 study, conducted by the Internet and Mobile Association of India (IAMAI) and KANTAR consulting group (ANTAR group of companies which is known for its market research and analysis across various industries globally), rural India has witnessed a 37% year-on-year (YoY) increase in Internet penetration (Kaur, 2022). The study has revealed that there were 351 million active users in 2021. Conversely, the utilization of the Internet in metropolitan areas of India has experienced a marginal increase of 2% YoY, resulting in 341 million active users during the same timeframe. According to the report, it is projected that by 2025, rural areas of India may exhibit a greater prevalence of Internet users in comparison to urban centers, thereby suggesting the expansion of the digital ecosystem into the country's hinterlands. This illustrates the enrichment of the ecosystem in rural and suburban parts with the unlimited potential of business in general and start-up activities in particular. Enthusiastic entrepreneurs and start-ups have begun investing in rural India. The new start-up ecosystem has emerged on the rough roads of far-flung towns. India is a developing nation, and this growth process depends heavily on its rural people.

According to Hudson Breen and Leung (2020), entrepreneurship in various forms, including production, exhibits a spatial dimension. Rural and urban areas have distinct factors impacting entrepreneurial activities in those regions. Korsgaard *et al.* (2015) stated that rural entrepreneurship involves a distinct engagement with the rural-natural milieu, resulting in unique obstacles for these entrepreneurs, including limited human and financial resources, relatively modest markets, and inadequate communication channels.

Some scholars discuss the entrepreneurial activities in the rural, interior parts in terms of subsistence entrepreneurship pertaining to business endeavors in impoverished environments. Subsistence entrepreneurs engage in entrepreneurial pursuits as a result of necessity. The acquisition of an active set of attitudes, behaviors, and legitimacy by impoverished individuals may enhance their empowerment, enabling them to transcend subsistence living and aspire to become subsistence entrepreneurs. Therefore, an additional aspect of poverty alleviation involves prioritizing the establishment of novel enterprises and fostering innovation. The objective of entrepreneurship development in these areas must be to foster sustainable development at the individual and household levels by utilizing local enterprise development, microfinance, and the implementation of fundamental innovations, such as those outlined in the base of the pyramid (BoP) research (Prahalad and Hammond, 2002).

Entrepreneurship Ecosystem Dynamics in Bengaluru

The structural framework of entrepreneurship players, social dynamics, human capital, cultural conditions, and social capital have sustained the value of innovation and start-up action in Bengaluru, and this is why this city continues to be attractive to unicorns and cockroach start-ups (Kantis *et al.*, 2020). The city's entrepreneurship ecosystem has been influenced and enriched by distinct factors for a significant amount of time, which has in turn transformed the way the city works to accommodate its status as India's "Start-up Capital," even though the tag officially belongs to New Delhi (Kapturkiewicz, 2022).

Bengaluru, Delhi, Mumbai, Chennai, and Hyderabad continue to offer excellent support infrastructure, the best of technology, education, extensive networking and connectivity opportunities, as well as investment and funding potential. These cities offer tremendous opportunities for Tier 2 and Tier 3 cities to harness their entrepreneurship ecosystems for their own growth. Business and investment dynamics, combined with entrepreneurial dynamics and governmental policies (Sunny & Shu, 2019), have positively intervened to support entrepreneurial activity in Bengaluru.

These opportunities, as observed by De Bernardi *et al.* (2020), are available in the form of coworking spaces (Fuzi, 2015), incubators, accelerators, and mentoring networks (Tripathi & Oivo, 2020). A sustainable entrepreneurship ecosystem with well-planned infrastructure and better access to a large number of investors, both VCs and angel investors, is what fledgling start-ups and aspiring entrepreneurs from smaller cities are looking for (Ratten, 2022).

Harnessing Existing Entrepreneurship Ecosystem Resources to Support Entrepreneurship Action in Tier 2 and Tier 3 Cities and Townships

The small towns and villages have been innovating and ideating in recent times with renewed fervor (Yin *et al.*, 2022). Whether it is a solution to protein deficiency or solar-powered equipment or identifying diseases in crops using technology, these prototypes are finding traction and visibility in Bengaluru, but the need is for hyperlocal ecosystems that can enable scaleup in these small locations. The ideation process eventually propels the development of a start-up ecosystem anywhere, which, when leveraged by an established ecosystem, can significantly speed up the effort (Greco & Tregua, 2022).

Busch and Barkema (2022) stated that growth is a reality in how the entrepreneurial focus extends beyond the metropolitan hubs. Digital skilling, apprenticeships, and nurturing innovations in smaller towns and cities are a reality today due to initiatives such as Code Unnati, a United Nations Development Program-Sytems, Applications and Products in Data Processing (UNDP-SAP) partnership project, which recognizes and leverages the entrepreneurship potential in youngsters. Karnataka's Raichur, Dakshina Kannada, Gulbarga, Dharwad, Udupi, and even rural Bengaluru need to access Bengaluru's entrepreneurship ecosystem for its youth to innovate and dream big. In developing multiple start-up hubs in the smaller cities and villages, there exists the imperative to improve infrastructure, network connectivity, quality of living, skilling, upskilling, and education and create a scalable network infrastructure (Lakshmanan *et al.*, 2022).

The Economic Survey 2020–2021 found that nearly half of the recognized start-ups were from smaller cities in India (Choudhary *et al.*, 2022). These start-ups are essentially solving local problems for basic issues such as healthcare, education, agriculture, and services. The quality of life in smaller cities and townships is improving due to the development of localized, decentralized, and grass-roots-level start-up ecosystems, which will generate jobs and wealth subsequently (Surana *et al.*, 2020). The global digital revolution has made technology and digital platforms accessible to all, and youngsters in smaller cities are increasingly pessimistic about traditional business models. They wish to explore new business models and leverage technology and these platforms, thereby creating start-up hubs in smaller cities such as Mysore, Mangaluru, Dharwad, Hubli, and Chitradurga, where initial costs for new ventures are low, labor costs are more affordable, the cost of living is lower, and operational costs including rentals are attractive. Unifying and scalable programs and missions, such as the ones in Kerala, can accelerate the growth of sustainable, localized ecosystems for entrepreneurship in smaller cities (Ghosh, 2020).

The reason why the growth of a vibrant start-up ecosystem in smaller cities is slow or not happening at all is due to a lack of foresight in extending the strength of a Tier 1 city's entrepreneurship ecosystem to the smaller cities (Roundy, 2017). There are many hurdles that prevent smaller cities and townships from moving ahead, such as investor hesitancy, underdeveloped markets, the perception of a limited customer base, and a lack of funding (De Silva *et al.*, 2020). This has led to the absence of robust infrastructure and limited or no access to ecosystem resources. Because aspiring entrepreneurs from smaller towns and cities do not have access to the ecosystem resources in Bengaluru, the ecosystem there has remained static, and there is evidently no infrastructure development or resource utilization there. It is imperative, therefore, to leverage the strengths of Bengaluru's entrepreneurship ecosystem to support and build hyperlocal sustainable start-up ecosystems in Karnataka's smaller cities by implementing programs and missions that would encourage youngsters to realize their start up dreams.

Leveraging Incubators, Accelerators, and Co-working Spaces as Mini-ecosystems

Start-up incubators support entrepreneurial foundational activities during the early stages of firm formation. In their study, Allen and Rahman (1985) claimed that the "business incubation" process could help start-ups with some of their problems. By creating a nurturing environment to improve the chances of survival in the early stages of their lives, this process may aid entrepreneurs in overcoming significant challenges and promote the growth of new businesses. The practice of start-up incubation involves creating welcoming environments for such businesses in order to increase the likelihood that recently or soon-to-be-launched private businesses will endure in the market long enough to develop their own networks and resources and operate independently. Start-up accelerators offer resources to those attempting to launch their own businesses or those who have just begun their operations but quickly realize they need assistance (Arteaga & Hyland, 2013). Legal counsel, office space, infrastructure, administrative support (access to computers and secretarial staff), and, perhaps most importantly, networking and training, are just a few of the services that the start-up incubators can offer. Since many university business programs have affiliations with start-up incubators, they can help new business owners fill in any skill gaps they might have in areas such as marketing, human resource management, accounting, and other related fields.

Case Instances: Examples of Start-ups in Smaller Cities

Many start-ups have garnered unique advantages through their embeddedness in the ecosystem in smaller cities. Shaandhar E-commerce Private Limited, an e-retailer headquartered in Hubli, North Karnataka, realized in its early days that only relying on consumers would not help the start-up as consumer behavior in smaller cities differs from that of major cities. Initially, the start-up was in a dilemma about whether it would survive in the Tier 2 market but adopted a multifold strategy of venturing into the B2B and B2C markets. The start-up Shaandhar, whose founders are from the Gangavathi region (known as the rice bowl of Karnataka), and their families, who are rice farmers, helped the firm start their operations in the rice business. The company started its brand and started supplying other regional retailers. Shaandhar Ecommerce Private Limited has not only survived its initial phase with this strategy but has also prospered in recent years. The start-up now owns an offline store with the same name.

Pallavi, who runs a start-up called **GULBONDA**, offering personalized, handcrafted toys and illustrations and which operates out of Kozhikode's start-up hub, utilizes every opportunity to create visibility for GULBONDA, leveraging the strengths of a developed entrepreneurship ecosystem in Kochi, Kerala. Tier 2 and 3 cities and townships account for nearly 50% of recognized start-ups.

A case in point is **Kerala's Start Up Mission (KSUM)**, which has progressively encouraged entrepreneurs from Tier 2 and Tier 3 townships to utilize the strengths of Kochi's entrepreneurship ecosystem to realize their dreams. Kerala has emerged as one of the best start-up hubs in India. The state offers a robust entrepreneurship ecosystem supported by an enabling social and intellectual milieu.

PHONOLOGIX is a Kochi-based start-up in the wellness space which is partnering with KSUM to run a start-up accelerator program for women in Kerala. KSUM has emerged as a bridge between entrepreneurship dynamics in Tier 2 and Tier 3 cities and townships and Kochi's entrepreneurship ecosystem.

Noureen Aysha from Kasaragod in Kerala decided to move to Kochi to set up and scale their start-up **FEMISAFE** because the city offered a supportive ecosystem, and entrepreneurs in Tier 2 and Tier 3 townships and cities struggle with guidance and mentorship. Under KSUM, cities such as Kozhikode, Kannur, and Kasaragod have customized hybrid incubation programs that promise to benefit budding entrepreneurs there.

Today, while Kochi accounts for more than 36% of start-ups, Kozhikode with 10% and Thiruvananthapuram with 23% are emerging as vibrant start-up hubs in Kerala, fueled mostly by Kochi's vibrant ecosystem, which includes Maker Spaces-Fablabs, IOT labs, Future Sparks-Students in Technology and Innovation, K-Accelerator Program, and start-ups in niche sectors, such as cancer research, space tech, and biotech.

Gurugram-based **Allegra Fashion** got an excellent response when they launched their innovative idea of "virtual sizing," wherein inputs such as height, weight, and age are obtained from the customers, and with the help of AI-based applications, suitable options are made available for customers to choose from. The optimal size options are provided based on the individual's body type. The start-up provides a comprehensive range of approximately 500 products that fall under various categories, such as ethnic and Western wear, nightwear, athleisure, swimwear, footwear, and accessories. Allegra utilizes its online platform and social media outlets for sales purposes. It aspires to place Indian designers on the global map by 2025. The start-up has leveraged the advantages of operating in small cities. The start-up can source the raw materials easily and have a close-knit relationship with its suppliers.

Six childhood friends from Surat staked everything to launch Alpino Health Foods in 2016. India's annual peanut butter consumption at that time was quite moderate and stood at around 1 kiloton. Having a good understanding of the availability of raw peanuts in the locality made them see the vast potential in the market. For most of their products, peanuts are sourced from Junagadh in Gujarat, and products are developed in-house in Surat. The local embeddedness in the region and networks with suppliers and distributors facilitated their venture. They could easily relate to their customers and make a pitch to stakeholders. The start-up has implemented an omnichannel strategy by offering its products through various online platforms, such as its own website as well as e-commerce marketplaces, including Amazon, Flipkart, and JioMart. Alpino has reported that its products have been consumed by over 600,000 individuals as of 2022. The company has outlined its intention to focus on online sales in order to achieve a revenue target of Indian Rupee (INR) 44 crore for the fiscal year 2023.

Mubeen Masudi, the entrepreneur who established Rise, was motivated by personal sentiments to initiate his venture in Srinagar. Following his graduation from IIT Bombay in 2011, Mubeen made the decision to establish his own company, Rise, in his hometown of Srinagar. Mubeen's establishment of Rise was motivated by the scarcity of educational prospects in Srinagar. The organization offers courses and mentorship to Kashmiri students with the aim of enhancing their likelihood of gaining admission to esteemed academic institutions both domestically and internationally.

These cases are testimony to the passion of young entrepreneurs and the growing possibilities of starting up on their own in the smaller cities of the country. Their numbers are growing, and this may just be the initial stages of a much-needed transformation in the overall entrepreneurship movement the country is witnessing.

Conclusion

Entrepreneurs' actions lead to the country's economic progress, and currently, the entrepreneurs of start-ups in India are leading the charge, with our country emerging as one of the top three start-up ecosystems in the world. Although India has abundant resources and economically skilled labor, entrepreneurial growth however hasn't reached the expected heights and, more surprisingly, the expected spread across the landscape. This anomaly can be corrected by the participation of young entrepreneurs from the smaller towns and cities in the country's interior parts, which are often aloof or isolated from the mainstream of economic activities.

There are challenges for start-ups, such as access to critical information, a smaller market size as compared to metros, skilled human resources, the availability of adequate finance, and a lack of efficient managers. The chapter also discusses many opportunities available for start-ups, as a new market, lack of competition in smaller cities, economical labor, lower operational costs as compared to metro cities, and government initiatives in the smaller cities to promote entrepreneurship. Many of the challenges mentioned above can be overcome with an ecosystem that recognizes the special needs of entrepreneurs and provides a supportive environment for start-ups to flourish.

Although the challenges are plentiful, there are many unique advantages too for start-ups in smaller cities, such as ease of contacting their customers, suppliers, vendors, and other business associates and the greater emotional bond between the enterprise and its employees. Operational costs are lower when compared to metropolitans, and smaller cities provide a close-knit community for start-ups. The embeddedness of start-ups in their local roots gives them access to some vital resources and unique advantages unavailable to those outside the ecosystem. In many smaller towns, incubation centers and academic institutions are emerging as critical constituents of the start-up ecosystem. One more significant reason for start-ups to initiate their operations in smaller cities is that entrepreneurs belonging to these cities have a strong emotional connect, being the "sons of the soil" and wanting to see the city prosper in entrepreneurial activity.

For an entrepreneurial venture to be successful, both internal (firm-level factors) and external factors (such as the social context and ecosystem) must be favorable. In order to improve the ecosystem, action will be required from the government; local governing authorities, business associations (such as Nasscom in India), educational institutions (colleges and universities), community organizations, professional associations, private businesses, Public Sector Units (PSUs), Non-Governmental Organizations (NGOs), intellectuals, and regular residents are all included. It demands the creation of local institutional support systems as well as the formulation of policy.

The trends are changing for good, and start-up activity is on the rise in smaller cities in India. India's Tier 2 and Tier 3 cities (many of those have been identified as "smart cities" of the future by the government, providing support for infrastructure development and economic activities) are observing rapid growth in start-up activity. The COVID-19 pandemic also provided an impetus to the latent enterprising nature of youth to express itself and has led to the development of start-ups in smaller cities. The start-up scenario in smaller cities is undergoing a major transformation and may change India's entrepreneurial activity landscape.

References

Acs, Z. J., Desai, S., & Hessels, J. (2008). Entrepreneurship, economic development and institutions. *Small Business Economics*, 31, 219–234.

Ács, Z. J., Szerb, L., Ortega-Argilés, R., Aidis, R., & Coduras, A. (2015). The regional application of the global entrepreneurship and development index (GEDI): The case of Spain. *Regional Studies*, 49(12), 1977–1994.

Aidis, R., Estrin, S., & Mickiewicz, T. (2009). Entrepreneurial entry: Which institutions matter? (CEPR Discussion Paper No. DP7278). http://papers.ssrn.com/sol3/papers.cfm?abstract_id=1405075.

Allen, D. N. & Rahman, S. (1985). Small business incubators: A positive environment for entrepreneurship. *Journal of Small Business Management*, 23(3), 12–22.

Arteaga, R. & Hyland, J. (2013). *Pivot: How Top Entrepreneurs Adapt and Change Course to Find Ultimate Success*. Canada: John Wiley & Sons.

Bakshi, A. J. & Fernando, B. J. (2022). Intersectionality of rural community, geography and gender in the careers of young adults. *British Journal of Guidance & Counselling*, 50(6), 966–984.

Bakshi, C. (2021). Size matters: Smaller cities can be perfect for start-ups. *The Financial Express*. https://www.financialexpress.com/industry/sme/size-matters-smaller-cities-can-be-perfect-for-startups/2290360/.

Batjargal, B. (2003). Social capital and entrepreneurial performance in Russia: A longitudinal study. *Organization Studies*, 24(4), 535–556.

Belitski, M., Guenther, C., Kritikos, A. S. *et al.* (2022). Economic effects of the COVID-19 pandemic on entrepreneurship and small businesses. *Small Business Economics*, 58, 593–609. https://doi.org/10.1007/s11187-021-00544-y

Bhatt, A. K. *et al.* (2022). Management of E-waste: Technological challenges and opportunities. In Chinnappan Baskar, Seeram Ramakrishna, Shikha Baskar, Rashmi Sharma, Amutha Chinnappan, Rashmi Sehrawat (Eds.), *Handbook of Solid Waste Management: Sustainability through Circular Economy*, pp. 1523–1557. Springer Nature, Singapore.

Burt, R. S. (1992). *Structural Holes: The Social Structure of Competition.* Cambridge, MA: Harvard University Press.

Burt, R. S. (2000). The network structure of social capital. *Research in Organizational Behavior*, 22, 345–423.

Busch, C. & Barkema, H. (2022). Planned luck: How incubators can facilitate serendipity for nascent entrepreneurs through fostering network embeddedness. *Entrepreneurship Theory and Practice*, 46(4), 884–919.

Chang, C. (2010). The immune effects of naturally occurring and synthetic nanoparticles. *Journal of Autoimmunity*, 34(3), J234–J246.

Chortareas, G. E., Girardone, C., & Ventouri, A. (2013). Financial freedom and bank efficiency: Evidence from the European Union. *Journal of Banking & Finance*, 37(4), 1223–1231.

Choudhary, L., Taparia, K., Pandey, A., & Kakkar, A. (2022). Indian startup ecosystem 2021. *Hans Sodh Sudha*, 2(4), 9–20.

Codeunnati Admin. (2021). United Nations Development Programme (UNDP), in partnership with SAP, launched the Project Code Unnati, to promote digital skilling and entrepreneurship development for youth and women across three districts in Karnataka. https://codeunnati.org/united-nations-development-programme/.

Coleman, J. S. (1990a). *Foundations of Social Theory*, Cambridge, MA: The Belknap Press of Harvard University.

Coleman, J. S. (1990b). Commentary: Social institutions and social theory. *American Sociological Review*, 55(3), 333–339.

De Bernardi, P., Azucar, D., De Bernardi, P., & Azucar, D. (2020). Innovation and entrepreneurial ecosystems: Structure, boundaries, and dynamics. Innovation in food ecosystems. *Entrepreneurship for a Sustainable Future*, 73–104. ISBN 978-3-030-33502-1.

De Silva, M., Khan, Z., Vorley, T., & Zeng, J. (2020). Transcending the pyramid: Opportunity co-creation for social innovation. *Industrial Marketing Management*, 89, 471–486.

Deo, P. (2023, February). India Population: Is India's rapidly growing youth population a dividend or disaster? *TimesofIndia.com*. https://timesofindia.indiatimes.com/india/is-indias-rapidly-growing-youth-population-a-dividend-or-disaster/articleshow/97545222.cms.

Dinh, H. T., Mavridis, D., & Nguyen, H. (2010). The binding constraints on firm's growth. World Bank Policy Research Working Paper 5485, Washington, DC. http://documents.worldbank.org/curated/en/966571468137388733/pdf/WPS5485.pdf.

El Hanchi, S. & Kerzazi, L. (2020). Startup innovation capability from a dynamic capability-based view: A literature review and conceptual framework. *Journal of Small Business Strategy*, 30(2), 72–92.

Fingar, C. T. (Ed.). (2009). *Global Trends 2025: A Transformed World*. Diane Publishing.

Fuzi, A. (2015). Co-working spaces for promoting entrepreneurship in sparse regions: The case of South Wales. *Regional Studies, Regional Science*, 2(1), 462–469.

Gage, D. (2012). The venture capital secret: 3 out of 4 start-ups fail. *Wall Street Journal*, 20.

GEM. (2021). https://www.gemconsortium.org/file/open?fileId=50900.

Ghosh, A. & Raha, S. (2020). Jobs, growth and sustainability: A new social contract for India's recovery. In Ghosh, A. & Raha, S. (Eds.) *Jobs, Growth and Sustainability: A New Social Contract for India's Recovery*. New Delhi, India: Council on Energy, Environment and Water (CEEW).

Greco, F. & Tregua, M. (2022). It gives you wheels: The university-based accelerators in start-up ecosystems. *International Journal of Entrepreneurship and Small Business*, 45(2), 235–257.

Gionchetti, E. (2022). Twitter, social corporate responsibility and economic performance: How multinational companies exploit social media.

Hudson Breen, R. & Leung, A. (2020). Choosing mothering and entrepreneurship: A relational career-life process. *International Journal of Gender and Entrepreneurship*, 12(3), 253–271.

Ip, C. Y., Zhuge, T., Chang, Y. S., Huang, T. H., & Chen, Y. L. (2022). Exploring the determinants of nascent social entrepreneurial behaviour. *International Journal of Environmental Research and Public Health*, 19(6), 3556.

Isenberg, D. J. (2011). *The Entrepreneurship Ecosystem Strategy as a New Paradigm for Economy Policy: Principles for Cultivating Entrepreneurship*. Babson Park, MA: Babson Entrepreneurship Ecosystem Project, Babson College.

Jain, G., Shrivastava, A., Paul, J., & Batra, R. (2022b). Blockchain for SME clusters: An ideation using the framework of Ostrom commons governance. *Information Systems Frontiers*, 24(4), 1125–1143.

Jain, N., Sanghi, K., & Balaji, N. (2022a). Ten things you should know about e-commerce in India, BCG report. https://www.bcg.com/publications/2022/e-commerce-in-india-ten-things-you-should-know.

Jayadatta, S. (2017). Major challenges and problems of rural entrepreneurship in India. *IOSR Journal of Business and Management*, 19(9), 35–44.

Kantis, H. D., Federico, J. S., & García, S. I. (2020). Entrepreneurship policy and systemic conditions: Evidence-based implications and recommendations for emerging countries. *Socio-Economic Planning Sciences*, 72, 100872.

Kapturkiewicz, A. (2022). Varieties of entrepreneurial ecosystems: A comparative study of Tokyo and Bangalore, *Research Policy*, 51(9), 104377.

Kau, J. (2022). Rural India drives internet penetration with 351 Mn users: IAMAI report. *iNC42.Com*. https://inc42.com/buzz/rural-india-drives-internet-penetration-with-351-mn-users-iamai-report/#:~:text=IAMAI%20and%20KANTAR.-,The%20ICUBE%202021%20report%20named%20'Internet%20in%20India'%20covered%20over,growth%20of%20rural%20internet%20users.

Khan, S. & Magd, H. (2022). Identifying the barriers and drivers to agriculture entrepreneurship in India. In *Driving Factors for Venture Creation and Success in Agricultural Entrepreneurship* (pp. 261–272). IGI Global. Driving Factors for Venture Creation and Success in Agricultural Entrepreneurship, United Kingdom.

Korreck, S. (2019). The Indian startup ecosystem: Drivers, challenges and pillars of support. *ORF Occasional Paper*, 210, 04–44.

Korsgaard, S., Müller, S., & Tanvig, H.W. (2015). Rural entrepreneurship or entrepreneurship in the rural–between place and space. *International Journal of Entrepreneurial Behavior & Research*, 21(1), 5–26.

Krajcik, V. & Formanek, I. (2015). Regional startup ecosystem. *European Business & Management*, 1(2), 14–18.

Kumar, J. & Rai, R. (2023). Resilience and recovery of Indian start-ups. Managing and Strategising Global Business in Crisis: Resolution, Resilience and Reformation.

Lakshmanan, V. I., Murty, V. K., Chandrashekhar, V. S., & Singh, M. (2022). *Smart Villages: Bridging the Global Urban-Rural Divide*. Springer, Canada.

Madanaguli, A., Kaur, P., Mazzoleni, A., & Dhir, A. (2022). The innovation ecosystem in rural tourism and hospitality–a systematic review of innovation in rural tourism. *Journal of Knowledge Management*, 26(7), 1732–1762.

Makridakis, S., Hogarth, R. M., & Gaba, A. (2009). Forecasting and uncertainty in the economic and business world. *International Journal of Forecasting*, 25(4), 794–812.

Mason, C. & Brown, R. (2013). Entrepreneurial ecosystems and growth oriented entrepreneurship. *Final report to OECD, Paris*, 30(1), 77–102.

Mason, C. & Brown, R. (2014). Entrepreneurial ecosystems and growth oriented entrepreneurship. *Final Report to OECD, Paris*, 30(1), 77–102.

McEvily, B. & Zaheer, A. (1999). Bridging ties: A source of firm heterogeneity in competitive capabilities. *Strategic Management Journal*, 20(12), 1133–1156.

Mergemeier, L., Moser, J., & Flatten, T. C. (2018). The influence of multiple constraints along the venture creation process and on start-up intention in nascent entrepreneurship. *Entrepreneurship & Regional Development*, 30(7-8), 848–876.

Mukul, K. & Saini, G. K. (2021). Talent acquisition in start-ups in India: The role of social capital, *Journal of Entrepreneurship in Emerging Economies*, 13(5), 1235–1261. https://doi.org/10.1108/JEEE-04-2020-0086.

Mukul, K., Pandey, N., & Saini, G. K. (2022). Does social capital provide marketing benefits for start-up business? An emerging economy perspective. *Asia Pacific Journal of Marketing and Logistics,* 34(9), 1864–1879. https://doi.org/10.1108/APJML-02-2021-0142.

Müller, S., & Korsgaard, S. (2018). Resources and bridging: the role of spatial context in rural entrepreneurship. *Entrepreneurship & Regional Development*, 30(1–2), 224–255.

NASSCOM. (2020). https://nasscom.in/knowledge-center/publications/indian-tech-start-ecosystem-%E2%80%93-march-trillion-dollar-digital-economy, https://nasscom.in/knowledge-center/publications/nasscom-idc-report-technology-sector-india-building-capabilities-win.

NASSCOM. (2021). NASSCOM PGA labs tech start-ups: Quarterly investment Factbook (Q3 CY21). https://nasscom.in/knowledge-center/publications/nasscom-pga-labs-tech-start-ups-quarterly-investment-factbook-q3-cy21.

Ojha, S. (2023, January 11). Why Tier 2, 3 cities are rising as India's most rapidly growing start-up hub. *Mint*. https://www.livemint.com/news/india/why-tier-2-3-cities-are-rising-as-india-s-most-rapidly-growing-startup-hub-11673415892047.html.

Portes, A. (1998). Social capital: Its origins and applications in modern sociology. *Annual Review of Sociology*, 24(1), 1–24.

Prahalad, C. K. & Hammond, A. (2002). Serving the world's poor, profitably. *Harvard Business Review*, 80(9), 48–59.

Rasmussen, M. T. (2022). Welcoming newcomers in start-ups: Challenges for strategic internal communication. *International Journal of Strategic Communication*, 16(2), 273–290.

Ratten, V. (2022). Toward a theory of strategic entrepreneurial ecosystems and business model innovation. In *Strategic Entrepreneurial Ecosystems and Business Model Innovation* (pp. 1–15). Emerald Publishing Ltd., USA.

Roundy, P. T. (2017). "Small town" entrepreneurial ecosystems: Implications for developed and emerging economies. *Journal of Entrepreneurship in Emerging Economies*, 9(3), 238–262.

Stuart, T. E., Hoang, H., & Hybels, R. C. (1999). Interorganizational endorsements and the performance of entrepreneurial ventures. *Administrative Science Quarterly*, 44(2), 315–349.

Sunny, S. A. & Shu, C. (2019). Investments, incentives, and innovation: Geographical clustering dynamics as drivers of sustainable entrepreneurship. *Small Business Economics*, 52, 905–927.

Surana, K., Singh, A., & Sagar, A. D. (2020). Strengthening science, technology, and innovation-based incubators to help achieve Sustainable Development Goals: Lessons from India. *Technological Forecasting and Social Change*, 157, 120057.

Sushma UN, qz com. (2017). India's smaller towns are the new it destination for start-ups [Text]. *Scroll.In*. https://scroll.in. https://scroll.in/article/857830/indias-smaller-towns-are-the-new-it-destination-for-startups.

Sushma, U. N. (2017). Morgan Stanley explains why India's e-commerce market is a hot investment opportunity. Retrieved March, 18, 2018.

Tripathi, N. & Oivo, M. (2020). The roles of incubators, accelerators, co-working spaces, mentors, and events in the startup development process. In A. Nguyen-Duc, J. Münch, R. Prikladnicki, X. Wang, P. Abrahamsson (Eds.), *Fundamentals of Software Startups*. Cham: Springer. https://doi.org/10.1007/978-3-030-35983-6_9.

Wang, M., Xu, Q., He, N., Zhang, L., & Zhang, X. (2022). Materialism and problematic social network sites use among Chinese adolescents: The mediating role of self-esteem and self-control. *Psychological Reports*, 00332941221130230.

Wiesenberg, M., Godulla, A., Tengler, K., Noelle, I. M., Kloss, J., Klein, N., & Eeckhout, D. (2020), Key challenges in strategic start-up communication. *Journal of Communication Management*, 24(1), 49–46.

Yin, X., Chen, J., & Li, J. (2022). Rural innovation system: Revitalize the countryside for a sustainable development. *Journal of Rural Studies*, 93, 471–478.

Websites

https://economictimes.indiatimes.com/tech/startups/over-50-of-indian-startups-belong-to-non-metros-govt-informs-parliament/articleshow/93159161.cms?from=mdr.

https://web-assets.bcg.com/09/9e/3cf5c702473fa0c5bb1008c7498e/bcg-ten-things-you-should-know-about-e-commerce-in-india-jun-2022.pdf.

https://www.livemint.com/news/india/why-tier-2-3-cities-are-rising-as-india-s-most-rapidly-growing-startup-hub-11673415892047.html.

Chapter 9

Frugal Innovation with Bricolage Mindset for Organizational Evolution

Geo P Bose

Entrepreneurship Development Institute of India, Gujarat, India

geo05@ediindia.org

Abstract

Frugal innovation has become necessary while considering the mindset of addressing the emerging issues of organizational evolution under resource constraints. An innovation is successful when it is commercialized, enabling an organization to evolve into consecutive life cycles. Innovators who are frugal at the grassroots level are individuals or groups who use local resources to solve problems and find new solutions. This perspective sees innovation as a result of the interaction between human creativity and frugality. A bricolage innovation process is one where resources are combined to solve new problems as they arise. This process could be a new perspective driven by the need to solve problems rather than a consumption focus. It starts with the problem itself rather than being planned from the outset. The Prime Minister of India called on the nation on May 12, 2020 to become more self-sufficient to combat the COVID-19 pandemic. The most prevalent slogan during the pandemic has been "Vocal for Local," meaning that people should value and buy local products. The Prime Minister stated,

"The free India mindset should be 'voice for local.' We should value our local products; if we don't, our products get discouraged and denied the opportunity to grow. An extension of this motto is 'local for global,' meaning Indian products should have worldwide appeal and reach." Thus, this approach of focusing on strengthening skill sets rather than heavy investment in land, capital, and human resources will help to transverse the organizational life cycle.

Keywords: Frugal innovation, commercialization, entrepreneurial bricolage, stakeholder engagement, organization evolution.

Introduction

In a resource-constrained environment, a firm's success is directly dependent on exploiting and exploring untapped opportunities. The main concern for today's and future markets is how to strategize diffusion and commercialization of innovation through the lens of a frugal approach. Our entrepreneurship field is basically anxious with understanding how, with the non-existence of current markets for upcoming goods and services, these goods and services cope for the survival (Venkataraman, 1997). Dawar and Chattopadhyay (2002) and Karnani (2007) said that the cost of serving the markets at the bottom of the pyramid is the lack of good infrastructure, ultimately leading to shattered markets. Other scholars contend that companies tend to build new business ecosystems due to weak institutional arrangements and the absence of many important services (Khanna & Palepu, 1997; Seelos & Mair, 2007). Despite the presence of adverse choices and moral hazard issues, some entrepreneurs can surpass the hurdles and succeed. The innovations at the bottom of the pyramid were the outcome of the diffusion of innovation from developed markets. As time passes, the availability of raw materials for production declines gradually, eventually forcing the producers to strategize a diffusion and commercialization pattern. This resource-constrained situation tempts entrepreneurs to serve better with less to a mass market. The bottom of the pyramid market greatly influences converting sophisticated, expensive innovation to site-specific, simple, low-cost, sustainable innovation. This research is done to understand and analyze whether community engagement through a frugal approach will enhance the diffusion and commercialization strategies of a particular innovation.

A few academic researchers have discussed the diffusion of frugal innovation. A few research works have dealt with the diffusion of frugal products, but not much on frugal services. The diffusion of creation is a process "in which an innovation is communicated through certain channels over time among the members of the social system and spreads in a market" (Rogers, 2010). The literature related to the diffusion of innovation includes widely accepted models, such as Rogers' model, Moore's crossing-the-chasm model, and Bass's model, Di Benedetto (2015). The diffusion pattern of innovation in developed countries is different from that in developing countries. Scholars raised some criticism against Rogers's model of diffusion (Strang & Meyer, 1993, 1998). The nature of innovation, influence, the speed of diffusion, local needs, communication channels, weak institutional arrangements, lack of advanced and specific skills, time, and social contexts were the characteristics taken into account which had an impact on the diffusion of innovation in developing countries (Zanello *et al.*, 2015). Most consumers of frugal products and services are focused on affordability in developing economies. The developed economies are also gradually becoming price-conscious. Thus, pricing had become one of the criteria for the diffusion of frugal innovation.

The aspiration to find solutions for local challenges has motivated a number of people to innovate frugally (Douglas, 2013). In emerging markets, major success factors are recognizing the core value and localization of multi-national companies. The proximity to the local markets throughout the value chain, team formulation, and marketing are the key requirements for successfully creating, developing, and commercializing frugal innovation (Agarwal, 2012).

Developing and emerging economies are facing severe challenges with the scarcity of investment capital, technological innovation, and skilled human resources. Hence, entrepreneurs in such economies need to come up with solutions to their problems with limited resources. The frugal mindset to tackle this situation by strategizing the diffusion and commercialization pattern is keen on the successful implementation of these innovations. These innovations are mainly sustainable, low-cost, site-specific solutions focusing on core functionalities addressing the needs of targeted customers. Therefore, if the strategy of diffusion and commercialization of innovation works, then this typical frugal approach can be adopted in countries with similar socioeconomic conditions. We selected three illustrative cases to explore and analyze the effectiveness of community engagement through frugal innovation. Instead of selecting cases from different sectors, we choose cases from the same sector to tap the diffusion and commercialization strategies of frugal innovations through community engagement.

Even though the frugal approach to innovation is becoming a phenomenon of great significance in the present scenario, academic research on it from many dimensions hasn't been explored much. The effectiveness of community engagement through frugal innovation in different regions and socioeconomic contexts is one of the unexplored research areas (Hossain *et al.*, 2016). This chapter aims to understand and analyze whether a frugal approach to community engagement will enhance a particular innovation's diffusion and commercialization strategy. To achieve the objective, we selected three cases, which determine how far community engagement by the frugal approach has enhanced the diffusion and commercialization strategies of respective firms. The use of three cases is a common approach in various studies. The minimum sample size recommended for doing the case study research method can be 3–5 participants (Creswell, 2002).

Theoretical Background

Entrepreneurs in resource-scarce situations develop more realistic solutions with much effort to seek out many challenges. While considering these views, many scholars have developed advanced and distinct theoretical stands describing the behavioral aspects and facts within a resource-constrained context. Many scholars have cited these theories a number of times, and some of them are entrepreneurial bricolage (Baker & Nelson, 2005), user entrepreneurship (Shah & Tripas, 2007), and effectuation (Sarasvathy, 2001). Their considerable shades of differences and similarities have been pointed out reasonably by Fisher (2012), Salimath and Jones (2011), Selden and Fletcher (2015), Stinchfield *et al.* (2012), and Welter *et al.* (2016).

It was in 1967 that Levi-Strauss, an anthropologist, coined the term "bricolage" in the literature, with some enlightenment. Baker and Nelson (2005) defined bricolage as "making do by applying combinations of the resources at hand to new problems and opportunities" (p. 333) and gave it immense reach in the field of entrepreneurship. The three attributes of bricolage, as per Baker and Nelson (2005), are: (a) making do, (b) using resources at hand, and (c) recombining resources.

Bricolage gives insights into how entrepreneurs exploit resources they do not have and are not within their direct influence (Sonenshein, 2014). Some of the reviews of entrepreneurial bricolage which have been done at various levels during recent times are as follows: at the level of a business or firm (Baker & Nelson, 2005; Perkmann & Spicer, 2014), at the network level (Mckague & Oliver, 2016), at the community level (Di Domenico *et al.*, 2010), at the industrial level (Garud & Karnøe, 2003), at the institutional level (Mair & Marti, 2009), and at the individual level (Duymedjian & Rüling, 2010; Hmieleski & Corbett, 2008; Rai, 2015; Zahra *et al.*, 2009). Some of the contexts within which bricolage has been assessed include developed economies (Davidsson *et al.*, 2017; Plowman *et al.*, 2007; Senyard *et al.*, 2014; Stinchfield *et al.*, 2012), developing economies (Bond, 2014; Linna, 2013; Mair & Marti, 2009; Ros-Tonen *et al.*, 2013), social entrepreneurship (Desa, 2012; Di Domenico *et al.*, 2010; Sunley & Pinch, 2012; Zahra *et al.*, 2009), and service entrepreneurship (Salunke *et al.*, 2013).

The context within which recent research on entrepreneurial bricolage has been done is developed economies where resource scarcity doesn't have a predominant picture compared to developing or emerging economies (Xu & Meyer, 2012). When further research has been extended to emerging or developing economies, entrepreneurial bricolage has given insights into the interpretation of social entrepreneurship (Linna, 2013; Zahra *et al.*, 2009) instead of the diffusion or commercialization of innovation. Most recently, it has been found that bricolage capability is positively related to both cost innovation and affordable value innovation by emerging market firms (Cai *et al.*, 2019), which were considered the two types of frugal innovation.

With this theoretical background, this research explores the question, "how to foster collaboration among different actors involved in the frugal innovation process and specifically on community engagement for diffusion and commercialization?" It aims to explain the dynamics of the bricolage behavior of entrepreneurs and firms within the context of an engaged community. It adds to theoretical explanations and predictions by conducting qualitative research to fill up missing shades of frugal innovation (Pisoni *et al.*, 2018) and entrepreneurial bricolage.

Frugal Innovation and Community Engagement

Frugal innovation has become a relevant topic for academicians in recent years. There have been significant efforts to define the phenomenon of frugal innovation. But there hasn't been much work done on how frugal innovation is diffused and commercialized among the markets through community engagement.

Frugal approach to diffusion

A frugal approach to diffusion is possible only if a proper strategy is adopted along the channel with which the market has to be developed. According to Rogers, diffusion is a peculiar kind of communication consisting of the following elements: an innovation, two individuals or other units of adoption, and a communication channel. In brief, the diffusion of innovations model defines diffusion as a process by which an innovation is communicated through channels over time among members of a social system and spreads in the market (Rogers, 2010). Some of the characteristics which affect the diffusion of innovation in developing countries include the type of innovation, influence, diffusion speed, regional needs, communication channels, the strength of institutional arrangements, the degree of advanced and specific skills, duration, and social contexts (Zanello *et al.*, 2015).

Entrepreneurs adopt community engagement as a frugal strategy to reduce the risk of return on investment and accomplish sustainable growth with positive social impact. In this era of sharing ownership, the frugal approach has a significant role in accelerating the diffusion of innovation. The primary focus of innovations developed in developing economies is to solve socially pressing local problems (Sinkovics *et al.*, 2014).

Sustainability by community engagement

Developing programs and processes that promote social interaction and cultural enrichment are the main focus points for social sustainability. Social sustainability is more about safeguarding the vulnerable, considering social diversity, and is linked to more basic needs such as happiness, safety, freedom, dignity, and affection (Vavik & Keitsch, 2010). For sustainable development within a societal context, there is a significant influence on economic and environmental facets. The frugal approach or mindset to innovation has greatly helped economically backward regions to solve various issues such as unemployment, health issues, illiteracy, and living standards. The frugal approach to innovation has helped many communities facing economic distress. Entrepreneurs' frugal mindset has led to a remarkable contribution to uplifting the bottom of the pyramid while solving societal problems and generating revenue. From past studies, it has been found that in attaining sustainable development, entrepreneurs play a critical role. To analyze the relationship between frugal innovation and sustainable development, researchers argue that in-depth studies with better tools should be adopted (Levänen *et al.*, 2016).

We purposefully selected three illustrative cases to explore the effectiveness of diffusion of frugal innovations and to find out linkages between frugal innovation, community engagement, and sustainability. We selected cases from the water sector instead of selecting from different sectors to capture extensive diffusion patterns of frugal innovations through community engagement for sustainable growth.

Method

Case Illustration

We have followed the case study approach, which is apt for capturing a preliminary understanding of upcoming phenomena in real-life contexts (Yin, 2013). As our objective was to get insights into the effectiveness of community engagement through a frugal approach to innovation for sustainable diffusion, we applied purposive sampling (Sofaer, 1999). We selected the sample in the water sector on purpose so that more dimensions of community engagement can be explored as closely intertwined with society's sustainable growth. We aimed to determine the effectiveness of community engagement by selecting the following three cases. The frugal approach has become a widely accepted innovation in both emerging and developed economies. It will not be sufficient for firms to scale up and run the enterprise sustainably by having frugal innovation in design alone. To strategize and execute with the aim of a fruitful outcome on a measurable scale is the real challenge of frugal innovation. Even though there has been a great leap in defining frugal innovation, there is still much more to explore regarding the notion of the impact of community engagement through the frugal innovation approach. There is a lack of empirical evidence which substantiates a frugal perspective on community engagement that greatly impacts innovations. The relationship between community engagement practice through the frugal approach and social sustainability was also a less explored topic. This chapter demonstrates how Indian entrepreneurs have put forward the frugal approach to community engagement practices in their sector. Qualitative data were drawn from the case study on entrepreneurs who were in the water sector. These firms are from the states of Kerala, Gujarat, and Maharashtra. Interviews were conducted with these entrepreneurs at various levels, and site visits to their plants were also done subsequently. The first entrepreneur was in the business of water cans and bottles. The second entrepreneur was in the business of rainwater harvesting techniques. The third entrepreneur was in the reverse osmosis (RO) water plant business in the mode of A.T.M. cards with and without water.

To validate the interview, feedback was drawn from different stages of the execution of projects undertaken by the respective entrepreneurs. The different entrepreneurial traits processed by respective entrepreneurs to overcome their hurdles with a frugal mindset were also analyzed to establish a link between entrepreneurial competencies and the effectiveness of community engagement through frugal innovation. How far these entrepreneurs were able to successfully overcome the hurdles in their entrepreneurial journey through sustainable community engagement practices was analyzed from the case study. This study helped reveal that the sustainability of frugal innovations in ecological, social, and economic dimensions is related to community engagement practices. The practical implication of the work is that the frugal mindset of the community can be triggered in the respective sector to a commendable position through community engagement. In the literature, the various aspects of the effectiveness of community engagement through frugal innovations have not been articulated adequately. This research provides more insights in that direction. This work could offer valuable insights for entrepreneurs who could benefit from this knowledge, which can be practically implemented in their firms. Most often, entrepreneurs innovate frugally to solve a socially pressing problem. Products and services can be marketed better, and entrepreneurs can portray these impacts if they observe the linkages between frugal innovation, community engagement, and sustainability. These entrepreneurs can easily and effectively evaluate the pros and cons of the association between these concepts and use this knowledge while promoting a frugal approach in their respective fields.

Water A.T.M.: Diffusion by Community Engagement through a Frugal Approach

Water A.T.M. gives the required amount of water as chilled or normal water by swiping the allotted prepaid card. The Piramal Foundation, the corporate social responsibility branch of the global business conglomerate Piramal Group, developed this technology. Water A.T.M., or vending machines, can be found in numerous places, ranging from rural under-privileged villages to urban cities and railway stations. This setup has strengthened and raised these regions' standard of living and health toward becoming a sustainable society.

The case we are considering is how Prarabda Multi-Business Corporation (PMBC) has effectively used community engagement through a frugal approach for the sustainable diffusion of innovation. PMBC was established in 2015, and they got their first order of an RO plant a year later from Shahada Tehsil of Nandurbar District, which has a population of 15,000. PMBC had a total team size of 12. This team followed a hierarchy, with Dhananjay at the top as a proprietor, followed by four main direct sales agents (DSA) covering the Dhule, Pulghar, and Mumbai regions. These main DSAs had sub-DSAs, forming a group of 5 altogether. Thirdly, the DSAs of PMBC include a technical team of size 2. These technical members in charge of technical issues will have communication and intimation across entire levels of the hierarchy. PMBC, instead of giving salaries to the team members consisting of DSAs, gave a specific amount per installation. Thus, it avoided the burden of wages to be paid at the end of each month. PMBC had three methods of execution of its business of RO plant installation. The initial one is commonly known as a self- or privately operated plant. PMBC installs the plant upon request by private parties or by themselves. They deliver water through tumblers with 20 L capacity, charging 10 Rs/tumbler to the mar-ket. The second one, the build, operate, and transfer (BOT) model, involves installation and operation in partnership with PMBC. Once the plant has stepped into the track of operation and revenue generation, PMBC transfers the plant to the partner for further operation; the profit is shared equally between them. The third one is a government-operated plant. In this type, the village head, or *sarpanch*, will lead the project. They install the project through any government fund or scheme. Water is distrib-uted to the villagers through a mechanically metered A.T.M. The customers were provided with an A.T.M. card, which can be recharged as per requirement. This card can be swiped at the machine for hot or cold water. PMBC delivers customized plants to customers, with capacities ranging from 10 to 5,000 L/h.

PMBC had an ideology while doing their business operations, whether B2B or B2C. They took a keen interest in ensuring that the delivered plant would benefit the poorer sections of society. Its plants are mostly owned or operated by retired military officers, unemployed youth, women, widows, and physically disabled people. As of March 10, 2019, 45 projects were running under PMBC, including BOT projects and others as government- or private-operated projects. Some of these projects benefited either as a business option or as an employment opportunity for these sections of society. These sections benefited both economically and health-wise. Their feedback revealed that their health and economic standards have improved promisingly.

During the initial phase of PMBC's business operation, they could gain trust among the suppliers, which helped them install plants using the materials supplied on credit. With the quality and standard of service delivered, PMBC increased the customer base to 45 installations within 3 years. PMBC charges 50% of the project before installation and 50% when the plant is ready for operation. PMBC assured the repair and maintenance of the plant for 10 years. Their business was monetized based on profits. The company has achieved a growth percentage of 5% in the last three financial years, from 2015–2016 to 2017–2018. PMBC carried out market research before developing the customized product for the site-specific plants. The target audiences for PMBC were villages, small towns, and municipalities. PMBC promoted products through word-of-mouth publicity as they believed that the hands-on trust of products was among the best ways to convince customers at a higher rate. Each member of the hierarchy at PMBC also took on the role of the marketing team. They kept process charts and service blueprints of the course of business operations. Every 3 months, PMBC performs the routine procedure of checking the installed plants. Log books kept at each plant were recorded with support from the area in charge of the specific plant.

PMBC, being registered as a Micro, Small & Medium Enterprise (MSME), has been growing at a steady rate. Its sales had grown to an average of 2–8 installations of RO plants per year by each DSA. On average, a DSA sold 3–4 installations during the summer and 1–2 installations during the winter. One of the projects of PMBC was undertaken by the Central Bank for women at Paroda Tehsil, Jalgav District, Maharashtra.

There were 7 methods adopted through which funds were raised for the implementation of the projects. The first is generally categorized as self- or privately owned plants in which individuals would raise funds. Here, PMBC usually gives emphasis on employment generation. In the second one, 50% of the funds will be raised by the BOT partner and 50% by the company itself. The third method adopted by them involves a government scheme known as Prime Minister Employment Generation Programme (PMEGP). The fourth method adopted was by the direct investment from government institutions, such as government banks, or was headed by the *sarpanch* of a village. The fifth method adopted a path in which plants were owned and run by Mahila Bachat Gat, a group of 12 women. The sixth method was adopted via non-government organizations. The seventh method was implemented by adopting a village through private invest- ment. Even though PMBC has tried these methods of implementation of projects, they are facing challenges in the smooth execution of projects due to the complexity of government policy in allocating subsidized funds. Many bank rejections had occurred, stating varied issues at differ- ent times of approach. One of the issues stated was that they could not avail of loans for machinery. This factor caused a significant delay in the purchase of instruments and the execution of the project. Assurance of the quality of products and services is the main aspect that PMBC never com- promises on. Its competitors, which provide RO machinery accessories at low rates that don't produce the desired output, had encouraged a prefer- ence to opt for cheaper accessories among his customers. An ex-army officer, one of its customers, had opted to purchase filters from its com- petitor at a low price to reduce the initial cost of installation. With the increased demand for water, the filters were unable to deliver quality water. This issue forced the officer to change the filters sooner than antici- pated. This led not only to an increase in expenses but also to the need for a technician on time. The lack of skilled technicians to operate, maintain, and repair the plant in an emergency, especially in remote villages, remained a significant challenge for PMBC.

RAINTAP: Diffusion by Forming an Association with the Community

RAINTAP rainwater filter for rooftop rainwater harvesting is a simple, smart, and sensible unit that works round the clock to capture, filter, and collect rainwater. RAINTAP has more than 25,000 installations across

India and abroad. RAINTAP is a highly efficient, cost-effective, and user-friendly unit requiring no maintenance. Simple cleaning under a running tap is enough. A flexible T connector makes it suitable for varied installation requirements; an SS 304 filter element keeps the dirt and debris out; and a strong flush valve flushes out impurities. RAINTAP is ideal for our modern way of living, where we don't need human intervention while harvesting rainwater (RAINTAP, 2015). An interview was conducted with Vardhman Envirotech, the company that developed RAINTAP. Vardhman Envirotech has made its presence felt in Western India and is involved in projects in 10 states. The company is a preferred choice for plumbing consultants, architects, town planners, and municipal corporations for rainwater harvesting.

The company had used a differentiator strategy as an entry strategy and had used contract manufacturing as a medium. The company provides the molds of the rainwater harvesting unit to third-party manufacturers. The company uses product development (launching a new product in an existing market) as a growth strategy. They are launching a new product, "NeeRain," another rainwater harvesting unit with a new and transparent design. Such a strategy helps the enterprise capitalize on the existing distribution system. The entrepreneur has formed partnerships with distribution channels and manufacturers, effectively serving as an angel community for the respective firm for the diffusion of its products. Vardhman Envirotech is actively associated with industry, trade bodies, and management associations, such as Jain International Trade Organization, Ahmedabad Management Association, the Indian Plumbing Association, the Indian Plastics Manufacturers Association, Alert Vyapar Organization, JITO Business Network, Amazon India Inc., Sheth Shri Anandji Kalyanji Jain Shwetambar Pedhi, Maratha Chamber of Commerce, Industry and Association (MCCIA), the Indo African Chambers of Commerce (IACC), and Indo-American Chambers of Commerce (IACC). The enterprise functions on zero debt. Their return on investment is about 10%. The revenues for the years 2016, 2017, and 2018 are INR 15 lakh, INR 26 lakh, and INR 40 lakh, respectively. The company has witnessed growth in revenues at a rate of 25% and 50% in the years 2017 and 2018, respectively.

DOW: Diffusion by Community Engagement

Bluemount Foods and Beverages is a quality-driven firm offering a wide range of mineral water. Registered in 2017, the firm supplies mineral water within a present time limit. This firm is situated in the Kozhikode district of Kerala. They were selling water in the form of bottles and cans under the label DOW. They have tried to maintain quality standards in their mineral water by following a series of 13 steps in manufacturing their product. They collect water in tankers from contract suppliers. These suppliers supply water in tankers from bore holes according to demand. The firm produces an average purified quantity of 6,000 L per month. Then, this processed water is filled in 20 L cans, 1 L bottles, and so on. These are then sent to the distribution channel to be transported to the prevailing market.

Even though Kerala was seriously affected by heavy monsoon rains in 2018 and 2019 and is blessed with 44 rivers, we could see many water tankers and water can suppliers helping during the summer season. The reason for this scenario was the sheer negligence of the authorities in charge and communities in preserving rainwater. Bluemount Foods and Beverages had relied completely on the water supply contractors rather than community involvement. The entrepreneur is solving the socially pressing problem of the scarcity of drinking water by innovating the process of purification. Timely checkups are done to ensure processed water quality, and filters are changed accordingly. The wastewater, after treatment, is released from the plant. The entrepreneur is engaged in serving drinkable water to schools, offices, hotels, restaurants, and residential buildings. Even though the market size is large, they could not scale up. Their investment was huge in setting up the plant. Bluemount was not able to scale up in 2019 compared to 2018 because the capital investment declined from INR 4.4 million in 2018 to INR 2.9 million in 2019.

Cross-case Analysis & Discussion

Impact of Community Engagement through Frugal Approach to Diffusion by Water A.T.M.

The emerging concept of shared ownership, or community engagement, has become an important dimension in emerging entrepreneurship theories. This concept falls in line with the bricolage concept of "involving customers, suppliers, and hangers-on in providing work on projects" (Baker & Nelson, 2005). Community members engaged in entrepreneurial action serve as evangelists for new products and services. The sales and diffusion of products and services have increased at a better rate compared with a firm where no such community exists. Word of mouth from each community enhanced the diffusion rate of water A.T.M.

Impact of Community Engagement through Frugal Approach to Diffusion by RAINTAP

In the case of RAINTAP, diffusion was possible through community engagement by forming associations with groups such as the Indian Plumbing Association, the Indian Plastics Manufacturers Association, and many more, as listed above. Through this frugal approach, they were able to capture markets over a wide range within a short span of time. This approach enabled them to reduce the cost of ownership. The association with a specific community helped channel toward targeted markets sustainably. Another important aspect is that the association with a third party for manufacturing by simply providing the required mold helped reduce the costs of plant, machinery, maintenance, and labor to a significant extent.

Impact of Community Engagement through Frugal Approach to Diffusion by DOW

DOW Water Bottles is a case that faced difficulty scaling up sustainably, even though it was solving a social problem. Bluemount Foods and Beverages had engaged with a very small community of contractors which supplied water. They had a huge investment in plants and machinery. Their cost of ownership increased substantially because they depended mainly on their own capital investment instead of customers' and laborers' investments, which form the major market share. The avoidance of customer community engagement, which forms the major share of venture growth, could be the reason for the low diffusion rate.

Limitations & Future Research

Some limitations of this research need to be acknowledged. The first limitation of this research is the sample size itself. As the purpose of this research is not to generalize but to get insights on the effectiveness of community engagement through the frugal approach, only 3 cases were chosen. The second limitation pertains to the depth of the discussion in relation to the psychological perspective of the entrepreneur who engages actively with the concerned community.

These limitations pave the path for future researchers to research this field, considering different industries. The observation from the three cases leads to the following proposition. Entrepreneurs who actively engage with the community as a strong base for diffusion could explore: (1) how far will the collective cognition of the community to launch a product or service be effective; (2) how can the collective cognition of a community help in creating frugal products and services; and (3) how collective cognition differs among entrepreneurs who do not engage with the community from those who engage in venture growth once the product or service is launched.

Conclusion

The main objective of this chapter was to explore the effectiveness of community engagement through frugal innovation based on three cases of entrepreneurs who were in the water sector. In these cases, each entrepreneur came up with a different strategy for the diffusion of their products and services through community engagement. All three entrepreneurs were trying to solve the socially pressing problem of the scarcity of drinking water. In this emerging era of shared ownership, such a frugal mindset is significant for budding entrepreneurs to pitch, launch, and nurture a new venture. In this research, we found that the entrepreneurs dealing with Water A.T.M. and RAINTAP were successful and were able to scale sustainably. Even though the entrepreneur dealing with water cans under the brand DOW wasn't able to scale up through community engagement, it gives insights into the fact that he could have scaled up if he focused on a frugal approach to community engagement and customers who form the major beneficiaries of his venture. In the future, researchers could extend this research to a new dimension by exploring the effectiveness of collective cognition in community engagement, which might give a psychological perspective to the frugal approach to diffusion.

References

Baker, T. & Nelson, R. E. (2005). Creating something from nothing: Resource construction through entrepreneurial bricolage. *Administrative Science Quarterly*, 50(3), 329–366.

Bond, J. (2014). A holistic approach to natural resource conflict: The case of Laikipia County, Kenya. *Journal of Rural Studies*, 34, 117–127.

Cai, Q., Ying, Y., Liu, Y., & Wu, W. (2019). Innovating with limited resources: The antecedents and consequences of frugal innovation. *Sustainability*, 11(20), 5789.

Davidsson, P., Baker, T., & Senyard, J. M. (2017). A measure of entrepreneurial bricolage behavior. *International Journal of Entrepreneurial Behavior & Research*, 23(1), 114–135.

Dawar, N. & Chattopadhyay, A. (2002). Rethinking marketing programs for emerging markets. *Long Range Planning*, 35, 457–474.

Desa, G. (2012). Resource mobilization in international social entrepreneurship: Bricolage as a mechanism of institutional transformation. *Entrepreneurship Theory and Practice*, 36(4), 727–751.

Di Benedetto, C. A. (2015). Diffusion of innovation. *Wiley Encyclopedia of Management*, 13, 1e5.

Di Domenico, M., Haugh, H., & Tracey, P. (2010). Social bricolage: Theorizing social value creation in social enterprises. *Entrepreneurship Theory and Practice*, 34(4), 681–703.

Duymedjian, R. & Rüling, C. C. (2010). Towards a foundation of bricolage in organization and management theory. *Organization Studies*, 31(2), 133–151.

Fisher, G. (2012). Effectuation, causation, and bricolage: A behavioral comparison of emerging theories in entrepreneurship research. *Entrepreneurship Theory and Practice*, 36(5), 1019–1051.

Hmieleski, K. M. & Corbett, A. C. (2008). The contrasting interaction effects of improvisational behavior with entrepreneurial self-efficacy on new venture performance and entrepreneur work satisfaction. *Journal of Business Venturing*, 23(4), 482–496.

Karnani, A. (2007). The mirage of marketing to the bottom of the pyramid: How the private sector can help alleviate poverty. *California Management Review*, 49(4), 91–111.

Khanna, T. & Palepu, K. (1997, July/August). Why focused strategies may be wrong for emerging markets. *Harvard Business Review*, 75, 41–51.

Levänen, J., Hossain, M., Lyytinen, T., Hyvärinen, A., Numminen, S., & Halme, M. (2016). Implications of frugal innovations on sustainable development.

Linna, P. (2013). Bricolage as a means of innovating in a resource-scarce environment: A study of innovator-entrepreneurs at the BOP. *Journal of Developmental Entrepreneurship*, 18(03), 1350015.

Mair, J. & Marti, I. (2009). Entrepreneurship in and around institutional voids: A case study from Bangladesh. *Journal of Business Venturing*, 24(5), 419–435.

McKague, K. & Oliver, C. (2019). Network bricolage as the reconciliation of indigenous and transplanted institutions in Africa. In *Entrepreneurship in Africa* (pp. 66–95). Routledge.

Perkmann, M. & Spicer, A. (2014). How emerging organizations take form: The role of imprinting and values in organizational bricolage. *Organization Science,* 25(6), 1785–1806.

Pisoni, A., Michelini, L., & Martignoni, G. (2018). Frugal approach to innovation: State of the art and future perspectives. *Journal of Cleaner Production,* 171, 107–126.

Plowman, D. A., Baker, L. T., Beck, T. E., Kulkarni, M., Solansky, S. T., & Travis, D. V. (2007). Radical change accidentally: The emergence and amplification of small change. *Academy of Management Journal,* 50(3), 515–543.

Rai, A. S. (2015). The affect of Jugaad: Frugal innovation and postcolonial practice in India's mobile phone ecology. *Environment and Planning D: Society and Space,* 33(6), 985–1002.

Rogers, E. M. (2010). *Diffusion of Innovations.* Chicago, IL: Simon and Schuster.

Ros-Tonen, M. A., Insaidoo, T. F., & Acheampong, E. (2013). Promising start, bleak outlook: The role of Ghana's modified taungya system as a social safeguard in timber legality processes. *Forest Policy and Economics,* 32, 57–67.

Salimath, M. S. & Jones III, R. J. (2011). Scientific entrepreneurial management: bricolage, bootstrapping, and the quest for efficiencies. *Journal of Business & Management,* 17(1).

Salunke, S., Weerawardena, J., & McColl-Kennedy, J. R. (2013). Competing through service innovation: The role of bricolage and entrepreneurship in project-oriented firms. *Journal of Business Research,* 66(8), 1085–1097. http://doi.org/10.1016/j.jbusres.2012.03.005

Sarasvathy, S. D. (2001). Causation and effectuation: Toward a theoretical shift from economic inevitability to entrepreneurial contingency. *Academy of Management Review,* 26(2), 243–263.

Seelos, C. & Mair, J. (2007). Profitable business models and market creation in the context of deep poverty: A strategic view. *Academy of Management Perspectives,* 21(4), 49–63.

Selden, P. D. & Fletcher, D. E. (2015). The entrepreneurial journey as an emergent hierarchical system of artifact-creating processes. *Journal of Business Venturing,* 30(4), 603–615.

Senyard, J., Baker, T., Steffens, P., & Davidsson, P. (2014). Bricolage as a path to innovativeness for resource-constrained new firms. *Journal of Product Innovation Management,* 31(2), 211–230.

Shah, S. K. & Tripsas, M. (2007). The accidental entrepreneur: The emergent and collective process of user entrepreneurship. *Strategic Entrepreneurship Journal,* 1(1-2), 123–140.

Sinkovics, N., Sinkovics, R. R., & Yamin, M. (2014). The role of social value creation in business model formulation at the bottom of the pyramid–implications for MNEs? *International Business Review*, 23(4), 692–707.

Sofaer, S. (1999). Qualitative methods: What are they and why use them? *Health Services Research*, 34(5 Pt 2), 1101.

Sonenshein, S. (2014). How organizations foster the creative use of resources. *Academy of Management Journal*, 57(3), 814–848.

Stinchfield, B. T., Nelson, R. E., & Wood, M. S. (2012). Learning from Levi–Strauss' legacy: Art, craft, engineering, bricolage, and brokerage in entrepreneurship. *Entrepreneurship Theory and Practice*, 37(4), 889–921.

Strang, D. & Meyer, J.W. (1993). Institutional conditions for diffusion. *Theory and Society*, 22(4), 487–511.

Strang, D. & Soule, S. A. (1998). Diffusion in organizations and social movements: From hybrid corn to poison pills. *Annual Review of Sociology*, 24(1), 265–290.

Sunley, P. & Pinch, S. (2012). Financing social enterprise: Social bricolage or evolutionary entrepreneurialism? *Social Enterprise Journal*, 8(2), 108–122.

Vavik, T. & Keitsch, M. M. (2010). Exploring relationships between universal design and social sustainable development: Some methodological aspects to the debate on the sciences of sustainability. *Sustainable Development*, 18(5), 295–305.

Venkataraman, S. (1997). *Advances in Entrepreneurship, Firm Emergence and Growth*, Vol. 3, pp. 119–138.

Welter, C., Mauer, R., & Wuebker, R. J. (2016). Bridging behavioral models and theoretical concepts: Effectuation and bricolage in the opportunity creation framework. *Strategic Entrepreneurship Journal*, 10(1), 5–20.

Xu, D. & Meyer, K. E. (2013). Linking theory and context: 'Strategy research in emerging economies' after Wright *et al.* (2005). *Journal of Management Studies*, 50(7), 1322–1346.

Yin, R. K. (2013). Validity and generalization in future case study evaluations. *Evaluation*, 19(3), 321–332.

Zahra, S. A., Gedajlovic, E., Neubaum, D. O., & Shulman, J. M. (2009). A typology of social entrepreneurs: Motives, search processes and ethical challenges. *Journal of Business Venturing*, 24(5), 519–532.

Zanello, G., Fu, X., Mohnen, P., & Ventresca, M. (2016). The creation and diffusion of innovation in developing countries: A systematic literature review. *Journal of Economic Surveys*, 30(5), 884–912.

Chapter 10

Entrepreneurial Organization of Social Innovations in the Diverse Indian Culture

Preeti Aagneya (alias Avani Bharadwaj)[*,‡],
Soumitro Chakravarty[*,§], **and Umesh Prasad**[†,‖]

[*]*Department of Management, BIT Mesra Lalpur Off-Campus, Ranchi, Jharkhand, India*

[†]*Department of CSE, BIT Mesra Lalpur Off-Campus, Ranchi, Jharkhand, India*
[‡]*bharadwajavani@gmail.com*

[§]*soumitro@bitmesra.ac.in*

[‖]*umesh@bitmesra.ac.in*

Abstract

Indian culture aligns with social entrepreneurship through values such as optimism, quality focus, karma, long-term relationships, environmental care, and acceptance of diversity. This alignment is essential for achieving social development goals.

The evolution of social responsibility in Indian businesses went through phases of philanthropy, support for independence, state-led initiatives, and, most recently, strong civil society engagement.

India needs more social entrepreneurs to address persistent social issues, including poverty, unemployment, environmental degradation, and gender disparity. Social entrepreneurs can create inclusive societies, tackle environmental challenges, innovate for social impact, build sustainable businesses, and serve as change agents.

Social entrepreneurship in India faces challenges such as a lack of financial support, resource constraints, difficulties in measuring social impact, gender discrimination, and the need to overcome traditional gender roles. Despite these challenges, social entrepreneurship remains a promising avenue for addressing India's complex social problems.

Keywords: Social entrepreneurship, India, entrepreneurship, social impact, social impact enterprises, challenges, sustainable businesses.

Introduction

Mulgan (2006, p. 146) has defined "social innovation" as involving all those creative "activities and services" which are focused on meeting an unmet social need or gap. The earliest reference to the term social innovation has been found to be made in 1998, when Rosabeth Kanter identified the change in path taken by private entities from that of corporate social responsibility toward corporate social innovation. Here, Kanter viewed how a few organizations were utilizing their workforce and business skills to innovate products and services which not only entered new markets but were also socially impactful, thereby creating the idea of community payoff. A social innovator comes up with an idea, which can be either a model of business, a product, or a service which has the capabilities to meet a social gap (Dro *et al.*, 2011).

Social innovation is different from business innovation. Business innovations are market-driven and focus on the needs of an individual consumer. On the other hand, social innovation caters to the unmet needs of the community as a whole and leads to their growth in a certain way (Lettice & Parekh, 2010). One of the most commonly used definitions of social innovation, as given by Phills *et al.* (2008), states that social innovation is "a novel solution to a social problem that is more effective, efficient, or just than existing solutions and for which the value created accrues primarily to society as a whole rather than private individuals."

As a method of organizing social innovation, social entrepreneurship, as defined by Zahra *et al.* (2009, p. 519), involves "the activities and processes undertaken to discover, define, and exploit opportunities in order to enhance social wealth by creating new ventures or managing existing organizations in an innovative manner."

A look at the definitions of social innovation and social entrepreneurship makes us understand that both concepts are inclined toward solving a social issue by recognizing the social gap or the unmet need to be a business opportunity.

Social innovators might be facing barriers related to a lack of financing for their ideas or a suitable network for promoting the same (Lettice & Parekh, 2010; Moore *et al.*, 2012). The resources are generally scarce, and sometimes, the social innovations also belong to varied categories. This is where social entrepreneurship gains importance. It provides the necessary resources to the social innovators and, in turn, get access to their knowledge and capabilities. A partnership is built in which both parties recognize a social opportunity and work toward creating social value. Hence, social innovation requires partnerships which are aimed at benefiting the public as a whole and not only a private individual, i.e. bringing entrepreneurs, investors, and the community into one profitable venture (Phills *et al.*, 2008). It is important to remember that though social innovations generate wealth, they are not market constructs, but are primarily aimed at bringing about social change (Pol & Ville, 2009). The financial performance of a social entrepreneurship venture should be sufficient for its survival (Groot & Dankbaar, 2011).

The skills required for running a social venture are not the same as those needed to run a typical business venture. The day-to-day running of a social venture is different too. The institutional environment greatly influences how a socially impactful business is run. At times, new organizational systems are also built to effectively run a social entrepreneurship venture.

The concepts of social innovation and social entrepreneurship are not standalone concepts. These are based on interactive and continuous learning. Such interactions involve the collective sharing of knowledge and often lead to the generation of fresh knowledge and insights, the development of new capabilities, and further social development in other underdeveloped sectors.

Therefore, it is seen that the interplay of social innovation and social entrepreneurship leads to collective social learning and paves the path for networking for social good. The two concepts have been found to overlap in their objectives of solving unmet social needs. Social entrepreneurs

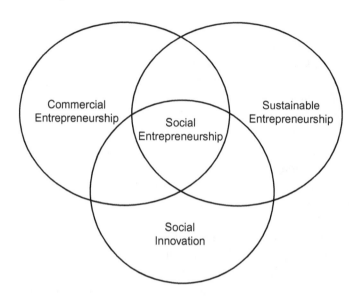

Figure 1.   Social entrepreneurship and India.

focus on the "double bottom line" (Phillips *et al.*, 2014) of doing social good and earning profits, which are reinvested as capital.

Figure 1 (Cardella *et al.*, 2021) indicates how social entrepreneurship derives its characteristics from commercial entrepreneurship, sustainable entrepreneurship, and social innovation.

The phenomenon of social entrepreneurship has always been a part of the Indian value system, though not in an institutional form. In ancient India, the emperors were loved by their people for voluntarily indulging in social welfare activities. All the religions thriving in India have emphasized providing the needy with whatever help one in a better position can afford to give.

At present, India has earned itself a respectable position in the world for the astounding number of social entrepreneurs it has currently working toward the rehabilitation of marginalized sections of people by utilizing their skills and simultaneously generating revenue (Tiwari *et al.*, 2017). Some of the most notable people in this field are Padma Shri Saalumarada Thimmakka (founder of the Saalumarada Foundation, an Non-Governmental Organizations (NGOs) working for orphans and vulnerable women), Urvashi Sahni (founder and CEO of Study Hall Education Foundation, working for providing financial support and mentorship to underprivileged students), Sharad Vivek Sagar (founder of Dexterity Global, working toward providing job opportunities to children in remote areas), Ria Sharma (founder of the Make Love Not Scars NGO, working for rehabilitating acid attack survivors), Sunil Bharti Mittal (chairman and founder of the Bharti Foundation, one of the biggest philanthropic units in India), Jeroo Billmoria (founder of Childline, which provides crisis relief to children), Anshu Gupta (founder of Goonj, a social organization working for the poor and needy), Santosh Parulekar (founder of Pipal Tree, working for creating livelihood generation opportunities for the Indian youth in rural areas), Dhruv Lakra (founder of Mirakle Couriers, which employs people with disabilities), and many more unsung heroes.

These social entrepreneurs have shown the world that business can be used to solve many of the toughest social challenges that our country faces, and it is possible to do so without any external funding.

Fundamental Values of Indian Culture

Before trying to build a connection between the diverse Indian culture and social enterprises, it is necessary to first understand the roots of Indian culture (Jain, 2018). The age-old tradition of India is deeply connected with nature. Indian culture is fundamentally different from the cultural values of many developed nations. In this section, we deal with some of the basic features of Indian culture and the connection between them and social entrepreneurship. This comparison would go on to show how the nurturing nature of Indian culture is resonant with the basic goals of the process of social entrepreneurship.

The youth of the country are increasingly getting associated with such initiatives, which means higher participation, greater innovation, and more use of technology in the field. The strength of Indian culture needs to be combined with the goals of social entrepreneurship and therefore reach the social development goals of the country.

Focus on Optimism

Indian culture believes that our thoughts drive our actions. It is not always by chance that acts of goodness are performed. Noble thoughts motivate us to engage in noble actions. Therefore, it is considered important to fill the mind with positive thoughts. Indian families consider *teerthayatras*, *satsangs*, *goshthi*, etc., as important.

Focus More on Quality than Quantity

The Indian system of life focuses more on creating value. Looking at the traditional business practices in India, we find that most of those were into small-scale production, which made it easier for them to maintain the quality of production. Being quality-obsessed is beneficial for innovation and the performance of an entity in general.

The Concept of Karma

The Indian philosophy is rooted in the concept of karma: What happens to us is because of what we do. Because of this belief, we are generally conscious of the effects our decisions and actions will have on our surroundings, which in turn is also evident in our business decisions. We consider it our duty to behave well. Since the concept of karma is deeply rooted in Indian culture, so is the motive behind social entrepreneurship ventures, i.e. to do what is right. It does not focus solely on material gains but on the overall development of society.

Focus on Long-Term Associations

The Indian tradition of forging life-long bonds in social relationships is a much-required feature for the present scenario. We talk about our gods and goddesses by a single name. Our festivals are all about cooperation and mass celebrations. When employees are valued and preserved for longer periods of time, they become like family to the entrepreneurs and are as concerned about the overall development of their employers' firms as the owners themselves.

Care for the Environment

Our traditional practices were environment-friendly in nature. We used and continue to use leaf-based disposable plates in our feasts; festival decorations mostly involve the use of flowers and leaves; cow dung was used for mopping the clay pathways in houses; rangoli, or *kolam*, which uses rice powder, was drawn to beautify house entrances; and so on. These practices are not as prevalent in today's families but are needed to keep the environment safe.

Acceptance of Diversity

India is a perfect example of unity in diversity. Our culture is an amalgamation of languages, practices, rituals, ideas, etc. This makes our country a breeding ground for creativity and opportunities to innovate.

Phases of Social Responsibility of Business in India

According to Sundar (2000), business social responsibility among Indian businesses passed through four phases:

(i) The early industrialization phase (1850–1914):
This phase saw social responsibility in business in the form of business philanthropy. The affluent business houses would run hospitals and educational institutions for the needy through various trusts.

(ii) During the Indian struggle for independence (1914–1960):
During this phase, the rich business families showed support for the movement for Indian independence and other related social causes.

(iii) During 1960–1980:
This phase saw a decline in business philanthropy and the rise of state-led developmental schemes.

(iv) After the economic liberalization of 1991:
This phase saw the birth of a strong civil society, where entrepreneurs began to take social causes very seriously, and we witnessed improvements in industry returns.

Why India Needs More Social Entrepreneurs?

In the past few decades, India has seen rapid growth in the areas of technological advancement, sanitation, education, and healthcare facilities.

However, there doesn't seem to be much improvement in the social issues that have been plaguing the country for a long time. Some of the social issues that need to be dealt with with the utmost urgency are poverty, unemployment, environmental deterioration, and gender disparity. According to the Global Multidimensional Poverty Index, India is home to the highest number of poor people and children in the world. Social entrepreneurs are characterized by their sustainable ventures, where they convert innovative ideas into business models for solving problems in the community or bringing about positive change. They have an important part to play in this regard (Dubey, 2023).

The following section discusses some of the major reasons why we need more social entrepreneurs in India (Dubey, 2023).

Creating an Inclusive Society

Social entrepreneurs include local communities in their workforce. They inherently focus on leveraging the skills of those from marginalized communities by creating opportunities for them and training them in the skills which are in high demand. This would go a long way toward bridging the gap between the rich and the poor in India.

Environmental Challenges

As India can be seen quickly climbing up the ladder of advancement, the numerous environmental challenges that tag along cannot be ignored. Social ventures are found to be working on maintaining environmental balance as the core of their objectives. They aim for sustainability in all their practices. Thus, the country stands to gain immensely if social entrepreneurship is promoted.

Tackle Societal Problems on a Larger Scale

The products or services offered by social entrepreneurs are solutions to issues affecting whole communities. Their focus on addressing social gaps while generating revenue is bound to bring about major social transformation, which is not possible to achieve solely through government policies. Their socially impactful business models can be easily replicated on a larger scale because of their locally sustainable nature.

Innovating for Social Impact

Utilizing the resources at hand, social entrepreneurs form social structures that work with the aim of solving grass-roots-level issues. India requires such socially conscious structures which not only contribute to its economic growth but also solve its social challenges. According to a report by the Impact Investors Council (IIC), approximately 600 Indian social entrepreneurs have so far attracted a capital of around USD 9 billion and have contributed to improving almost 500 million lives through their ventures (Agarwal, 2022).

Create Sustainable, Impactful and Commercially Successful Businesses

The world at large has become increasingly conscious of how important sustainability is. Social entrepreneurs are adept at commercial tactics and can draw from their commercial caliber to create value for their ventures, which is again invested in the business. They have become successful in attracting private capital to the objective of social innovation. The generation of their own funds for their operations and not depending on external grants appears to be a helpful approach for a nation like India, where the majority of the population is working day and night for personal sustenance.

Social Change Agents

Social entrepreneurs are hailed as changemakers or social catalysts, who influence others to engage in social causes. People and business houses feel attracted to their mission and business models and are therefore inspired to contribute in some way or, better yet, start similar ventures of their own. Looking at the vastness of the population living under the shadows of social issues, such as exclusion, discrimination, or vulnerability, India needs more and more social changemakers in the form of social entrepreneurs.

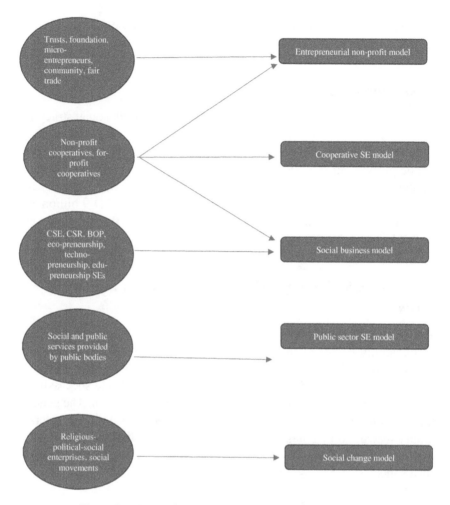

Figure 2.   Types of social entrepreneurship ventures in India.

Types of Social Entrepreneurship Ventures in India

Figure 2 shows the five classifications of Indian social entrepreneurship ventures (Agrawal & Khare, 2019):

   (i)   entrepreneurial non-profit (ENP) model,
  (ii)   social business (SB) model,
 (iii)   cooperative model,
 (iv)   public-sector social enterprise (PSE) model, and
  (v)   social change model.

(i)   The ENP Model

The ENP model is defined as made up of "all non-profit organizations developing any type of earned income business activities in support of their social mission" (Defourny & Nyssens, 2017, p. 12). These include NGOs, foundations, non-profit organizations, micro-entrepreneurs, small self-help groups, foundations, and societies. These institutions are registered institutions. The various acts under which these might be registered are: the Societies Registration Act (1860), the Co-operative Societies Act (1904), the Companies Act (2013), or the Indian Trusts Act (1882). Most of these institutions invest the earnings from their commercial activities in their social development activities. Some examples of this type of model are CRY (Child Rights and You), Smile Foundation, and HelpAge India.

(ii)   The SB Model

The SB model includes corporate social enterprises, healthcare firms, "edu-tech" firms, and "clean-tech" firms (Agrawal & Sahasranamam, 2016). These institutions focus on social development as well as on individual profit motives. These can be registered under the Societies Registration Act (1860), the Indian Trusts Act (1882), the Companies Act (2013), or the Cooperative Societies Act (1904). These firms operate as private organizations, earning profit as well as creating social value. Some examples of this model are Patanjali and SKS Microfinance.

(iii) The PSE Model

The PSE model includes the programs run by the government of India mostly in collaboration with private players in the areas of education, sports, healthcare, buying rural produce, employment, social equality, etc., which are focused on uplifting the underprivileged (Defourny & Nyssens, 2017, p. 16). Some examples of this type of social venture include online education programs provided free of charge by Indian universities, collaborative entities (privately owned but government-funded) working for "re-skilling" marginalized communities, and entities selling subsidized health insurance schemes.

(iv) The Cooperative SE Model

This model was primarily launched for the benefit of Indian farmers and later started providing services to the needy and poor at low costs. These are mostly registered under the Cooperative Societies Act (1904). These institutions are structures where the decision-making authority remains with a board of members, composed of elected members, volunteers, employees, citizens, donors, relevant field experts, members of other public bodies, etc. Some examples of social entrepreneurs belonging to this category are the Amul dairy cooperative and the IFFCO (Indian Farmers Fertilizers Co-operative Limited).

(v)   The Social Change Model

The social change model plays a significant role in the Indian scenario. This model includes all such organizations which specifically work for the greater social good (Dees, 1998). They largely rely on volunteers for their running. The various stakeholders in this model are religious institutions, political organizations, the media, the general public, and legal institutions. These are typically public-funded and do not accept government grants. Some examples of social entrepreneurs belonging to this category are the Chipko movement activists, Mahatma Gandhi, and Nelson Mandela.

Social Entrepreneurship and Diverse Indian Culture

The wide diversity in India lends a unique identity to the country. The country is home to many ways of life, customs, languages, traditions, ethnicity, religions, attires, castes, and food habits. These differences make our lives colorful and enriched. Political collisions, which are a result of the diversity, cannot be overlooked. However, the enrichment in our lives in the form of festivals, recipes, art and craft, hospitality, and media overpowers such collisions. We boast a cultural heritage that is also our strength. This makes the nation attractive to millions of tourists flocking for a taste of our diverse culture. It provides a platform for social entrepreneurs who can leverage the opportunities created by this cultural diversity in the fields of tourism and handicrafts. The preservation of cultural heritage and sharing it uplift the communities engaged in the mentioned activities. Therefore, these enterprises fall under the umbrella of social entrepreneurship models (Dhesi, 2010).

The social enterprises which help in preserving the cultural heritage while simultaneously creating social value are called culture-based social enterprises (Agrawal & Khare, 2019). These are mostly non-profit in nature.

Challenges of Social Entrepreneurship in India

The success stories of social entrepreneurship in India are not the only face of the phenomenon in the country. They have been facing numerous challenges in their establishment, operations, and survival (*Top 10 Social*, 2023).

Lack of Financial Support

Social innovators are often faced with a lack of sufficient funds for putting their ideas into practice, as well as, in later stages, for carrying on with their goals until they become a known face in the market. The corporate houses are mostly driven by profits and private gains, which is a deterrent to achieving the social impact that social entrepreneurship works for. Lack of financial backing does not make it possible for the social entrepreneurship operations to scale up and thus help more people in the long run.

Lack of Resources and Market

To begin with, the needy communities might be doubtful of the intentions of the social entrepreneurs about whether they actually aim to bring prosperity to them or for their own selfish motives. Looking at the situation they have been living in, this is not surprising. It requires perseverance and communication to convince them of the motives of social enterprises. In the face of distrust and many times due to their locations, the marginalized sections of society become inaccessible to social entrepreneurs.

Another challenge faced by social entrepreneurs is finding partners with shared values who agree to help them reach the market with their products and services.

Measuring Their Value

In a traditional business, measuring success or failure is simply through profits made. A social enterprise works toward the "double bottom line," i.e. earning profits as well as creating social impact. Measuring the social change caused is a complex task and often requires studying multiple qualitative metrics.

Gender Discrimination

The Indian culture puts a lot of pressure on women in the household in the form of domestic duties, most of which remain unshared by other members of the family. Although now they are seen demolishing the cultural barriers, many are still unable to rise above the stereotypical roles that are expected of them and feel the lack of family support. Additionally, Indian female social entrepreneurs have been found to be struggling with a lack of investment and mentorship in pursuing their ventures.

References

Agarwal, A. (2022, March 3). How can India boost social impact investment to touch billion lives. India Today. https://www.indiatoday.in/business/story/how-can-india-boost-social-impact-investment-to-touch-billion-lives-1920257-2022-03-03.

Agrawal, A. & Khare, P. (2019). Social Entrepreneurship in India: Models and Application. In E. Bidet & J. Defourny (Eds.), *Social Enterprise in Asia: Theory, Models and Practice* (pp. 56–78). Routledge: New York. https://doi.org/10.4324/9780429265761-4.

Agrawal, A. & Sahasranamam, S. (2016). Corporate social entrepreneurship in India. South *Asian Journal of Global Business Research*, 5(2), 214–233.

Cardella, G. M., Hernández-Sánchez, B.R., Monteiro, A. A., & Sánchez-García, J. C. (2021). Social entrepreneurship research: Intellectual structures and future perspectives. *Sustainability*, 13, 7532. https://doi.org/10.3390/su13147532.

Dees, J. G. (1998). Enterprising nonprofits. *Harvard Business Review*, 76, 54–69.

Defourny, J. & Nyssens, M. (2017). Fundamentals for an international typology of social enterprise models. *Voluntas*, 28(6), 2469–2497.

Dhesi, A. S. (2010). Diaspora, social entrepreneurs and community development. *International Journal of Social Economics*, 37(9), 703–716.

Dro, I., Therace, A., & Hubert, A. (2011). *Empowering People, Driving Change: Social Innovation in the European Union*. Brussels: European Commission. http://dx.doi.org/10.2796/13155.

Dubey, A. (2023, April 13). Why India needs more social entrepreneurs. Forbes India Blogs. https://www.forbesindia.com/blog/entrepreneurship/why-india-needs-more-social-entrepreneurs/#:~:text=There%20is%20a%20significant%20gap,creating%20opportunities%20for%20marginalised%20communities.

Groot, A. & Dankbaar, B. (2014). Does social innovation require social entrepreneurship? *Technology Innovation Management Review*, 4(12), 17–26.

Jain, T. K. (2018). Social entrepreneurship: Indian roots. https://ssrn.com/abstract=3284943 or http://dx.doi.org/10.2139/ssrn.3284943.

Lettice, F. & Parekh, M. (2010). The social innovation process: Themes, challenges and implications for practice. *International Journal of Technology Management*, 51, 19–158.

Moore, M., Westley, F. R., & Nicholls, A. (2012). The social finance and social innovation nexus. *Journal of Social Entrepreneurship*, 3, 115–132.

Mulgan, G. (2006). The process of social innovation. *Innovations: Technology, Governance, Globalization*, 1, 145–162.

Phillips, W., Lee, H., Ghobadian, A., O'Regan, N., & James, P. (2015). Social innovation and social entrepreneurship: A systematic review. *Group & Organisation Management*, 40(3), pp. 1–34. https://doi.org/10.1177/1059601114560063.

Phills, J. A., Deiglmeier, K., & Miller, D. T. (2008). Rediscovering social innovation. *Stanford Social Innovation Review*, 6, 34–43.

Pol, E. & Ville, S. (2009). Social innovation: Buzz word or enduring term. *Journal of Socio-Economics*, 38, 878–885.

Sundar, P. (2000). *Beyond Business: From Merchant Charity to Corporate Citizenship: Indian Business Philanthropy Through the Ages*. Tata McGraw Hill: New Delhi.

Tiwari, P., Bhat, A. K., & Tikoria, J. (2017). An empirical analysis of the factors affecting social entrepreneurial intentions. *Journal of Global Entrepreneurship Research*, 7(9). https://doi.org/10.1186/s40497-017-0067-1.

Top 10 Social Entrepreneurs in India in 2023. (2023, December 5). Chegg. https://www. cheggindia.com/earn-online/social-entrepreneurs-in-india.

Zahra, S. A., Gedajlovic, E., Neubaum, D. O., & Shulman, J. M. (2009). A typology of social entrepreneurs: Motives, search processes and ethical challenges. *Journal of Business Venturing*, 24, 519–532.

Part V

Subaltern Approach

https://doi.org/10.1142/9789811296444_0011

Chapter 11

Digital Revolution in Indian SMEs and a Regenerative Managerial Mindset

Manu Shukla[*,‡] **and Purvi Pujari**[†,§]

Independent Researcher, Zurich, Switzerland

†*Professor, Vijay Patil School of Management,*
DY Patil University, Navi Mumbai, Maharashtra

‡*manupandey81@gmail.com*

§*purvipujari@gmail.com*

Abstract

India is a land of diversity, where diverse cultures, religions, languages and ethnicities have increasingly driven innovation and creativity, giving a boost to the development of small- and medium-sized enterprises (SMEs) in the country. Given that 70% of India's rural population still primarily depends on agriculture for their livelihood and most of the population lives in villages and Tier 1 and Tier 2 cities, SMEs in these areas have been playing a pivotal role in the inclusive growth of the Indian economy since independence. From cottage industries to the Internet of Things (IoT) and smart technologies or large manufacturing industries, SMEs account for the majority of enterprises worldwide, contributing two-thirds of employment opportunities. Studies conducted in the past show that SMEs have constantly been confronted with various challenges, such as lack of timely access to credit facilities, shortage of manpower and skills, and adoption of new technologies. The outbreak of the COVID-19 crisis in the past few years has crippled their regular activities. However, the crisis has fundamentally changed not only the mindsets, perceptions, and the way businesses, SMEs, organizations, institutions, and individuals operate but also given an opportunity amid the crisis to be more resilient and embrace the digital platforms to survive and eventually achieve success. The aim of this chapter is to identify the future prospects of SMEs through thriving digitization while proposing a framework with a new managerial mindset as a strong force of SME specificities. It also focuses on policy intervention to optimize businesses in order to achieve sustainable economic growth.

This chapter is divided into three main parts. The first part focuses on defining and explaining the purpose of SMEs in India, wherein the significant benefits of digitization as a strategy for driving improved performance and productivity of SMEs are explained. The second part deals with describing the challenges and struggles of Indian SMEs from a managerial perspective while focusing on the new mindset of SME managers and owners toward the organic development of their businesses. The third and most crucial part examines policy interventions and support for SMEs and a new entrepreneurial mindset, and it suggests a model for inclusive growth in an economy.

Keywords: Small and medium enterprises, digitization, strategy, challenges, new managerial mindset.

Introduction to Indian SMEs

The decline in many large-scale industrial operations in the 1980s stimulated the importance of small and medium enterprises in generating employment (Greene *et al.*, 2008) and adding value to emerging markets for new growth opportunities. From the Khadi, village, and coir industries to large manufacturing units, small- and medium-sized enterprises (SMEs) are an important productive driver of employment, gross domestic product (GDP), and exports. Although the corporates, or the large-sized sector, continues to attract a major workforce, the economic model of our country is such that there is a need to encourage and promote entrepreneurship as a step toward reducing regional disparities. Broadly, the SME sector, with its widespread capability to create 10 million job opportunities over the next 4–5 years, has the potential to serve as a key contributor to help India achieve its five trillion dollar economy by 2026–2027.

At the beginning of 1991, SMEs were finding it very difficult to survive due to a lack of advanced technology, resources, and competitiveness, but with the forces of globalization and technological advancements in the last half-decade, India has witnessed an accelerated growth in SMEs, accounting for 45% of total industrial output and nearly 40% of total exports, thereby representing an increase in the national income (GDP), growth, job creation, and balanced economic development. However, many researchers have highlighted that economic globalization has impacted the prosperity of SMEs both positively and negatively, for instance, the closing down of SMEs within a short span of time (Prasanna *et al.*, 2019), a lack of timely access to credit facilities, a lack of awareness of the existing government policies (Alqassabi, 2020), entrepreneurial orientation, size of businesses (Bhalerao *et al.*, 2022), shortage of manpower and skills, and adoption of new technologies. While the SMEs were already facing significant headwinds due to the challenges of globalization, they became the victims of the COVID-19 crisis later in the past few years, creating dramatic and immediate changes to the way these businesses work. These small business owners are more vulnerable to crises (Shane, 2011) due to fewer assets, lower productivity, and lower capital reserves (Organization for Economic Cooperation and Development (OECD, 2020)).

But their unique and unleashing innovative nature helped SMEs thrive amid the pandemic. The crisis has changed the mindsets, behaviors, and attitudes of our personal, professional, and societal lives by incorporating greater flexibility into the way we think, act, work, take decisions, and learn. The pandemic presents an enticing transformational opportunity by offering new perspectives on tech platforms and sustainability. Many researchers argued that the adoption of digital, or new-age, technologies is critical for SMEs (Pujari *et al.*, 2022) to mitigate the impact of the pandemic crisis (Kumar & Ayedee, 2021) and to improve their performance (Papadopoulos *et al.*, 2020). It is in this view that this chapter highlights the importance of the adoption of more sophisticated technologies while focusing on the mindsets of managers in achieving a resilient recovery and sustainable economic ecosystem.

Definition of SMEs

Although in entrepreneurship research, the term small and medium sized enterprises (SMEs) has been a central concept, there is no standard definition of these SMEs; it varies significantly across countries, sectors, and industries based on traits such as size (number of employees), market capitalization, and assets. According to the Micro, Small and Medium Enterprises Development (MSMED) Act 2006, micro, small, and medium enterprises were classified into two sectors, i.e. manufacturing and service, based on investment in plant, machinery, and equipment. However, considering the dynamic impact of inflation, globalization, and digitization on the development and growth of this sector, a revised definition of MSMEs in India was announced on May 13, 2020, as a part of the "Atmanirbhar Bharat" scheme. This new criterion of classification was officially introduced on July 1, 2020, based on turnover while eliminating the distinction between manufacturing and service enterprises. Table 1 shows the changes in criteria for classification and the definition of MSMEs.

Table 1 highlights the quantitative features considered in defining small- and medium-sized firms. However, it is also imperative to incorporate qualitative criteria, such as organization structure, corporate social responsibility, ownership structure, financial management, and other unquantifiable criteria, to foreground the importance of SMEs in today's era and also to differentiate them from large businesses.

Table 1. Definition of micro, small, and medium enterprises.

Existing and Revised Definition of MSMEs

Existing MSME Classification			
Criteria : Investment in Plant & Machinery or Equipment			
Classification	Micro	Small	Medium
Mfg. Enterprises	Investment<Rs. 25 lac	Investment<Rs. 5 cr.	Investment <Rs. 10 cr.
Services Enterprise	Investment<Rs. 10 lac	Investment< Rs. 2 cr.	Investment<Rs. 5 cr.
Revised MSME Classification			
Composite Criteria : Investment And Annual Turnover			
Classification	Micro	Small	Medium
Manufacturing & Services	Investment< Rs. 1 cr. and Turnover < Rs.5 cr.	Investment< Rs. 10 cr. and Turnover < Rs.50 cr.	Investment< Rs. 20 cr. and Turnover < Rs.100 cr.

Source: Ministry of MSME.

Characteristics of SMEs

Under the "Start-up India" scheme of the government of India (GOI) for the development of entrepreneurship, the culture of innovation, and sustainability, SMEs, through their unique characteristics, have the potential to lay the foundation of a global sustainability agenda and meet their future aspirations for sustainable domestic and economic growth. Some of the characteristics are included in Figure 1.

Apparently, this paints a picture of which characteristics make a successful SME, which depends largely on the mindset of the owners or

Figure 1. Key attributes of small and medium-sized enterprises (SMEs).

managers. In today's era of economic globalization, different variations in the performance and productivity of small and medium businesses trigger the need to investigate the mindset of the SME owner or managers. The mindset here refers to the mental bandwidth, traits, awareness, clarity, and priorities of the owners at different development stages of their businesses, viz. start-up, survival, growth, expansion, and maturity. This growth mindset has long been acknowledged as a key quality cultivated by owners and managers to create momentum for future growth. Success is not simply about getting bigger; rather, it is often about having a valuable growth strategy, self-awareness, turbocharging your core business with the available resources and technology, and being a hero in a particular geographic area. In short, the success of small businesses depends largely on the perceptions of their owners.

Role of SMEs

In an era where small and medium businesses represent the majority of firms globally, India is no exception. With more than 6.3 crore Micro, Small and Medium Enterprises (MSMEs) in the country, contributing nearly 30% to GDP and generating 50% of the income from total exports, the government continues setting up growth agendas and policies to strengthen SMEs' performance and make our country self-reliant. As per the data from the Ministry of MSME, there were 12,201,448 registered MSMEs in 2022. The accelerated growth shows that India is all set to meet its ambitious target of becoming a five trillion dollar economy in the next few years and becoming the world's third-largest economy. To achieve the development goals in a more systematic manner, the government has announced various reforms to unleash the potential of SMEs. A few of these initiatives are included in Table 2.

Besides the above-mentioned schemes, there are other initiatives for providing credit, including financial-marketing assistance, infrastructure development, skill development training, technology upgradation, competitiveness, and other services for SMEs across the country.

From the above table, it is evident that digitization has greatly affected all sizes of businesses across industries; therefore, all of the governments' strategies are directed toward technological transformation in SMEs. However, is it purely the government's responsibility?

Table 2. Government of India's initiatives for the growth of SMEs.

S. No.	Initiatives	Objectives
1	Credit Guarantee Trust Fund for Micro and Small Enterprises (CGTSME)	Encouraging first-time entrepreneurs to establish SMEs Providing collateral-free credit to the MSME sector
2	Pradhan Mantri Mudra Yojana	Fund the refunded Offers up to INR 10 lakhs to business enterprise Hassle-free loan disbursement
3	Zero Defect Zero Effect (ZED) Certification Scheme	Provides both financial and technological support to MSMEs to enhance productivity and manufacturing of high-quality products with zero defects Ensuring environmental consciousness
4	Udyam, e-Shram, National Career Services (NCS), Aatamanirbhar Skilled Employee Employer Mapping (ASEEM)	Interlinked portals to generate a centralized database of workers for delivering services related to credit facilitation, skilling, and recruitment
5	Design Clinic	Encouraging small businesses to experiment, learn, and implement new design expertise into their functions
6	Credit Linked Capital Subsidy Scheme (CLCSS)	Facilitates technological upgradation by providing 15% subsidy for investments up to INR 1 crore Promoting competition
7	Creation and Harmonious Application of Modern Processes for Increasing the Output and National Strength (CHAMPIONS)	Promoting a empowered, unified, and technology-driven platform to help MSMEs in terms of management, permissions, finance, etc. Grievance redressal

No business defines its own transformational path or how the managers should act or perform; rather, it is the manager or the owner who must first learn how to grow and transform their mindset to respond flexibly to changes and to be able to drive digitalization with maturity. Establishing an enterprising and resilient mindset provides them with the opportunity to influence the performance and socioeconomic lifestyle of their local people and the economy at large.

Digitization as a Strategy

The COVID-19 pandemic has forced the adoption of digital technologies (e.g. artificial intelligence, robotics, big data, machine learning, and adaptive learning) by businesses and organizations more urgently than ever. There's no doubt that the crisis has had a devastating impact on individuals, societies, businesses, organizations, and economies as a whole and has dramatically changed the way we live, work, think, behave, and communicate and also the way businesses, whether large or small, operate. In a nutshell, everything has been impacted. Overall, small and medium enterprises could no longer escape the extraordinary and threatening impact the pandemic has had on their existence. However, the post-COVID-19 recovery provided opportunities for SME managers to replace conventional tried-and-tested business models with more versatile, resilient, and innovative models driven by the adoption of high-end modern technologies to improve their competitiveness in the global market.

Prior to the pandemic, a pattern of flexibility, such as remote working, had started to emerge slowly in large businesses due to technological advancements, but the abrupt disruptions caused by the shutdown in 2020 forced industries and sectors to reinvent their business plans and strategies as a step toward a resilient recovery. This is when and where the SMEs went into disconnected silos due to their inability to seamlessly work from remote locations and communicate efficiently with customers, suppliers, and people. Many of these businesses face the toughest market environment due to data integration challenges. At this moment, small businesses realized the importance of establishing a common platform where all the information is accumulated in an integrated manner as a source of innovation and productivity growth.

The main pillars of job creation, poverty reduction, social inclusion, innovation, and economic growth are undergoing massive transformation by creating big data through the adoption of Industry 4.0 technologies. However, together with the support of government initiatives, schemes, and financial incentives, many small businesses have successfully transitioned from being low-tech to complete digital strategy adoption to improve the socioeconomic standards of the country. The important role of the government and other external service providers in the adoption of technology in SMEs has been identified as a critical element in the literature (Maroufkhani *et al.*, 2020). Moreover, due to economic globalization, businesses need to introduce innovative and digital technologies into their operations to maintain a competitive advantage in the long term (Manhart, 2013) and to stay alive in today's dramatically changing business environment (Chen *et al.*, 2016). The outcome has been very encouraging.

All the research studies conducted so far and the statistics from different sectors provide evidence that the adoption and deployment of Industry 4.0 technologies, such as artificial intelligence (AI), big data, robotics, cloud computing, blockchain, e-commerce, and social media, have undoubtedly been accelerated by many years. Also, these digital technologies have helped SMEs facilitate interconnection, interaction, communication, innovation, optimization, customization, adaptation, and energy efficiency of their products and services (Roblek *et al.*, 2013; Zezulka *et al.*, 2016). Building a digital transition has other advantages as well, such as market expansion (Malhotra, 2020), exponential improvement in products and services at a reduced cost, decreased human errors, and improved financial performance and productivity (Shaikh *et al.*, 2021), flexible approaches to work management, improved customer engagement and satisfaction, better collaboration, and increased competitiveness.

The concept of digitization, or digital transformation, is not limited to the adoption of smart technologies, paperless operations, data analytics, software, etc.; it's more about an agile and growth mindset, or a "digital transformative mindset," by managers, together with the business processes. We have defined digital transformative mindset as the process of cultivating positive thoughts and attitudes, embracing changes, learning to learn through effective management of energy (not just time and information), and thriving on challenges. The owners' commitment and consistency have a great influence on transitioning to new automated technologies (Gandhi & Patel, 2018). To create a foundation for successful digitization in small or large businesses, it is therefore very essential to transition to a digitally mature mindset.

Challenges and Struggles of Indian SMEs

Small and medium enterprises represent the majority of businesses operating in India and around the world. They play a crucial role in creating an ecosystem for inclusive and sustainable socioeconomic development. However, various research and statistics highlight that these businesses have always been facing challenges for decades due to their outdated practices and policies, whether conventional or novel.

Al-Shanfari (2012) identified education as one of the major obstacles to promoting SMEs. Yarahmadi and Magd (2016) also noted that there has been a gap between educational institutions and business-related skills curricula, which hinders the survival of SMEs. Furthermore, many researchers argued that cultural issues, such as fear of failure and a risk-taking attitude, affect the success and performance of small businesses (Al-Mataani, 2017; Kabir *et al.*, 2022). Bunte *et al.* (2021), in their study on SMEs, found that initial cost and time investment, lack of expertise, resources, and size of the business are some of the barriers to the adoption of high-end technologies such as AI. SMEs have also been struggling considerably due to unpredictable financial markets (Kale *et al.*, 2010) and, most importantly, to perceived mindsets (Nieman, 2006). Johnson (2009), in the same light, elaborated that individuals with fixed mindsets show a helpless pattern of thoughts, behaviors, and feelings when faced with challenges, and this contributes to the high risk of failure of SMEs.

Taking the above-discussed challenges into account, we have deduced some of the common challenges faced by traditional and digitally transformed SMEs in India (Table 3).

However, the integration of smart technologies and tools into business models and processes, as an outcome of the COVID-19 recovery, has

Table 3.   Challenges faced by small and medium enterprises.

S. No.	Traditional SMEs	Digitally transformed SMEs
i	Infrastructural issues	Shortage of skilled workforce
ii	Capital and funding problems	Resistance to change
iii	Lack of educated, skilled workforce and zero mindset with inability to innovate	Lack of change in management strategy due to poor communication, workers involvement, and business culture
iv	Non-availability of resources, financial/non-financial	Inadequate information and knowledge about adoption of tools and processes
v	Inability to cater to customer demands and balancing growth and quality	Lack of well-defined transformation strategy
vi	Lack of upgraded ICT tools and complicated government policies on export/import	Supply chain challenges due to data quality, inventory shortage, and relationship with suppliers
vii	Poor networking and collaboration	Absence of an affirmative mindset

proved quite helpful in bringing significant benefits to small businesses, such as reduced transaction costs, better access to information, resources, innovation, and government services (OECD, 2019). Since small and medium enterprises act as ancillary units for large businesses, it is very essential to upgrade them with the technological infrastructure for them to remain competitive in the global market (Kale *et al.*, 2010; Pollard, 2006; Sadagopan, 1999). In more general terms, 2022 has been a year of profound change for SMEs. Automation and digitalization in small and medium business strategies have enabled them to exploit the opportunities to remain competitive with regard to manufacturing, administrative, and procurement processes.

With increasing globalization and digitalization across businesses and industries, it is imperative for owners to reorient their thinking to have a long-term and holistic view of designing and aligning processes and systems with a new digital culture. As it is rightly said that there is always continuity in culture (Hofstede *et al.*, 2005), so is the current digital era, where millennials and Gen Z represent the generation of digital wizards. However, as with any other shift initiative, resistance comes naturally, which has been one of the owners' major challenges. Therefore, with investment in technology upgradation to scale up the business, owners with an innovative, inquisitive, and risk-averting mindset are better able to create a momentum shift to a more formalized innovation process by creating a completely integrated structure where employees work together as a team in real time. However, there is a need for additional research to understand the relationship between a growth mindset and other factors such as education, motivation, creativity, and risk-taking propensity to understand its impact on the performance of small and medium enterprises.

Suggested Model and Policy Interventions

India's digitization is rising toward the best, and SMEs in India are undergoing a massive digital transformation, right from the adoption of automated tools and technology in the processing stage to the final delivery of products and services. This shift not only provides them with better access to their operations but has also given them a bigger brand establishment and recognition. After a thorough literature review, we can infer that there are three common practices, roles, and functions to increase the agility and flexibility of SMEs in India and make them digitally mature eventually. We have labeled this as the "S-M-E" growth model (Table 4).

Table 4.   S-M-E growth model.

Practices	Roles	Strategies to foster longevity
S: Sustainability	Enhancer	Go digital Remote working/flexibility Awareness and proactive approach Collaboration and commitment
M: Mindset	Crafter	Embrace challenges Cultivate resilience Perseverance and tenacious attitude Practicing gratitude

E: Exposure
   Marketing
	Facilitator	Branding and showcasing
		Facilitates long-term customer relationship and perception
		   through visibility and consistency

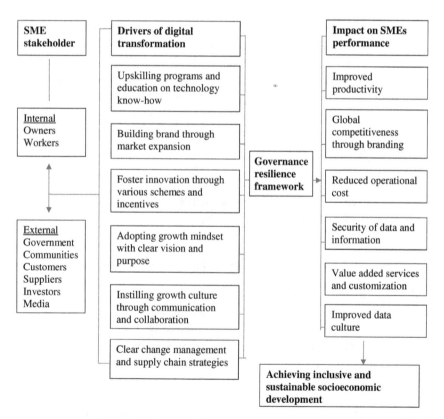

Figure 2.   Suggested SME digitalization framework.

Simply put, by their nature, SMEs are better poised to reap the benefits of digitalization and sustainability. Their success is very well rooted in their capabilities for innovation, flexibility, the utilization of local resources, exclusivity, adaptability, customer relationships, commitment, and, no less importantly, consistency.

Thus, the framework defined by us for an inclusive growth of an economy is presented in Figure 2.

Figure 2 implies that the growing levels of globalization and competitive heterogeneity have made it essential for SME stakeholders to invest in smart and autonomous technologies, together with governments' strong resilience initiatives and interventions, to have a positive impact on SMEs' productivity, competitiveness, data security, culture, small size, market visibility, and customization, and, eventually, achieving the goals of sustainable development.

The suggested framework in Figure 3 highlights the policy actions of the government and other external partners taken together in

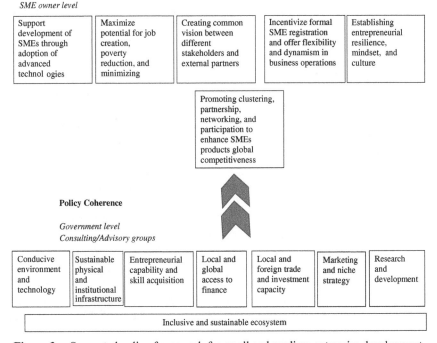

Figure 3. Suggested policy framework for small and medium enterprise development.

creating synergies toward achieving common objectives of sustainability in a digital ecosystem.

India, a country with a population of 1.4 billion in 2022, has around 658 million active Internet users, which shows a deep penetration of digital services both in rural and urban areas. Demonetization in November 2016 and the aftershocks of the COVID-19 pandemic in March 2020 proved to be a turning point in accelerating the digital transformation and technological adaptation in small and medium enterprises by several years, fundamentally changing the SME landscape and enabling SMEs to transform from small manufacturing units to more globally competitive firms. Various government campaigns such as Self-reliant India, Vocal for Local, Local for Global, Make in India, and Start-up India for trade, investment, employment, advanced technology adoption, tax benefits, compliance, etc., provide SMEs with the opportunities to showcase India's local culture and tradition globally.

References

Al-Mataani, R. N. (2017). Examining the entrepreneurial context of Oman: Multi-layered perspective using the institutional lens. Ph.D. Thesis, University of Southampton, Southampton, UK.

Al-Shanfari, D. A. (2012). Entrepreneurship in Oman: A snapshot of the main challenges. In *Proceedings of the United Nations Conference on Trade and Development: Multi-Year Expert Meeting on Enterprise Development Policies and Capacity-Building in Science, Technology and Innovation (STI)*, Geneva, Switzerland, 16–18 January.

Alqassabi, M. A. (2020). Insights on sustainability of small and medium enterprises in Oman: A conceptual framework. *International Journal of Finance & Economics*, 10, 209–218.

Bhalerao, K., Kumar, A., Kumar, A., & Pujari, P. (2022). A study of barriers and benefits of artificial intelligence adoption in small and medium enterprise. *Academy of Marketing Studies Journal*, 26(S1), 1–6.

Bunte, A., Richter, F., & Diovisalvi, R. (2021). Why it is hard to find AI in SMEs: A survey from the practice and how to promote it. In *Proceedings of the 13th International Conference on Agents and Artificial Intelligence (ICAART 2021)* in Heidelberg, Germany. Volume 2, pp. 614–620. SCITEPRESS — Science and Technology Publications, LDA.

Chen, Y.-Y. K., Jaw, Y.-L., & Wu, B.-L. (2016). Effect of digital transformation on organisational performance of SMEs. *Internet Research*, 26(1), 186–212. doi: 10.1108/IntR-12-2013-0265.

Gandhi, R. D. & Patel, D. S. (2018). Virtual reality opportunities and challenges. *International Research Journal of Engineering and Technology*, 5, pp. 482–490.

Greene, F., Mole, K., & Storey, D. J. (2008). *Three Decades of Enterprise Culture? Entrepreneurship, Economic Regeneration and Public Policy.* Houndmills: Palgrave Macmillan.

Hofstede, G., Hofstede, G. J., & Minkov, M. (2005). *Cultures and Organizations: Software of the Mind.* New York: McGraw-Hill.

Johnson, D. V. (2009). Growth mindset as a predictor of smoking cessation. Thesis Submitted in Partial Fulfillment of Requirements for the Degree Doctor of Philosophy in Urban Education at the Cleveland State University.

Kabir, I., Abdullahi, Y. A., & Naqshbandi, M. M. (2022). Measuring entrepreneurial orientation and institutional theory for informal enterprises: Scale validation. *Quality & Quantity*, 57, 1–25. doi:10.1007/s11135-022-01357-1.

Kale, P. T., Banwait, S. S., & Laroiya, S. C. (2010). Performance evaluation of ERP implementation in Indian SMEs. *Journal of Manufacturing Technology Management*, 21(6), 758–780. doi:10.1108/17410381011064030.

Kumar, A. & Ayedee, N. (2021). Technology adoption: A solution for SMEs to overcome problems during COVID-19. *Academy of Marketing Studies Journal*, 25(1), 1–16.

Internet Usage in India — Statistics & facts. https://www.statista.com/topics/2157/internet-usage-in-india/#topicOverview (Accessed on January 22, 2023).

Malhotra, A. (2020). Making the one-sided gig economy really two-sided: Implications for future of work. In S. Nambisan, K. Lyytinen, & Y. Yoo (Eds.), *Handbook of Digital Innovation*. Northampton, MA: Edward Elgar Publishing.

Manhart, K. (2013). Industrie 4.0 could soon be reality. https://computerwelt.at/knowhow/industrie-4-0-konnte-schon-bald-realitat-sein/ (Accessed January 17, 2023).

Maroufkhani, P., Tseng, M. L., Iranmanesh, M., Ismail, W. K. W., & Khalid, H. (2020). Big data analytics adoption: Determinants and performances among small to medium-sized enterprises. *International Journal of Information Management*, 54, article 102190.

MSME Industry in India, https://www.ibef.org/industry/msme (Accessed January 13, 2023).

Nieman, G. (2006). Managing the small business. In G. Nieman (Ed.) *Small Business Management: A South African Approach* (p. 1724). Pretoria: Van Schaik.

OECD. (2019). *OECD SME and Entrepreneurship Outlook 2019*. Paris: OECD Publishing. https://dx.doi.org/10.1787/34907e9c- en.

OECD. (2020). Coronavirus (COVID-19). SME policy responses. https://read. oecd-ilibrary.org/view/?ref=119_119680-di6h3qgi4x&title=Covid-19_ SME_Policy_Responses (Accessed January 22, 2023).

Papadopoulos, T., Baltas, K. N., & Balta, M. E. (2020). The use of digital technologies by small and medium enterprises during COVID-19: Implications for theory and practice. *International Journal of Information Management*, 55, 102192.

Pérez Perales, D., Alarcón, F., & Boza, A. (2018). Industry 4.0: A classification scheme. doi:10.1007/978-3-319-58409-6_38.

Pollard, D. (2006). Promoting learning transfer: Developing SME marketing knowledge in the Dnipropetrovsk Oblast, Ukraine. *South East European Journal of Economics and Business* (1840118X), 1, 97–106.

Prasanna, R. P. I. R., Jayasundara, J. M. S. B., Naradda Gamage, S. K., Ekanayake, E. M. S., Rajapakshe, P. S. K., & Abeyrathne, G. A. K. N. J. (2019). Sustainability of SMEs in the competition: A systemic review on technological challenges and SME performance. *Journal of Open Innovation: Technology, Market and Complexity*, 5, 100.

Pujari, P., Arora, M., Apoorva, B., Jyotsana, S., & Kumar, A. (2022). Scope of industry 4.0 components in manufacturing SMEs. doi:10.1016/B978-0-323-91854-1.00003-0.

Roblek, V., Pejić Bach, M., Meško, M., & Bertoncelj, A. (2013). The impact of social media to value added. *Kybernetes*, 42, 554–568.

Sadagopan, S. (1999). *Enterprise Resource Planning — A Guide to Indian Managers*. New York, NY: Tata McGraw Hill.

Shaikh, A. A., Kumar, A., Syed, A. A., & Shaikh, M. Z. (2021). A two-decade literature review on challenges faced by SMEs in technology adoption. *Academy of Marketing Studies Journal*, 25, 1–13.

Shane, S. (2011). The great recession's effect on entrepreneurship. *Economic Commentary*. https://www.clevelandfed.org/newsroom-and-events/ publications/economic-commentary/economic-commentary-archives/2011-economic-commentaries/ec-201104-the-great-recessions-effect-on-entrepreneurship.aspx (Accessed January 20, 2023).

The ten rules of growth. https://www.mckinsey.com/capabilities/strategy-and-corporate-finance/our-insights/the-ten-rules-of-growth (Accessed January 12, 2023).

Top 5 government schemes for startups and MSMEs in India. https://www.msmex.in/learn/government-schemes-for-startups-and-msmes-in-india/ (Accessed January 12, 2023).

Yarahmadi, F. & Magd, H. A. E. (2016). Entrepreneurship infrastructure and education in Oman. *Procedia — Social and Behavioral Sciences*, 219, 792–797.

Zezulka, F., Marcon, P., Veselý, I., & Sajdl, O. (2016). Industry 4.0 — An introduction in the phenomenon. *IFAC — PapersOnLine*, 49, 8–12. doi:10.1016/j.ifacol.2016.12.002.

Chapter 12

Digital Technologies for Sustaining SME Growth in India

Namrata Pancholi[*,¶], Seema Garg[†,], Madhu Khurana[‡,††], and Vinita Sharma[§,‡‡]**

Amity University, Noida, UP, India

†*University of Gloucestershire, Cheltenham, UK*

¶*namratapancholi@gmail.com*

****Sgarg3@amity.edu*

††*iamkhurana669@amity.edu*

‡‡*vsharma12@amity.edu*

Abstract

SMEs play a very important role in the economic development of a country, contributing to almost 30% of the gross domestic product and 40% of total exports. They offer huge employment opportunities with minimal capital investments. There are several schemes providing financial assistance, skill development, infrastructure development, marketing assistance, and technological upgradation. Like any other sector, SMEs were badly affected by the mobility restrictions during the pandemic. E-commerce and digitization were key to the survival and growth of SMEs during and after the pandemic era.

In the year 2020–2021, more than 60% of the SMEs sold their products through online channels. Technology played a pivotal role in helping SMEs combat competition from large enterprises. There are also challenges for technological upgradation and innovations for SMEs. The positive point for SMEs is that they are inspired and rooted deeply in culture. This helps in generating employment while working in unison with the environment. This chapter aims to discuss how SMEs are deeply rooted in the Indian cultural background, providing business opportunities and employment in the local regions. Being close to nature, they also tend to fulfill the Sustainable Development Goals of the United Nations. Green innovations have played an important role in sustainable innovations in the SME sector. Further, the adoption of new technologies by SMEs has helped them enhance their overall efficiency.

Keywords: SMEs, digital technology, economic development.

Introduction

Small and medium enterprises (SMEs) play a very important role in the economic development of a country. SMEs are deeply rooted in culture and the natural environment. There are various factors which promote and influence small business in India, and culture is one of them. Culture is a set of traditions, beliefs, ways of life, values, and behaviors which are passed from one generation to another. Culture plays a very crucial role in shaping small-scale businesses and entrepreneurial activity in a society but is often ignored. Success in SMEs comes only through an understanding of culture and the related demands of a specific region. Culture guides the establishment of small business activities and aligns them with society. From Jammu & Kashmir to Tamil Nadu and from Punjab to Rajasthan to Nagaland, each has a unique tradition and culture. One can buy woolen shawls on the mall road of Shimla, Phulkari suits from an Amritsar market, silver jewelry from Udaipur; the list is endless. This is all an amalgamation of culture and entrepreneurship, promoting small-scale business activities in the region (MSME Insider, 2021). The adoption of modern technologies by SMEs can accelerate their digitization journey toward improving efficiency, productivity, and skills. Technology is also key to competitiveness in the SME sector.

Credit Rating Information Services of India Limited (CRISIL) conducted a survey in November 2020, which showed 55% of micro enterprises and 45% of small enterprises have adopted digital sales platforms in India. This shows a steep increase in the use of digital technologies in the post pandemic world.

The small, and medium enterprises (SMEs) are divided into two classes under the Micro, Small and Medium Enterprises Development (SMED) Act of 2006: manufacturing enterprises and service enterprises. The Indian SMEs manufacturing industry needs to be digitized to become competitive. The digitization can be done by adopting basic tools to create an online presence and by integrating technology into the business model. Efforts should also be made to reduce cybersecurity attacks, as Indian SMEs are vulnerable to cyberattacks and data leakage. Most of the SME models are inspired by the culture of the region. Along with the inspiration from culture, 5G technology, smart manufacturing, and Industry 4.0 processes will ensure the competitiveness of India's manufacturing sector and secure the vision of "Atmanirbhar Bharat."

SMEs and their Significance in the Economic Development of India

SMEs play a significant role in economies, specifically in emerging economies like India. SMEs contribute to a great extent toward job creation and the overall economic development of a country. Further, SMEs represent 90% of the businesses and more than 50% of the employment across the world. They are estimated to create around 600 million jobs by the end of the year 2030. Therefore, it is imperative for all nations, especially the emerging economies, to promote more SMEs and support them through technological integration and upgrades (World Bank, 2022). SMEs contribute very significantly to India's economic development. In 2022–2023, the SMEs' contribution was 30% of the gross domestic product (GDP), 45% of total industrial production, and 40% of total exports. SMEs contribute to 30.50% of total services and 7.09% of manufacturing (Goyal *et al.*, 2022). With more than 63 million SMEs registered (Figure 1) in the country, providing jobs to over 111 million people, SMEs can be a major contributor to realizing the dream of India becoming a five trillion dollar economy by 2025.

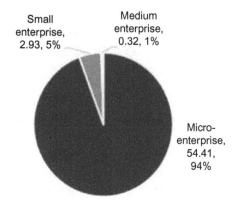

Figure 1.   Registered SMEs in India on March 31, 2022.

Source: Based on www.ibef.org.

SMEs and Indian Culture: A Recipe for Growth, Sustainability, and Self-Reliance

Indian culture acts as a backbone for SME's businesses. SMEs based on local culture and tradition, on the one hand, help in providing employment to the local community and, on the other hand, help preserve the age-old tradition of the region. Every region in India has its own specialty in food, textiles, and crafts, creating a demand for such differentiating products. Examples of such demand are related to annual events, traditions, and festivities. In Delhi, the annual procession of floral fans, *phool wallo ki sair*, from an ancient temple to a Sufi *dargah* is the cultural testimony of the region. It also gives a chance to the manufacturers of unique floral fans to generate economy besides keeping their tradition alive.

Pisi loon, a mix of spices and endemic Himalayan herbs popularly consumed by Uttarakhand locals, resulted in a women-oriented business, thus empowering women financially in the region.

In Chhattisgarh, the Gond tribe of Sarguja district was known for the art of tattoo-making on the body. The same art is now applied to clothing and apparel, resulting in innovative small-scale textile enterprises. Similar is the case with the magical mirrors made of an alloy metal, which is a specialty of Aranmula village in Kerala and is another emerging medium- and small-scale industry of Kerala. The small business has not only created employment opportunities but also utilized indigenous raw materials and sold them in local markets and fairs, creating a sustainable ecosystem.

Thus, the system of producing traditional goods results in self-reliance, *atmanirbharta*, and sustainability. The most important challenge for the Indian government is to make them more visible and promote them in national and international markets. For the above purpose, the government of India has made plans in Budget 2023–2024 to establish a "Unity Mall" in every state for the promotion of "one district, one product," selling GI products from different states all under one roof. Similarly, efforts are needed to promote the products through e-commerce sites to make them available to a larger pool of consumers.

Sustainability and SMEs

The concept of sustainability has recently gained considerable attention on a global scale. Since SMEs are contributing on the basis of social and economic gains, they have adopted strategies which were earlier adopted only by large enterprises. Lean and green manufacturing is one of them. Studies have shown that lean manufacturing is positively correlated with sustainability (Sajan *et al.*, 2017).

The Indian government has taken a number of actions, such as "Make in India" with the "Zero Defect & Zero Effect" initiative, balancing economic growth, sustainability, and social inclusion. It also encourages SMEs to continually improve the quality of their products and processes without harming the environment. To achieve the joint goal of constructing a sustainable nation, all economic sectors — agriculture, manufacturing, and services — must contribute. Enhanced efforts are being made to include the manufacturing sector as a key component of sustainable economic growth.

Two organizations — the Coir Board and the Khadi and Village Industries Commission (KVIC) — lead the path of eco-friendly SMEs. The Coir Board, which was set up under the Coir Industry Act, 1953, by the government of India for the overall sustainable development of the coir industry in India. KVIC is an organization under the Ministry of SMEs that seeks to plan, promote, facilitate, organize, and assist in the establishment and development of Khadi and village industries in the rural regions in coordination with other trusts and agencies engaged in the development of rural areas. Both the organizations, KVIC and the Coir Board, are labor-intensive and nature-friendly. In the wake of industrialization and mechanization, any coir unit or unit under KVIC requires little capital to set up, thereby making them an economically possible option for any individual or aspiring entrepreneurs.

Impact of Information Technology across Micro, Small and Medium Businesses

Although not many, a few SMEs have definitely started using new-age technologies, such as artificial intelligence (AI), for better growth (Soni, 2022). Technology is used by SMEs in the areas of marketing, production, improving productivity, competitiveness building, etc. The Ministry of SME is helping with many schemes, such as the Credit-Linked Capital Subsidy and Technological Upgradation Scheme (CLCS-TUS) for improving competitiveness and the Zero Defect Scheme (ZED) for waste reduction by way of lean manufacturing and design improvement. The ministry is also supporting innovations through incubation centers (Ministry of SMEs, 2023).

Objectives of the Study

(a) To understand the link between Indian culture and SMEs.
(b) To determine the importance of technology adoption by SMEs.
(c) To conduct a detailed review of existing literature for the purpose of understanding Indian culture, the importance of technological integration across SMEs, and sustainability.
(d) To study the latest and most recent developments in SMEs.

Review of Literature

The relationship between SMEs and Indian culture is a topic that has been explored in various literature and research studies. While there isn't a specific comprehensive literature review on this specific topic, several scholarly articles and reports have touched upon the influence of Indian culture on SMEs. Here are a few key points and references to consider.

Impact of Culture on Entrepreneurial Behavior: Indian culture has been found to influence entrepreneurial behavior and decision-making processes in the context of SMEs. Cultural values such as collectivism, hierarchical structures, respect for elders, and risk aversion have been identified as factors shaping the entrepreneurial mindset and business practices (Calja, 2020).

Work Ethics and Traditional Practices: Indian cultural values of discipline, hard work, and dedication have been linked to the work ethics observed within SMEs. Traditional practices such as joint family systems and community support networks have been found to influence the behavior and functioning of SMEs in terms of resource sharing, collaboration, and risk management (Srinivasan, 2002).

Role of Social Networks: Indian culture places high importance on social relationships and networks. Studies have highlighted the role of social networks in the success and growth of SMEs in India. Social ties and trust within networks facilitate access to resources, information sharing, and business opportunities.

Influence of Festivals and Rituals: Indian festivals and rituals have been examined in the context of SMEs, particularly in terms of their impact on marketing strategies and consumer behavior. Festivals serve as occasions for increased consumer spending and have been leveraged by SMEs to promote their products and services (Roemer, 2007).

To gain a more comprehensive understanding of the influence of Indian culture on SMEs, it is recommended to explore academic databases, such as JSTOR, Google Scholar, and Emerald Insight, using keywords like "SMEs," "Indian culture," "entrepreneurship," and "small business" in various combinations. Additionally, you may also consider looking into reports published by government agencies, industry associations, and research organizations focused on SMEs in India.

Role of Government in Promoting SMEs

The state governments, along with the central government, are working to make Indian states self-reliant. The government injected an INR 20 trillion (US$ 0.25 trillion) special economic package for SMEs under the Aatma Nirbhar Bharat scheme. The chief ministers launched self-employment schemes to assist young and aspiring entrepreneurs in the states of Uttarakhand, Rajasthan, Punjab, etc. The scheme offers financial assistance of up to INR 2.5 million to SMEs for manufacturing and INR 1 million for service businesses. Uttarakhand's CHAMPIONS portal stands for the "creation and harmonious use of contemporary procedures to increase output and national strength" (Kumar & Gajakosh, 2021).

The Hornbill Festival in Nagaland is attracting global attention. Along with the Azadi ka Mahotsav celebration, the state and central governments celebrated the 22nd Hornbill Festival in 2021. Nagaland is home to 16 different types of communities, with each type representing a unique culture and skills which can be converted into small business opportunities. Nagas are excellent craftspeople who can make beautiful shawls, unique furniture from bamboos, and other items, which has received attraction at international fairs. The governments' measures and handholding can transform the lives of local communities. With this view, the government has launched "Tech for Tribes," an Entrepreneur cum Skill Development Program (ESDP).

Other initiatives include food microlab development by the natives of Mizoram. This lab is developed for mushroom cultivation and also provides employment opportunities to the youth in the area. The state government, along with the central government, is making all efforts in transforming our agri-food systems into sustainable systems. India has taken measures to provide income support to farmers, improve rural incomes, and address the issues of undernutrition and malnutrition in the country (*Economic Times*, 2021). The recently announced Formalization of Micro Food Processing Enterprises Scheme by the Ministry of Food Processing Industry (MoFPI) aims to provide financial, technical, and business support to upgrade existing micro food processing enterprises.

The Ministry of Textiles has set up 7 PM Mega Integrated Textile Region and Apparel (PM MITRA) parks to position India on the global map. The prime minister's vision of "farm to fiber to factory to fashion to foreign" aims to establish state-of-the-art infrastructure for the attraction of Foreign Direct Investment (FDI) in the sector. This will not only help us achieve the United Nations Sustainable Development Goals (SDG) 9 but also boost local investment in the region India Brand Equity Foundation (IBEF, 2023).

Big companies, such as Aditya Birla Fashion and Reliance (ABFR) and Raymond, are sourcing Khadi fabric from Khadi village industries. Similarly, Bombay Rayon Fashion Textiles Pvt. Ltd. (BRFC) Textiles Private Limited is the first and largest fabric processing industry which is implementing a new sulfur dying process, making it an innovative, sustainable process.

There are many reasons for disposing an apparel. Some are inspired by Indian culture and traditions like marriage, childbirth, divorce, empty nest, etc. (Grigorian, 2018). Disposing of apparel in good condition can add to huge financial and environmental costs (Lisca *et al.*, 2021). SMEs like Doodlage are creating a revolution in the fashion industry by recycling and upcycling fabric to protect the environment and create sustainable products.

Big industries have sufficient funds to upgrade their technology, whereas SMEs have found themselves short of funds, especially after the pandemic period, and are unable to afford technological upgradation. This has made the Indian SME's sector a bit dormant when it comes to the use of the latest technology and knowledge of the global market. As a result, they are losing competition at the global level (Biswas, 2015).

Sustainability Adoption in SMEs

Micro-, small-, and medium-sized organizations contribute significantly to employment regulations that can help these enterprises adopt and upscale their operations without harming the environment in order to assist such SMEs in adopting new and green technologies (Kamble *et al.*, 2020). However, there are challenges to technology adoption by SMEs in this modern day (Dutta *et al.*, 2020). Therefore, sustainability in SMEs is also linked to their ability to innovate (Raghuvanshi & Agrawal, 2020).

A Scheme for Promoting Innovation, Rural Industry & Entrepreneurship (ASPIRE), Credit Linked Capital Subsidy for Technology Upgrading (CLCSS), and Design Clinic are just a few of the programs that the Ministry of SMEs and numerous other organizations and trade bodies offer to help SMEs take advantage of innovation and technology.

Technology Has Helped Enhance the Capabilities of the SME Sector

The number of online shoppers is estimated to increase from 150 million in 2020 to 300 million by 2025 (Malik, 2021). E-commerce can definitely help generate more employment in the SME sector in India. However, there is a steep decline in the percentage when it comes to e-commerce-based SMEs. While Multinational Corporation (MNCs) are able to reap the benefits of the increasing number of online shoppers, only 5% of SMEs have registered their online presence.

If gender-wise data are considered, the contribution of female entrepreneurs in the SME sector is 23.87%, as against 76.12% by their male counterparts. Females contributing to e-commerce in SMEs is only 10.04%, as against 89.96% contribution by male entrepreneurs (Annual Report of the Ministry of SMEs, Government of India, 2023). A low share of female employment is found in all sectors and in most of the states in India.

As highlighted above, the role of technology can be immense within an SME since it can add new dimensions of innovation and overall development. A new digital transformation is realized by the stakeholders (Mishra, 2019) for integration as well as enhanced knowledge about technology, software, equipment, and machinery, a combination of which can lead to long-term survival within the consumer market (Das *et al.*, 2020).

Researchers in the field of technology adoption highlighted how a firm's competitiveness is significantly influenced by technical innovation. A worldwide struggle for market share has been sparked by the interaction of globalization and technological innovation in global marketplaces. (Becheikh *et al.*, 2006). This is driving both larger corporate firms and smaller inventive entrepreneurial initiatives toward profitability and viability through enhanced competitiveness using the latest technology.

Conceptual Framework

The conceptual framework based on dependent and independent variables has been developed on the basis of the existing literature and is depicted in Figure 2.

Author's Work

Enhanced productivity, efficiency, and efficacy of SMEs are the dependent variables, which are based on a number of independent variables. A few of them have been used in the conceptual framework mentioned as follows:

(1) role of government in promoting SMEs;
(2) integrating new technologies;
(3) use of the latest payment methods;

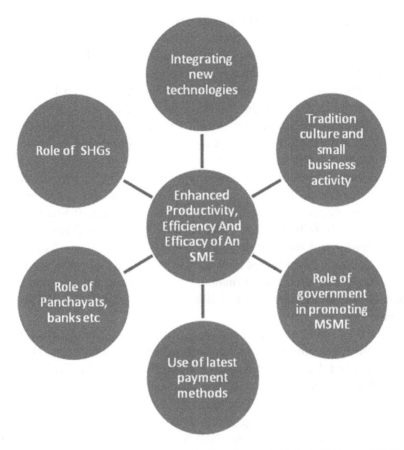

Figure 2.   Framework of dependent and independent variables of efficiency of SMEs.

(4) tradition, culture, and small business activities;
(5) role of panchayats, banks, and other financial institutions;
(6) role of self-help groups (SHGs) in economic activity.

   The above framework can be related to the following activities taken up by the government, panchayats, and corporates.

   The Ministry of Rural Development's National Rural Livelihood Mission (NRLM) has established around 8.2 million SHGs. The mission is to elevate these SHGs into sustainable enterprises by helping 88 million women throughout India. The mission is to connect formal banking services, form higher-level production clusters, enhance their branding, packaging, and marketing capabilities, and integrate them into supply chains with larger manufacturers and corporate entities.

Programs such as the Start-up Village Entrepreneurship Programme (SVEP) were launched under the National Rural Livelihood Mission to support 182,000 village enterprises in 24 villages, providing employment to over 10 million individuals. The program is supported by both the central and state government.

Similarly, the Leelavati Project, supported by the Japan Social Development Fund (JSDF) and managed by the World Bank, aims to enhance the digital and financial literacy of at least 500,000 women members across six Indian states: Gujarat, Rajasthan, Uttar Pradesh, Bihar, Meghalaya, and Assam. Under the Self-Employed Women's Association (SEWA), training is provided to women to showcase their work online. As a result, women have gained financial independence and are conducting basic online transactions using platforms such as Paytm, the BHIM App, Google, and UPI.

SHG-led micro and small enterprises are promoted by panchayats for economic development and income enhancement in rural areas. Here are a few successful examples: Kodariya Gram Panchayat, Madhya Pradesh; Digambarpur Gram Panchayat, West Bengal; Halduchaur Duna Gram Panchayat, Uttarakhand; and Belagavi Zilla Parishad, Karnataka.

There are several inspiring examples of successful SHG-led enterprises across India. A few examples are Nari Shakti Cluster Level Federation in Rudrapur, Balinee Milk Producers Company, and Nalla Panjanpatti Plastic Recycling Centre. SVEP establishes local markets (rural *haats*) to motivate entrepreneurs to take up demand-based production, advertise their enterprise, and increase earning opportunities.

In Jharkhand, under NRLM, a group of community resource persons known as "Tablet Didis" has been established. Their tablets handle all the financial activities of SHGs; additionally, they use their tablets to show short films to families, creating awareness about various livelihood opportunities, animal husbandry, and social issues. The government has introduced various online and IT-enabled platforms such as SME "Sampark," SME "Sambandh," SME "Samadhaan," SME Idea Portal, and Udyamimitra to reach out and support the intended beneficiaries. These platforms offer a range of services, including registration, easy access to financial and non-financial services, skilled worker provision, and assistance with grievances related to delayed payments. Limited access to computers and the Internet, as well as poor Internet connectivity in rural areas, remain significant concerns. Additionally, the majority of rural entrepreneurs lack the necessary skills to fully benefit from these digital services designed for them. Targeted funding, training, and capacity development enable rural entrepreneurs to navigate the digital ecosystem effectively.

Conclusion

In order to develop strategies that support the SMEs' sustained growth, it is necessary to comprehend and evaluate their actual demands. There are roadblocks related to infrastructure, technology, and trained labor which must be removed. Cultural diversity in India is an opportunity for small businesses to grow in their regions. A typical rural *haat* is mostly an indigenous, flexible, and multi-layered structure which accommodates the economic activities of various nature. The *haat* serves as an important economic platform where a range of products are traded. The products are derived from society, and hence sustainability should demonstrate how small businesses can help in providing employment, give economic gains, and build eco-friendly products. This is true sustainability, or real sustainability (Ravinder *et al.*, 2020).

References

Amara, N., Landry, R., Becheikh, N., & Ouimet, M. (2008). Learning and novelty of innovation in established manufacturing SMEs. *Technovation*, 28(7), 450–463.

Bipin, K. & Gajakosh, A. R. (2021). MSMEs issues and prospectus of Uttarakhand: A conceptual investigation with special reference to COVID-19. *Small Enterprises Development, Management & Extension Journal*, 48(3) 299–310.

Calza, F., Cannavale, C., & Nadali, I. Z. (2020). How do cultural values influence entrepreneurial behavior of nations? A behavioral reasoning approach. *International Business Review*, 29(5), 101725, ISSN 0969-5931, https://doi.org/10.1016/j.ibusrev.2020.101725.

CRISIL's Survey. (2022). Smaller enterprises in big digital shift to shore up sales in pandemic times. https://www.crisil.com/en/home/newsroom/press-releases/2020.

Das, S., Kundu, A., & Bhattacharya, A. (2020). Technology adaptation and survival of SMEs: A longitudinal study of developing countries. *Technology Innovation Management Review*, 10(6), 64–72.

Dutta, G., Kumar, R., Sindhwani, R., & Singh, R. K. (2020). Digital transformation priorities of India's discrete manufacturing SMEs — A conceptual study in perspective of industry. *Advances in Economics, Business and Management Research*, 192, 3204. *Complete Review: An International Business Journal*, 30, 289–314. https://doi.org/10.1108/CR-03-2019-0031.

Engidaw, A. E. (2022, January 10). Small businesses and their challenges during COVID-19 pandemic in developing countries: In the case of Ethiopia — Journal of innovation and entrepreneurship. *SpringerOpen.* https://innovation-entrepreneurship.springeropen.com/articles/10.1186/s13731-021-00191-3 (Accessed March 15, 2023).

EVOMA. (2017). SME sector in India Statistics, trends, reports. *EVOMA.* https://www.evoma.com/business-centre/sme (Accessed April 5, 2023).

Fade, L. (2022). Council post: Augmented reality in business: How AR may change the way we work. *Forbes.* https://www.forbes.com/sites/theyec/2019/02/06/augmented-reality-in-business-how-ar-may-change-the-way-we-work/?sh=774e5c7251e5 (Accessed March 26, 2023).

Goyal, T. M., Kukreja, P., & Kedia, M. (2022). By the India Council for Research on International Economic Relations (ICRIER). https://icrier.org/publications.

Grigorian, V. (2018). Symbolic consumption and the extended self during liminality of MBA students. [Master's thesis, University of Pretoria].

Guta, G. S., Sharma, S., & Sharma, U. (2019). *History & Culture of Rajasthan Significant Dimensions.* Jaipur: Centre for Rajasthan Studies, University of Rajasthan.

Ingram, D. (2019). Information technology for business success. *Small Business — Chron.com.* https://smallbusiness.chron.com/information-technology-business-success-4019.html (Accessed February 16, 2023).

Jalo, H., Pirkkalainen, H., Torro, O., Pessot, E., Zangiacomi, A., & Tepljakov, A. (2022). Extended reality technologies in small and medium-sized European industrial companies: Level of awareness, diffusion and enablers of adoption — Virtual reality. https://link.springer.com/article/10.1007/s10055-022-00662-2 (Accessed February 26, 2023).

Kamble, S., Gunasekaran, A., & Dhone, N.C. (2020). Industry 4.0 and lean manufacturing practices for sustainable organizational performance in Indian manufacturing companies. *International Journal of Production Research*, 58, 1319–1337. https://doi.org/10.1080/00207543.2019.16307.

Kumar, B. & Gajakosh, A. R. (2021). MSMEs Issues and Prospectus of Uttarakhand: A Conceptual Investigation with Special Reference to COVID-19. SEDME (*Small Enterprises Development, Management & Extension Journal*), 48(3), 299–310. https://doi.org/10.1177/09708464211073536.

Kumar, R., Singh, R. Kr., & Dwivedi, Y. Kr. (2020). Application of industry 4.0 technologies in SMEs for ethical and sustainable operations: Analysis of challenges. *Journal of Cleaner Production*, 275, 124063. ISSN 0959-6526.

Lisca, A., Feeley, J., Lozano, A. O., Wang, K., Hearn, B., Ropp, C.V.D., & Tung, R. (2021). Circular economy action agenda: Textiles. PACE. https://pacecircular. org/sites/default/files/2021-02/circular-economy-action-agenda-textiles. pdf.

Malik, B. (2021). India's e-commerce sector to clock USD 55 billion sales in 2021. *The New Indian Express*, 1 July. https://www.newindianexpress.com/ business/2021/jul/01.

Melanie. (2017). It challenges for small and medium enterprises. *Unleashed Software*. https://www.unleashedsoftware.com/blog/technological-hurdles-smes (Accessed March 17, 2023).

Ministry of MSME. (2023). MSME. https://msme.gov.in/technology-upgradation-and-quality-certification.

Mishra, P. (2019). Study on impact of digital transformation on MSME growth prospects in India. *International Journal of Research and Analytical Reviews*, 6(1), 611–613. Available at: http://ijrar.com/upload_issue/ijrar_issue_20543216.pdf (Accessed August 31, 2022).

MSME Insider. (2021). https://msme.gov.in/sites/default/files/December2021, vol. XXXIX.

Primasari, D., Magfiroh, S., & Sudjono, S. (2020). Cultivation of accounting-based financial management technology and e-commerce adoption on the development of MSMEs in Banyumas Regency (An Approach to Planned Behavior Theory). *Finance, Accounting and Business Analysis (FABA)*, 2(2), 119–126.

Raghuvanshi, J. & Agrawal, R. (2020). Revitalization of Indian SMEs for sustainable development through innovation. *Business Strategy & Development*, 3(4), 461–473.

Roemer, M. K. (2007). Ritual participation and social support in a major Japanese festival. *Journal for the Scientific Study of Religion*, 46(2), 185–200. http://www.jstor.org/stable/4621968.

Sajan, M.P., Shalij P. R., Ramesh, A., & Biju Augustine, P. (2017). Lean manufacturing practices in Indian manufacturing SMEs and their effect on sustainability performance. *Journal of Manufacturing Technology Management*, 28(6), 772–793. https://doi.org/10.1108/JMTM-12-2016-0188.

Singh, G., Maurya, A., & Goel, R. (2022). *Integrating New Technologies in International Business Opportunities and Challenges*. CRC Press, Taylor & Francis Group. https://www.crisil.com/en/home/newsroom/press-releases/ 2020/12/smaller-enterprises-in-big-digital-shift-to-shore-up-sales-in-pandemic-times.html.

Soni, S. (2022). How artificial intelligence is helping MSMEs to optimize processes, accelerate growth. *Financial Express*, 15 May. https://www. financialexpress.com/industry/sme/msme-tech-national-technology-day-how-artificial-intelligence-is-helping-mgrowth (Accessed March 31, 2022).

Srinivasan, V. (2009, December). CSR and ethics in MSMEs in India. *African Journal of Business Ethics*, 4(2), 32–36.

Sudjono, S. (2020). Cultivation of accounting-based financial management technology and e-commerce adoption on the development of MSMEs in Banyumas Regency (an approach to planned behavior theory). Academia. edu. (Accessed March 19, 2023).

Team MSMEx. (2021). Benefits & use of information technology in small businesses. How does information technology help small businesses? Explore benefits and multiple ways to use technology. https://www.msmex.in/learn/information-technology-in-small businesses (Accessed March 21, 2023).

World Bank. (2022). *World Bank SME Finance: Development.* World Bank https://www.worldbank.org/en/topic/smefinance (Accessed March 5, 2023).

Chapter 13

Catalyzing SME Growth in India

Rachetty Hariprasad* and D. Ashok†

VITBS, Vellore Institute of Technology, Vellore, India

*rachetty.hariprasad2020@vitstudent.ac.in

†dashok@vit.ac.in

Abstract

Small and medium enterprises (SMEs) are playing a vital role in the Indian economy. SMEs contribute significantly to the nation by providing employment, generating foreign exchange, contributing to the economy, and providing goods & services to the people at affordable costs. SMEs are very crucial to removing regional disparities in many areas. To promote and uplift SMEs, the government is providing support and encouraging citizens to set up their own companies through governmental-level schemes. Startup India and Make in India are some of the schemes launched to encourage students and citizens of India who have business ideas. SMEs act as catalysts for enhancing growth. They provide many benefits to the people and also to the nation. Hence, the authors formulated the following problem statement: How do SMEs foster growth and help our country become a developed one?

To answer this, the authors have set the following objectives as part of this study's scope: (1) to identify the opportunities and challenges for SMEs in the existing scenario; (2) to assess the level of governmental support to minimize the observed challenges to the growth of SMEs.

Keywords: Economy, development, employment, technology, finance & marketing.

Introduction

Small and medium enterprises (SMEs) in India are growing rapidly. Due to the policies framed by the government of India, this growth is one of the fastest among developing nations in the world. With changes in foreign direct investment (FDI) policy, it is observed that many nations have started investing and promoting industrial growth in India, which has resulted in the growth of SMEs. The government of India is also very keen on promoting SMEs by giving support and also strengthening them by providing required benefits and removing barriers to registering them. The Indian government is very keen on promoting young entrepreneurs by extending its full support through providing loans, technical support, and others that are required for setting up their enterprises. SMEs help in developing new products and services by adopting new technologies, which help in increasing production.

SMEs are small enterprises whose investment in plant and machinery or equipment does not exceed INR 10 crore and turnover does not exceed INR 50 crore. A medium enterprise is one whose investment in plant and machinery or equipment does not exceed INR 50 crore and turnover does not exceed INR 250 crore.[1]

SMEs are considered the backbone of India after agriculture because they make a significant contribution to the economy and they provide bulk employment opportunities to people who reside in the nearby areas. As per the data revealed by the government of India, SMEs employ

[1]*Source*: msme.gov.in.

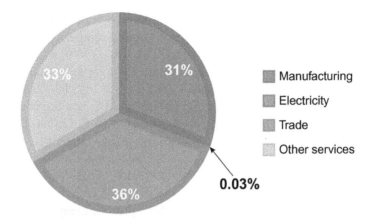

Figure 1. Estimated MSME distribution by sector.
Source: Ministry of Micro, Small and Medium Enterprises — Annual Report.

9,394,957 people and nearly 14,631,485 Micro, Small and Medium Enterprises (MSME) units are registered in India.[2]

Figure 1 illustrates the type of industries in which the SMEs in India have their presence. Manufacturing, electricity, trade, and service-oriented sectors are those sectors where they play a vital role. Many small- and medium-scale industries are part of these SMEs. The governments of states and at the center are giving top priority to these SMEs by supporting them through the provision of credit facilities, marketing, export promotion, technology upgradation, infrastructural development, and other related support that is required by them.

Review of Literature

Akter *et al.* (2020) report that SMEs help in the development of the nation by providing employment and thus maintaining regional growth (Revell *et al.*, 2010). SMEs are not receiving sufficient attention to maintain sustainability (Kumar *et al.*, 2014), despite contributing significantly to the economy of the nation, employing many, and helping in maintaining regional development (Kumar *et al.*, 2014).

---

[2]*Source*: Udyam Registration portal.

Indian SMEs in the manufacturing sectors are facing challenges of competitive product prices and quality to stay competitive in global markets.

SMEs in India are struggling in the manufacturing areas due to a lack of quality and technology (Thanki & Thakkar, 2014). They can attain sustainability if they implement it in their region of operation, which provides many benefits such as enhanced quality of products and services, good relationships with the community, and greater employee commitment (O'Laire & Welford, 1996).

Many local businesses are not aware of why, where, when, and how to implement sustainable practices in the development of their business strategy (Goldsmith & Samson, 2006). SMEs provide many opportunities in adopting regulations that are concerned with environmental responsibilities and manufacturing standards, which lead to producing low waste (Thanki *et al.*, 2016).

According to Naser (2013), SMEs play a major role in providing employment, contributing to Gross Domestic Product (GDP), and also playing an important role in the country's exports. Nearly 20% of the MSMEs are established in rural areas, and they are providing employment opportunities to about 40% of the workforce in India. MSMEs are playing a significant role by generating more job opportunities at fewer capital costs, as well as promoting industrialization in rural and remote areas, thus minimizing regional inequalities and income disparities among the poor people (MSME, 2019).

MSMEs are significantly contributing to the development of entrepreneurial efforts through business advancements (Drishti, 2020). More than 6,000 products, including traditional and high-tech goods, are produced by Indian MSMEs (Reserve Bank of India, 2019).

The main role of the MSME ministry is to extend its support to states in strengthening employment, entrepreneurship, and livelihood opportunities, which improves the economic conditions of the country (Srinivas, 2013).

In SMEs, management decisions play a major role in the adoption of sustainability. In a few cases, the managers/owners take responsibility for the environment and society because the environment impacts their businesses (Yu & Bell, 2007).

How Do SMEs Foster Growth?

There may arise a question of how SMEs help in fostering growth. SMEs are very easy to establish since they don't need much investment and infrastructure. They don't require many permissions and clearances from the government to start their operations. Moreover, SMEs operate in areas where raw materials are available.

SMEs help in accelerating the growth of the country by providing many advantages, which leads to providing facilities to the people as well as helping in removing the inequalities among them. Small businesses are performing exceptionally well; they are acting as the backbone of our economy after agriculture. SMEs are providing huge employment opportunities, earning substantial foreign exchange through exports, and becoming globally recognized by offering their products in different countries. SMEs are fostering growth in India and also help in developing the areas where they are established; therefore, governments are encouraging small businesses to grow and excel:

1. **Removing regional barriers:** Most of the small businesses are started in rural and underdeveloped areas, due to which the areas are developing. The functioning of SMEs enables many other companies to start next to them. In this way, they are removing regional barriers and helping in developing the areas where they are operating.
2. **Improving standard of living:** SMEs employ many people, most of whom are illiterate or do not have a good education. The wages that are provided for the workers in these companies help them meet their basic needs and also save money for the future, which enables people to raise their standard of living. This is true not only for those who are working in SMEs but also for the people who indirectly benefit from these SMEs.
3. **Reducing income disparities:** SMEs help in reducing income inequalities among workers, as they pay fair wages to all without any discrimination.
4. **Development in rural areas:** Governments are not able to develop all areas. So, whenever SMEs are established in rural areas, it helps in providing the basic infrastructure that is required in those areas. Most SMEs provide facilities such as roads, schools, drinking water, and other essential infrastructure under corporate social responsibility.

5. **Generating revenue to local authorities:** Local authorities/bodies, such as panchayats, collect taxes from these small businesses which are operating in their areas. These SMEs are generating revenue for local authorities, which helps them implement some developmental activities in these areas.

Opportunities for SMEs in India

There are plenty of opportunities available in India because of the vast geographical area, availability of manpower, availability of resources, etc., which are some of the factors that favor entrepreneurs to start their businesses in India. Some of the opportunities that are available in India are discussed as follows:

1. **Availability of manpower:** In India, human resources are easily available, and most of the educated youth are readily available for employment. So, companies can hire them and utilize their services at low costs, as they are ready to work with less remuneration.
2. **Availability of resources:** India is known for its abundant availability of resources, increasing the chances of starting new companies. Based on the availability, entrepreneurs can start their enterprises within that area. This helps reduce transportation and other allied investments.
3. **Government support:** The Indian government is supporting small businesses by providing training, finance, marketing, and technical expertise and also encouraging them to export their goods & services to other nations.
4. **Availability of technology:** Technology is one of the key factors for any business to become successful. In India, technology is easily accessible and can be acquired at cheaper costs. The usage of technology helps in reducing physical efforts by replacing manual labor, which increases productivity and also helps in reducing production costs.
5. **Export promotion:** The government of India has changed its foreign trade policy according to world trade requirements so that it can enable local businesses to export their goods and services to other nations. Many steps are being taken by the government to spread awareness among the businesses by giving certain incentives, lowering export taxes, and providing trade benefits to the SMEs, which in return brings huge foreign exchange and helps in maintaining the balance of trade.

Challenges for SMEs in India

The government of India is encouraging small enterprises; however, there are still many challenges that are acting as barriers to the growth of SMEs in India. Some of them are listed as follows:

1. **Changes in laws:** The government has introduced frequent changes in the laws and rules related to business while constantly increasing taxation. SMEs need to update their businesses according to these changes; otherwise, they face severe consequences imposed by the state and central governments, which may include paying fines and penalties and even the cancelation of permissions or licenses that are required for running businesses. It is one of the toughest challenges for SMEs to adopt those changes for their survival.

2. **External factors:** These factors include the change in Foreign Exchange (FOREX) values, global markets, laws and rules in foreign countries, etc., which play an important role in the functioning of SMEs.

3. **Socio-cultural factors:** Social and cultural factors constantly change from region to region, and it is the responsibility of SMEs to respect them and act accordingly. Otherwise, they might face opposition from the people. This may result in the closure of business or the failure of acceptance of that company's products, which affects the business operations of SMEs in the long run.

4. **High operational costs:** This is one of the main challenges faced by SMEs in India. Most SMEs are unable to procure raw materials that are required for manufacturing goods and services, as their prices are continually increasing due to the volatility of global markets and also changes in foreign trade policies. It is very difficult for SMEs to run their businesses with high operational costs.

5. **Cost of installation:** The latest technology needs to be installed by professionals, and most of the updated technologies have to be procured from foreign nations. To install these machines and technologies, SMEs need to spend a significant amount of money, which involves major investments and time-consuming processes. It may not be possible for most of the SMEs.

6. **Lack of skilled labor:** Most of the SMEs in India are facing this problem due to the availability of skilled labor being very minimal;

moreover, skilled labourers demand to be hired for high salaries, which is becoming one of the biggest challenges for SMEs. Even though the availability of manpower is high in India, SMEs need to train them according to their needs, which is much costlier when compared to hiring skilled workers.

7. **Increased production costs and reduced revenue:** Some SMEs are not in a position to continue their businesses due to increased production costs resulting from constant increases in infrastructural and electrical charges. Due to this reason, they are forced to keep their profits very minimal; otherwise, they have to face difficulties in the markets. Consequently, many SMEs are cutting down on their revenues to stay competitive.

8. **R&D-related problems:** Technology keeps on changing, and world markets are updating with new products on a regular basis, and it is the responsibility of businesses to keep up with the latest technologies and to procure the latest machinery. SMEs need to invest more money in R&D to procure updated technologies, which is quite difficult for most of them.

9. **Technology-related issues:** SMEs are mostly located in rural and underdeveloped areas where they are not in a position to acquire new technologies. They can run their businesses only with outdated technologies and are therefore not able to compete with global players. This is one of the foremost problems faced by many rural SMEs in India.

10. **Competition:** Due to the availability of technology, the availability of goods & services at cheaper rates, and more global players competing with local SMEs, major challenges are faced by SMEs. Competing with big businesses requires significant capital as well as the need to diversify their products as per the needs of their customers, which is not possible for SMEs. To run their business, they need to upgrade their technologies and goods & services to meet global standards, which is very difficult for SMEs.

11. **Procurement of funds:** SMEs are not in a position to procure funds that are required for their day-to-day needs. Most of the financial institutions are not ready to sanction loans to these SMEs, as they are not consistent in showing results, and these businesses involve a lot of risks.

12. **New customers:** Indian SMEs are not able to find new customers; there are many opportunities available in and around the world. Most

SMEs are not inclined toward the export option, as it involves many laws to be followed, so they fail to become recognized globally.

13. **Expansions:** In India, some SMEs are performing exceptionally well, but the main problem is that they are not in a position to expand their business since they are not aware of the possible opportunities that are available in and around the world. Most businesses are not able to diversify their businesses due to the high initial costs and risks involved in them.

Apart from these, many more challenges remain in India, which include social and political issues such as changes in government policies and laws. Social and societal sentiments and practices also remain a big challenge for SMEs in India.

Government Support toward SMEs

SMEs are facing many problems due to external forces, including the Ukraine war, the global economy, and changes in policies. It is the responsibility of the government to take care of these SMEs; otherwise, many employees and those who are dependent on these SMEs will suffer greatly. The government of India is giving more priority to SMEs by introducing special schemes to uplift them. To support SMEs, the government of India came up with many schemes:

1. **Emergency Credit Line Guarantee Scheme (ECLGS):** The government of India started this scheme in 2020 to support small businesses which are facing severe credit problems in running their businesses. Under this scheme, 1.2 crore businesses have applied for credit from banks, out of which 95% are MSMEs. Due to an increase in the growth of credit for MSMEs during the pandemic, this scheme was extended up to March 2023.

   Figure 2 shows the growth rate of credit to MSMEs, particularly during COVID-19.

2. **Credit Guarantee Trust for Micro and Small Enterprises (CGTMSE):** This is one more credit facility provided by the government to support SMEs, under which INR 2 lakh crore additional credit has been provided for micro and small enterprises.[3]

---

[3] *Source*: Economic Survey 2022–2023.

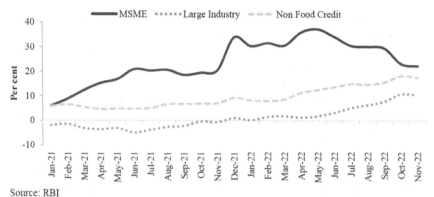

Source: RBI

Figure 2.   Double-digit credit growth in industry driven by MSMEs.

Source: https://www.indiabudget.gov.in/economicsurvey/.

3. To support SMEs, particularly during COVID-19, the **Aatma Nirbhar Bharat Package** was announced by the government to support SMEs that are severely affected by this pandemic. An amount of INR 50,000 crore was allocated through the Self-Reliant India fund.[4]

4. **Entrepreneurship and Skill Development Program (ESDP) scheme:** This scheme aims to promote and inculcate an entrepreneurial culture. The main objective of this scheme is to encourage new enterprises and also to enable and provide capacity-building for existing MSMEs. This scheme aims to expand entrepreneurship to different sections of society by providing skill development, motivation, and self-employment opportunities.[5]

5. **A Scheme for Promoting Innovation, Rural Industry, and Entrepreneurship (ASPIRE):** This scheme aims at setting up a network of incubation and technology centers to promote innovation and entrepreneurship to strengthen MSMEs in rural and underdeveloped areas. Under this scheme, the central government plans to provide an amount of INR 1 crore to government-run agencies and up to INR 75 lakhs to private institutions to promote incubators as well as support young entrepreneurs in rural areas.[6]

---

[4] *Ibid.*

[5] *Source*: investindia.gov.in/schemes-MSMEs.

[6] *Ibid.*

6. **Procurement and Marketing Support (PMS) scheme:** The intention behind this scheme is to provide marketing support to SMEs. This scheme helps SMEs get access to new markets and participate in national and international trade fairs, exhibitions, MSME expos, etc. It can also create awareness about developing the marketability of services and products in the MSME sector. Apart from this, it helps in providing awareness on marketing, the GeM portal, GST, and other related topics to upcoming entrepreneurs.[7]

SMEs can make use of the schemes that are launched by the government to facilitate technological, financial, infrastructural, and marketing-related support for them so that they can overcome the difficulties they are facing in operating their businesses.

Conclusion

SMEs are very much required for any developing nation, and it is the responsibility of the central and state governments to take the necessary steps to promote and support SMEs in their performance. Even though the government is providing all the possible support, this is not reaching all businesses because of the huge number of SME units present and operating all over the country.

References

Drishti. (2020). Role of MSMEs in Indian economy. https://www.drishtiias.com/daily-updates/daily-news-editorials/role-of-MSMEs-in-Indian-economy.

Goldsmith, S. & Samson, D. (2006). *Sustainable Development and Business Success*. Thomson.

Naser, A. (2013). A critical evaluation of the contributions made by the micro, small and medium enterprises in Indian economy. *International Journal of Marketing, Financial Services and Management Research*, 2(7), 151–158.

Reserve Bank of India (2019). Annual Report. Retrieved from: rbidocs.rbi.org.in/rdocs/.

Revell, A., Stokes, D., & Chen, H. (2010). Small businesses and the environment: Turning over a new leaf? *Business Strategy and the Environment*, 19(5), 273–288.

---

[7] *Ibid.*

Srinivas, K. T. (2013). Role of micro, small and medium enterprises in inclusive growth. *International Journal of Engineering and Management Research*, 3, 57–61. https://www.ijemr.net/DOC/RoleOfMicroSmallAndMediumEnterprises InInclusive Growth(57-61)e1655c8a-14e1-40ae-9924-124143f8f0fb.pdf.

Thanki, S., Govindan, K., & Thakkar, J. (2016). An investigation on lean-green implementation practices in Indian SMEs using analytical hierarchy process (AHP) approach. *Journal of Cleaner Production*, 135, 284–298.

Thanki, S. J. & Thakkar, J. (2014). Status of lean manufacturing practices in Indian industries and government initiatives: A pilot study. *Journal of Manufacturing Technology Management*, 25(5), 655–675.

Yu, J. & Bell, J. N. B. (2007). Building a sustainable business in China's small and medium-sized enterprises (SMEs). *Journal of Environmental Assessment Policy and Management*, 9(1), 19–43.

Websites

https://www.ibef.org/industry/msme-presentation.
https://my.msme.gov.in/MyMsme/Reg/Home.aspx.
https://www.indiabudget.gov.in/economicsurvey/.

Part VI

Historical Approach

Chapter 14

Corporate Organization in Ancient India — The Shreni System

Alka Maurya[*,‡], Veenus Jain[†,§], and Pallavi Mohanan[*,¶]

[*]*Amity University, Noida, UP, India*

[†]*Amity University, Mumbai, Mahasrashtra*

[‡]*amaurya@amity.edu*

[§]*Veenus.jain2607@gmail.com*

[¶]*Pallavimohanan2904@gmail.com*

Abstract

This chapter explores the structure and functioning of the *Shreni* system in ancient India. *Shreni* was an association of traders, merchants, and artisans, and generally, a separate *Shreni* existed for a particular group of persons engaged in the same vocation or activity. The guilds regulated manufacturing standards, trade, ethical codes, prices, and the quality of crafts. The chapter discusses the well-documented references to the existence of *Shreni* from the 5th century BC and how some *Shreni* became very wealthy with surplus resources, acting as custodians and bankers of religious and other endowments. The chapter also explores how each economic activity and craft had its own specific traditions and trade secrets, and how *Shreni* played a crucial role in regulating these activities. The study concludes that the *Shreni* system was an essential part of ancient Indian society and played a significant role in regulating the economy and society.

Keywords: *Shreni* system, ancient India, economy, ancient Indian society, business.

Introduction

The powers of a democratic government, a trade union, a court of justice, and a technological organization were all united in the ancient Indian guilds, which represent a distinctive and multifaceted type of organization. A pleasant work environment was supplied by the skilled guild employees. They found markets for the sale of manufactured items, managed the quality and pricing of the goods produced, and procured raw materials for manufacturing. They have been misunderstood owing to being observed with a Eurocentric lens. Due to a dramatic expansion in trade, it was considered that the Indian guild system also adopted the European feudal or manorial system of the High Middle Ages.

Although its prime was likely in the 13th and 14th centuries, these European organizations, known as "Merchant Organizations" and "Craft Guilds," persisted in some locations until the 19th and 20th centuries. The craft guilds held greater significance than the merchant guilds since they were the primary producers. However, compared to their European counterparts, Indian guilds were much more significant and sophisticated organizations. There has been some discussion regarding the authenticity and age of ancient Indian guilds.

"The ancient sources frequently refer to the system of guilds which began in the early Buddhist period and continued through the Mauryan period," says Romila Thapar. … Insofar as some districts of a city were typically occupied by all artisans of a particular profession, topography aided their development. Tradesmen's villages, where one specific craft was based and where raw materials were readily available, were also well known. The three main conditions required for the development of a guild system were present. First, it was feasible to localize one's occupation; second, it was acknowledged that some professions were inherited; and third, the concept of a guild master, or *jetthaka*, was widely accepted.

The development and stabilization of the guilds, which first served as a transitional group between a tribe and a caste, must have benefited greatly from the expansion of trade throughout the Mauryan period. They were later subjected to stringent laws, which led to some of them eventually becoming castes. Early guild formation must have been influenced by competition. Economically, it was preferable to work in a group than to work alone because doing so would give your company greater social status, and you could ask other members for help if you needed it. Guilds evolved into the most significant industrial organizations in their regions over time.

According to Thapar, the distribution of work was planned not only according to the professions that resided in the town but also according to the physical occupation of various professions in various regions of the town. Each *Shreni* had its own set of professional standards, workplace policies, responsibilities, and even religious observances. *Shreni*s would occasionally settle disputes over larger issues among themselves. Since there would be more economic opportunities for improving actual status, especially during periods of expanding trade, social mobility among such groups — where an entire group would seek to change its ritual status based on an improvement in actual status — would be more common. It is hardly a coincidence that periods of burgeoning trade were those during which heterodox sects and religious groups linked to social unrest engaged in their heaviest activity.

According to Ghosal, Narada forbids intergroup conflict as well as the wearing of illegal weapons and combined forces. For anyone who harms the public interest or disparages individuals who are versed in the Vedas, Brihaspati prescribes the severe punishment of exile. One who commits a horrible crime, causes a division in the community, or destroys their property is to be declared before the king and "destroyed," according to Katyayana. Brihaspati informs us, however, that all members share equally all assets obtained by the committee of advisers or rescued by them, all wealth received through the king's favor, and all obligations committed by members on behalf of the group. A specific sort of clay seal that was discovered during the excavations of Gupta sites at Basarh (the ancient Vaisali) and Bhita (near Allahabad) lends support to the evidence of the late Smriti legislation of guilds. These seals are inscribed with the legends *Shreni-kulikanigama* and *Shreni-sarthavaha-kulika-nigama* (Basarh), as well as *nigama* in Gupta letters (Bhita). These names are frequently combined with those of unidentified people. We have a possible allusion to agreements or agreements established between local industry and commerce groupings and private citizens or individual members. In the technical sense of the late Smritis, these records would be referred to as *sthitipatras* or *samvitpatras*.

In 2001, Thaplyal published a very thorough and critical study of the guilds (*Shreni*s) in ancient India. Thaplyal demonstrates how important a role the craft guilds played in the socioeconomic framework of ancient India's society as well as how prevalent merchant guilds were. His database consists of literary evidence from the Bible, other sources, and archeological discoveries. He covers the establishment of the guilds in four historical eras: the Vedic, Buddhist/Jain, Mauryan, and Post-Mauryan periods. In addition to discussing many aspects of the regulations, apprenticeship, organization, offices, and functions of these guilds, Thaplyal paints a brief historical overview. He also demonstrates how the guilds and the state are related. The oil millers' guild, the weavers' guild, the potters' guild, and the hydraulic engineers' guild are all mentioned.

According to Thaplyal, when Buddhism and Jainism first appeared in the 6th century BC, they were more egalitarian than the Brahmanism that came before them and offered a better setting for the development of guilds. In the Brahmanical yajnas, material possessions and animals were sacrificed. These yajnas were not performed by Buddhists or Jains. Animals and material wealth were therefore preserved and made accessible for trade and commerce. Buddhists and Jains felt less restricted in engaging in long-distance trade because they disregarded the social taboos of purity/pollution in mixing and eating with people of lesser *varnas*. In accordance with the Gautama Dharmasutra, which dates to the early 5th century BC, "cultivators, traders, herdsmen, moneylenders, and artisans have authority to lay down rules for their respective classes, and the king was to consult their representatives while dealing with matters relating to them." The Jataka stories mention 18 guilds, their leaders, the localization of business, and the inherited nature of vocations. The Jataka legends commonly mention a son continuing his father's trade. The suffixes "*kula*" and "*putta*" are frequently seen after craft names; the former denotes that the entire family accepted a specific craft, while the latter denotes that the son adopted his father's craft. This increased specialization and ensured consistent access to trained labor. The distinction between Indian guilds and European guilds of the Middle Ages, where membership was almost always determined by an individual's choice, is made here. The profession in Indian guilds is inherited. However, it should be noted that members of craftsmen's guilds were more likely to take a family profession than members of traders' guilds.

According to Thaplyal, there is disagreement among academics on whether the guild system existed in early Vedic times, before the Buddhist and Jain periods, in India. Some believe that Vedic society was sufficiently developed to justify the formation of these types of economic institutions, and they interpret phrases such as *"Shreni," "puga," "gana,"* and *"vrata"* in Vedic literature as referring to the structure of guilds, with *"sreshthi"* as the head of a guild. Others argue that early Vedic civilization was rural, with nomadism still being popular, and that the Aryans could not produce enough excess food grains, which were essential for allowing craftsmen to spend their entire time on practicing their skills since they were so obsessed with fighting wars. They contend that neither the names "guild" nor *"sreshthi,"* the "guild president," in Vedic literature suggest a guild. However, according to Thaplyal, the establishment of guild organizations may have been helped by the Varna system's division of employment. The three Vaisya occupations — agriculture, animal husbandry, and trade — evolved over time into distinct social groups. There are various pieces of evidence for the existence of guilds during that time period of the Upanishads (c. 6th century BC).

The detailed examination of guilds by Kautilya, who takes into account the possibility of guilds as organizations capable of becoming centers of power, highlights the Mauryan period. Thaplyal notes that better-maintained roads and greater mobility of people and goods were common under the Mauryan Empire (c. 320–c. 200 BC). The state took part in industrial and agricultural output. Indicating state involvement in guild matters, the government kept records on trades, crafts, and related transactions as well as guild conventions. The state assigned guilds specific locations in a town where they might conduct their business. Due to their inclusion in the vast Mauryan Empire, the citizens of the tribal republics who had lost their political clout turned to crafts and trades and established commercial organizations.

Thaplyal views the time between 200 BC and 300 AD as the peak of the guild system in ancient India. Guilds had a better chance to develop as a result of the political fragmentation and inadequate governmental authority brought on by the collapse of the Mauryan Empire (c. 200 BC). The epigraphs from the western Deccan sites, Sanchi, Bharhut, Bodhgaya, Mathura, and others, refer to gifts given by various artisans and merchants. The epigraphs make mention of guilds for maize traders, oil millers, potters, weavers, producers of hydraulic machines, etc. During this time, there was a closer commercial relationship between India and the Roman Empire, which brought in enormous riches for Indian traders.

In comparison to prior periods, the *Manusmriti* and the *Yajnavalkyasmriti* evidence reveal an increase in the authority of guilds. Epigraphic records from the time period mention the guilds' charitable and religious deeds as well as their bank-like activities.

Laws of *Shreni*s in Ancient India

Thaplyal uses many quotations from literature and scriptures to demonstrate the importance of guilds in ancient times, which must have included significant political influence as well. According to Thaplyal, guilds had their own regulations covering organization, manufacturing, fixing the prices of commodities, etc., which were based on usage and customs. The state largely acknowledged these laws. The laws served as a deterrent to government repression and meddling in guild matters. The *Gautama Dharmasutra* commands the king to consult representatives of the guilds before making decisions involving the guilds. A superintendent of accounts was tasked with documenting the practices and business dealings of organizations under Kautilya's plan. Manu commands the monarch to expel a guild member from the realm if they violate a contract. Profits and losses were to be divided among members in accordance with their shares, according to Yajnavalkya. There was no atonement for breaking guild laws, according to the *Mahabharata*. If someone steals from the guild, Yajnavalkya imposes harsh punishment. He claimed that the penalty for not depositing money acquired for the firm into the joint fund was 11 times the original amount. The guild rules aided in facilitating the smooth operation of the guilds and strengthening the bonds of solidarity among members.

Structure of *Shreni*s in Ancient India

According to Thaplyal, the guilds were made up of three parts: the general assembly, the guild chairman or head, and the executive officers, each with a clearly defined area of responsibility.

General assembly: The general assembly was made up of every guild member. Round numbers of 100, 500, and 1,000 are used in Jataka stories to represent members of various guilds. There is mention of 1,000 Varanasi carpenters working under two heads. Although it may be noted that there are a few references to 1,000 members of a guild without division, it is possible that this is because the number was deemed to be too big to make the guild manageable. Two weavers' guilds at Govardhana (Nasik) are mentioned in the Nahapana-era Nasik Inscription. Large guild disputes are frequently discussed, and it is likely that a location had multiple guilds practicing the same trade.

Guild head: In early Buddhist literature, the guild master is frequently referred to as the *jetthaka* or *pamukkha*. He is frequently referred to as the "head of the carpenters' guild" (*vaddhaki jetthaka*), "head of the garland makers' guild," etc., depending on his former profession. It appears that the guild head had a lot of control over the guild's members. *Setthis* frequently served as the head of merchant guilds and were also bankers. A guilty member could receive excommunication as punishment from the guild leader. Although there are positive references to both election and hereditary guild leadership, ancient texts do not appear to make a clear distinction between the two. It appears that the eldest son held the position of guild leader in the norm. The fact that succession is only discussed after the head's death and not while he is still alive suggests that the head held the position for his whole life. Two Damodarpur copper-plate inscriptions from the 5th century AD provide proof that one Bhupala held the position of *nagarasreshthi* for about 50 years.

Executive officers: Executive officers were chosen to support the guild leader and handle the day-to-day operations of the guild. The *Yajnavalkyasmriti* has the earliest mention of executive officers. Depending on the situation and requirements, their numbers changed. According to Yajnavalkya, they should be pure, avarice-free, and knowledgeable of the Vedas. The executive officers' election by the assembly or nomination by the guild leader is not particularly specified.

Functions of *Shreni*s in Ancient India

The guilds performed numerous helpful activities, such as administrative, economic, philanthropic, and banking duties, in addition to serving the objective of keeping the people of a trade together as a close community. According to Thaplyal, the strong guilds also served as courts of law. The administrative power over their members was largely in the hands of the guilds. Their top priority was to look out for the interests of their members and make things convenient for them. A pleasant work environment was provided by the skilled guild employees. They found markets for the sale of manufactured items, managed the quality and pricing of the goods produced, and procured raw materials for manufacturing. Even though there is no mention of guilds lending money to the common people in the *Arthasastra*, there are passages that imply the king's spies borrowed money from guilds under the pretense of buying various goods. This demonstrates that guilds also provided loans to merchants and craftspeople. The efficiency and integrity of guilds were established, and epigraphic evidence demonstrates that not only the ordinary population but also royalty deposited money with them. In contrast to contemporary banks, the guilds' ability to conduct banking was somewhat restricted. Here, Thaplyal alludes to a couple of epigraphs. The two permanent donations of 550 silver coins each with two guilds to feed Brahmins and the needy out of the interest money are mentioned in a Mathura inscription from the 2nd century AD. One of the two Nasik inscriptions from the second century AD mentions the endowment of 2,000 karshapanas at a rate of 1% (per month) with a weavers' guild for providing cloth to *bhikshus* and 1,000 karshapanas at a rate of 0.75% (per month) with another weavers' guild for providing them with light meals. Additional epigraphs and inscriptions are provided as supporting evidence. Furthermore, the guilds participated in charitable activities. Guilds performed acts of piety and charity out of a sense of obligation and worked to ease suffering. They were required to set aside a portion of their earnings to support widows, the needy, and the poor, as well as to preserve and maintain gathering places, such as watersheds, shrines, tanks, and gardens.

In addition to these duties, the guilds had the authority to prosecute members for offenses in line with their own traditions and usage, which grew to resemble the law in certain ways. Both guild and state laws had to be followed by a guild member. Guild testimony is recognized by the *Vasishtha Dharmasutra* as being admissible in resolving border disputes. Guild courts only had the authority to hear civil issues, nevertheless. All guilds served as courts for their members, but only the most important ones or individuals from different guilds with state authorization served as courts for the general public. Because guilds are associations of people from various castes who share a profession, they would have included Brahmin members as well. Some of these members would have served as executive officers, and it is likely that they helped create the courts of justice along with members or executive officers from other *varnas*.

Thaplyal contends that, although there are some similarities between caste and guild, they were fundamentally distinct groups. Castes were social organizations, while guilds were economic organizations. While guild membership is not necessarily hereditary, caste is. While one might belong to more than one guild, one could only belong to one caste. Guild and caste membership, however, corresponded in places where residents belonged to the same caste, and the guild leader presided over meetings of both the guild and the caste.

Last but not least, Thaplyal examines the relationship between the guild and the state and informs us that the guilds enjoyed a high degree of autonomy, which came not as a favor from the state but rather as a result of their intrinsic rights. The guilds protected the rights of merchants and craftsmen from the king's repression and the legal prejudice they frequently faced. Manu advises a king to educate himself on the *Shreni*s laws and other institutions while interacting with them. Yajnavalkya establishes that corporate regulations should be followed as long as they don't conflict with sacred laws. Even Kautilya, a supporter of state dominance in all areas of life, establishes guidelines for the defense of artisans. Due to the state's significant tax revenue from guilds, it was only reasonable for it to give facilities to them, such as maintaining highways for the transportation of goods and giving them loans and subsidies. In times of need, some wealthy merchants must have provided financial support to kings, whether as guild members or in other capacities. Kings would celebrate guild leaders with presents. During significant state ceremonies, guild heads were present. The leaders of the guilds accompanied Bimbisara's visit to the Buddha as well as Suddhodana's reception of the Buddha. Tradition holds that they, along with others, awaited Bharata's coronation and traveled with him to Chitrakuta to see Rama. At Rama's coronation, the *naigamas* took part.

There is no proof that any guild, or group of guilds, has tried to seize political control. The guilds of the time were regional in scope and lacked a centralized administration. Different guilds' interests varied and were occasionally at odds with one another, making it difficult for them to unite in opposition to the government. However, if there had been a contest for the royal throne, they might have assisted the contenders of their choice in winning. However, Kautilya urges the king to watch out for the leaders of various guilds banding together against him, acquire the support of the guilds through peacemaking and gifts, and undermine the ones that are hostile to him. He also suggests that the king give the guild of warriors access to land that is under hostile attack. Conflicts inside and between guilds gave the king the opportunity to appropriately meddle in guild affairs. Yajnavalkya advises a ruler to resolve disputes between guilds in accordance with their customs and force them to follow the established route.

Therefore, it can be elucidated that *Shreni*s performed a number of beneficial tasks, including the specialization of crafts, quality control of products, protection against state tyranny, composing differences between various social groups, delivering justice to the weak, and helping the destitute. The world's earliest democratic institutions may have been guilds.

Conclusion

In conclusion, the *Shreni* system was an essential part of ancient Indian society and played a significant role in regulating the economy and society. The *Shreni* system was a unique and multifaceted form of organization that existed in ancient India. The *Shreni* system was an association of traders, merchants, and artisans, and a separate *Shreni* existed for a particular group of persons engaged in the same vocation or activity. The *Shreni* system was a guild system that was egalitarian, and they worked together to promote their business interests. The *Shreni*s were responsible for procuring raw materials for manufacturing, controlling the quality of manufactured goods and their price, and locating markets for their sale.

The *Shreni*s were not only economic organizations but also sociopolitically dominant segments of ancient India that survived until the 12th century AD. The *Shreni*s were wealthy, and they acted as custodians and bankers of religious and other endowments. Through the successful management of their funds, some *Shreni*s became quite wealthy. They functioned as banks, lending money at lucrative interest rates to local merchants and other *Shreni*s. They also lent money to local rulers, thereby gaining political advantages for themselves and their members.

The *Shreni*s did not use their wealth exclusively to produce more wealth. They donated funds to construct religious buildings, such as the ivory workers' *Shreni* that donated funds to construct one of the stupa's four main gates. Furthermore, the ancient Indian *Shreni* compels us to move the date of the development of complex organizational structures to an earlier era. Studying the ancient Indian *Shreni* can teach us a lot about organizational structures and the corporate form.

In conclusion, the *Shreni* system was a unique and multifaceted form of organization that existed in ancient India. The *Shreni*s were responsible for regulating the economy and society, and they played a significant role in promoting business interests. The *Shreni*s were wealthy, and they acted as custodians and bankers of religious and other endowments. The *Shreni*s played a vital role in the socioeconomic structure of ancient India, and they had a deep understanding of how to arrange interactions in such a way that all those involved would benefit at large.

References

Bhaumik, P. K. (2015). Corporate governance in India. In *Corporate Governance, Responsibility and Sustainability: Initiative in Emerging Economies.* Palgrave Macmillan. pp. 24–25, https://doi.org/10.1057/9781137361851_3.

Buckingham, J. (2012). Guilds and governance in ancient India: Historical practices of corporate social responsibility. In *Managing Responsibility: Alternative Approaches to Corporate Management and Governance.* Routledge.

Ghosal, U. N., Majumdar, R. C., Pusalker, A. D., & Majumdar, A. K. (1997). *Economic Conditions in the Classical Age.* Bhartiya Vidya Bhavan, pp. 603–605.

Shah, M. & Agrawal, D. P. *Shreni (Guilds): A Unique Social Innovation of Ancient India.* Mandala of Indic Traditions. https://indicmandala.com/Shreni-guilds/.

Singh, G., Maurya, A., & Jain, V. (2017). Spirituality in Indian organizations. *Managing VUCA Through Integrative Self-Management: How to Cope with Volatility, Uncertainty, Complexity and Ambiguity in Organizational Behavior*, 171–181.

Thapar, R. (1996). *Ancient Indian Social History: Some Interpretations.* Orient Longman. pp. 129–130.

Thapar, R. (2000). *Asoka and the Decline of the Mauryas.* Oxford Publications, p. 73.

Thaplyal, K. K. & Pande, G. C. (2001). Guilds in ancient India (antiquity and various stages in the development of guilds up to AD 300). Life Thoughts and Culture in India, pp. 995–1006.

Verma, S. R. (2013, October–December). Women and her role in ancient Indian textile craft. *Journal of Eurasian Studies*, 5(4), 11–21. https://www.academia.edu/8128929/Women_and_Her_Role_in_Ancient_Indian_Textile_Craft.

Chapter 15

Corporate Governance in Shreni System: Glimpses from Ancient India

Veenus Jain* and Pallavi Mohanan†

Amity University, Noida, UP, India

*veenus.jain2607@gmail.com

†Pallavimohanan2904@gmail.com

Abstract

Ancient India had several ways of governing exchange, such as *gana*, *pani*, *puga*, *vrata*, *sangha*, *nigama*, and *Shreni*, in addition to family- and privately-owned companies. The terms *nigama*, *pani*, and *shreni* are most frequently used to describe commercial associations of traders, artisans, and potentially even paramilitary organizations. The aim of this chapter is to elaborate on the distinct characteristics of corporate governance in ancient India, especially highlighting the *Shreni* system, which resembles the modern corporate.

Keywords: *Shreni* system, business organizations, ancient India, economy.

Introduction

Businesspeople in the Indian subcontinent started using proto-corporate organizational structures fairly early on. The *Shreni*, a sophisticated organizational structure with parallels to companies, guilds, and producers' cooperatives, was in existence in India as early as 800 BC and continued to exist until the arrival of the Islamic conquests in the year 1000 AD. Complex organizational structures were in use much before the earliest Roman proto-corporations. These organizations were utilized in almost every aspect of business, politics, and local government in ancient India. These institutions' governance, structure, and regulation have many characteristics in common with companies, guilds, and other economic groups.

Examining the *Shreni* history reveals that the causes influencing its expansion are similar to those proposed for the expansion of organized entities in Europe. As with many other facets of the law governing corporate entities, the well-known concerns of agency costs and incentive effects are both present and addressed in relatively comparable ways. Increasing trade, strategies for controlling agency costs, and techniques for policing the borders between the assets of the *Shreni* and those of its members (i.e. to promote asset splitting or entity shielding and lower creditor information costs) are some of these reasons.

The powers of a democratic government, a trade union, a court of justice, and a technological institution were all united in the ancient Indian guilds, which represent a distinctive and multifaceted type of organization. A pleasant work environment was provided by the skilled guild employees. They found markets for the sale of manufactured items, managed the quality and pricing of the goods produced, and procured raw materials for manufacturing. "The ancient sources frequently refer to the system of guilds which began in the early Buddhist period and continued through the Mauryan period." (Shah & Agrawal).

Particularly, as some districts of a city were typically occupied by all artisans of a particular craft, topography aided their development. Tradesmen's villages were centered around one specific craft, and where raw materials were readily available was also well known. The three main conditions required for the development of a guild system were present. First, it was feasible to localize one's occupation; second, it was acknowledged that some professions were inherited; and third, the concept of a guild master, or *jetthaka*, was widely accepted. The development and stabilization of the guilds, which first served as a transitional group between a tribe and a caste, must have benefited greatly from the expansion of trade throughout the Mauryan period. They were later subjected to stringent laws, which led to some of them eventually becoming castes. Early guild formation must have been influenced by competition. Economically, it was preferable to work in a group than to work alone because doing so would give your company greater social status, and you could ask other members for help if you needed it. Guilds evolved into the most significant industrial organizations in their regions over time.

After reaching a stage where the guilds dominated practically all manufactured output, they discovered that they had to satisfy higher demands than their own labor and that of their families could handle; as a result, they began to use hired labor. This was divided into two groups: the slaves, known as *dasas*, and the *karmakaras* and *bhrtakas*, who were considered to be free laborers working for a regular wage. When Asoka speaks of the *bhatakas* and *dasas* in his edicts, he is referring to both classifications. As a result, by the time of the Mauryan period, the guilds had grown into major organizations that were acknowledged at least in the northern half of the subcontinent, if not the entire nation. A ban on guilds other than the neighborhood cooperative ones entering the villages suggests that they were registered by local authorities and had recognized status. This implies that a guild could not change locations without official consent.

According to Thapar, the distribution of work was planned not only according to the professions that resided in the town but also according to the physical occupation of various professions in various regions of the town. Each *Shreni* had its own set of professional standards, workplace policies, responsibilities, and even religious observances. *Shreni*s would occasionally settle disputes over larger issues among themselves. Since there would be more economic options for enhancing actual status, especially during periods of expanding trade, social mobility among such groups — where a whole community would attempt to modify its ritual position based on an improvement in actual status — would be more common. It is hardly a coincidence that periods of burgeoning trade were those during which heterodox sects and religious groups linked to social unrest engaged in their heaviest activity.

Corporate Governance in Ancient India

Ancient India had a variety of ways for governing business or group activity in addition to family-run and privately owned businesses, such as the *gana, pani, puga, vrata, samgha, nigama,* and *Shreni*. The *gana* and *samgha* appear to be more broad terms for political and religious bodies.

The *puga* and *vrata* refer to organizations whose members frequently had economic goals but were also citizens of a town or village that was entirely dedicated to a particular vocation. The terms *"nigama"* and *"Shreni"* are most frequently used to describe commercial, artistic, and maybe paramilitary organizations. Last but not least, *pani* is frequently viewed as a caravan of merchants traveling to trade goods. *Shreni, nigama,* and *pani* are those who engage in economic activity the most regularly.

In order to conduct longer-distance trade over land and water, there is evidence to show that traders frequently organized themselves into a partnership business structure. Typically, two or more people would get into one of these and choose a leader. Although the entity appeared to be able to own assets apart from its owners, it would be subject to the actions of the partners. These could all be organized simply. Additionally, over the years, rather intricate procedures for the separation of assets and obligations evolved. In the absence of an agreement, the laws in effect at the time that divided assets and liabilities equally or, occasionally, the proportionate contributions (talent, labor, and capital) made by members of the company might be used to determine how assets and liabilities should be shared. The latter was more typical of joint ventures between artisans.

Other issues were regulated by these early alliances. First, a partner's interest in a partnership could be left to his offspring. Second, guidelines and, in some cases, rules about who should enter partnerships are provided by the various textual sources. In general, collaborations between "learned" individuals with comparable socioeconomic circumstances and financial resources were promoted. This can be partially explained by the fact that it is simpler and less expensive to monitor conduct when partners are comparable, have nearly equal assets, and communicate well.

In addition, requiring partners to hold assets shows that they have an interest in the partnership, which should encourage them to be cautious when dealing with partnership issues. For instance, a partner in a trading caravan who has nothing to lose is probably going to be less careful and diligent than a partner who has something to lose. It is obvious that the ancient Indians were aware of some of the potential incentives included in this organizational structure.

The *Shreni* System of Ancient India

"*Shreni*" is the most popular term used to describe the economic entities in ancient India, but there are other terms that can also be employed. Generally, a *Shreni* is an organizational unit made up of a group of individuals who are typically involved in the same trade but who may or may not have the same caste.

*Shreni*s resembled corporations, guilds, and other types of organizational structures. Particularly, there are some similarities between the *Shreni* and the guilds of medieval Europe; however, the *Shreni* was more complicated and had rather specific internal organizational regulations. In fact, there is an example of a silk weaving *Shreni*, where some members also worked in other professions, demonstrating that a *Shreni* need not be dedicated to a particular profession (e.g. archery, astrology). The *Shreni*s were additionally mobile and were known to shift from one place to another without the danger of outside military intervention. Furthermore, in addition to economic activity, the *Shreni* was employed in political and municipal activities.

Widespread Usage & Legal Entity

There are some characteristics of the *Shreni* that have stayed quite constant over the many years that it was utilized in ancient India. The *Shreni* in particular was a distinct legal entity. There are numerous sources that attest to its capacity to keep property apart from its owners, create its own rules for regulating the conduct of its members, and contract, bring legal action, and be sued in its own name.

In fact, from at least the 6th century BC onward, some ancient texts mention a government official (Bhandagarika) who served as an arbitrator for conflicts among *Shreni*. These sources also provide regulations for suits between two or more *Shreni*. It was also abundantly apparent that changes to the *Shreni*'s membership or geographic location did not affect its obligations to third parties. With this distinct legal position, asset division should have been conceivable, which would have helped the *Shreni* expand by making it a more desirable contracting partner.

In addition, one intriguing aspect of the *Shreni* is how common it was in ancient Indian civilization. In ancient India, there were between 18 and 150 *Shreni*, who were involved in both trade and artisanship. This degree of occupational specialization is a sign of a developed economy, one in which the *Shreni* played a significant part. The *Shreni* was indeed employed by a wide range of tradespeople, including carpenters, ivory artisans, bamboo workers, moneylenders, barbers, jewelers, and weavers. Additionally, several of these vocations were split up even further into more specific categories.

Structure of the Shreni System

Although the *Shreni* was employed in a wide range of professions, its fundamental internal structure was rather constant. The general assembly of the *Shreni*'s members was its initial element, and some *Shreni* may have had over 1,000 members. It appeared that there were no restrictions on the maximum number of members.

One could anticipate that with so many participants, group action would be challenging without a smaller group being given greater daily operational and management authority. There were two groups of important figures in the *Shreni*, and management was heavily centralized. The first important figure was the headman of the *Shreni*, also known as a *jetthaka* or *sreshthi*. He was widely knowledgeable, skillful, and intellectual, and occasionally, he was also exceedingly wealthy. The headman's representation of the *Shreni*'s interests in the king's court and in several official business matters was another crucial role for him to play. The headman also held general administrative authority inside the *Shreni* and had the power to bind the *Shreni* in contracts as well as establish the terms of work there. The headman employed the *Shreni*'s adjudicative powers with regard to violations of the internal rules that bound all members, which gave him additional authority within the *Shreni*. It was typical for the headman to get a sizable pay in exchange for all of this.

However, it's not entirely clear if the headman was elected or not. When a headman passes away, according to some traditions, his son or other kin may succeed him. Other sources, however, state that the position is elected. Although this offers some evidence in favor of a hereditary position, there are grounds for skepticism about it. For instance, it is evident that the general assembly has the authority to dismiss a headman.

In such a case, it would be reasonable to assume that the incoming headman would not be a close relative or the headman's choice. It appears that an election may have been increasingly likely. In fact, it would seem that elections were the norm, and if the office was handed to the headman's son, it most likely did so with the *Shreni* members' consent.

Given how many issues the headman had to handle, it may not come as a surprise that he frequently managed the *Shreni* with the aid of two to five executive officers (*karya chintakah*), who also had the authority to bind the *Shreni* on topics pertaining to it. The written sources list the criteria for the executive officers, who were often elected by the assembly. They are typically anticipated to be knowledgeable about the Vedas (the oldest Hindu scriptures), not greedy, of noble heritage, and skilled in their trade. Additionally, some sources offer disqualifications (e.g. not too old or too young).

The *Shreni* had centralized management, with the headman and executive officers holding significant power, yet they were vulnerable to dismissal by the general assembly.

Internal Organization and Management

One may anticipate some way of regulating the relationships between the three layers of the *Shreni*, as well as even among the participants of the frequently enormous general assembly. Unless they were in conflict with the king's interests or the scriptures, the *Shreni*'s customs, traditions, and usage — which were frequently recorded in writing — generally had the force of law and were protected by the monarch. The division of assets and liabilities, the election and removal of headmen and officials, production procedures, prices, quality controls, and other issues could all be covered by these rules, or *Shreni* dharma. The *Shreni* dharma should also be recorded in a document (commonly called the *sthitipatra*) and registered with the government so that it can be used as evidence in future conflicts, according to many ancient scholars who encouraged (and even demanded) this.

In most cases, the general assembly's discussion and debate produced the *Shreni* dharma. The general assembly's members did, in fact, have a limited right to free expression. So, anyone who "opposed what was logical" or "interrupted a speaker during his speech and said something nonsensical" could be penalized. The goal was to maintain the *Shreni* in a relatively democratic position.

Once these regulations were established, it was mostly up to the *Shreni* to enforce them. The headman, along with the executive officials, had the power to act on behalf of the *Shreni* with regard to questions of *Shreni* dharma, which was the main means of enforcement. Thus, if a *Shreni* member violated the *Shreni* dharma, the headman or executive officers might punish him.

A member who was unhappy with the outcome had two options for redressal. First, the member had the option to appeal to the king if he believed that this punishment was motivated by the officers' or the headman's animosity toward him. The sentence could be reversed if the king believed it to be outside the *Shreni* dharma and was driven by animosity toward the member. This implies that there would need to be some ill will in order to repeal a sentence if the *Shreni* dharma was simply misapplied by the headman or officials.

The offended member may also seek restitution by approaching the *Shreni* assembly and asking them to censure the headman or officer. It is obvious that the assembly might penalize or remove the headman or officers for a variety of reasons, including breaking *Shreni* dharma and destroying *Shreni* property, without having the king's consent. Of course, if the headman or officer disobeyed the *Shreni* assembly's decision, the case would be brought before the monarch, who would decide in accordance with *Shreni* dharma and impose progressively worse punishments until the headman consented to removal or punishment. The king's authority may even include expelling the headman and seizing all of his belongings.

Despite the headman and officers' significant status within the *Shreni*, their power was not unchecked. In fact, there are some parallels to contemporary corporate governance.

First, management choices were respected, and a king would typically only get involved when the decision to punish a *Shreni* member could be seen as motivated by malice. Therefore, the king was unlikely to correct sincere errors of judgment.

Second, the assembly had the same authority to fire the management as American shareholders do today. The ability to fire management did exist, even if it seemed to require some sort of justification (such as a violation of *Shreni* dharma) as opposed to just the members' consent. Furthermore, the king may be contacted to have managers dismissed if they attempted to fight the removal. Therefore, it would have been challenging to try to maintain power against the wishes of the general assembly.

Third, the *Shreni* was aware of conflicts of interest and that some types of fraud were subject to harsh penalties. Stealing from the *Shreni* was a crime. Additionally, if a member obtains property for the *Shreni* and keeps it for himself, he must pay the *Shreni* 11 times the value of the item. A South Indian inscription specifies who is qualified to hold significant positions in a *Shreni* that performed a municipal function. It appears from those inscriptions, which are explored later in the chapter, that there has been considerable thought put into preventing conflicts of interest by preventing people with a conflict from holding important positions. This is comparable to the necessity for independence in contemporary boards. In addition, although not to the same extent as the municipal *Shreni*, some of the requirements for headmen and officers in the economic *Shreni* could be seen as fulfilling a similar purpose. A *Shreni* who understood the importance of independence, conflict of interest, harsh punishment for theft, and other wrongdoings governed the duty of allegiance situations very strictly. Conflict of interest situations were regulated, even though the sources rarely list the specifics of the *Shreni* dharma addressing such a situation.

Fourth, it is worth noting how *Shreni* dharma is enforced. The *Shreni* assembly would discuss any issues brought up unless they were ludicrous or simply illogical, in which case the member bringing up the problem would be punished. This serves as a restraint on the assembly's use for pointless matters of governance. Nobody can, however, stop a member from speaking unless they are expressing an outrageous or unreasonable issue; this offers, within reason, a pretty straightforward way to bring complaints before the general assembly.

Similar to this, only when the officers or headman acted unjustly in a case involving a decision made by the *Shreni* management would it be brought to the monarch. This aims to both limit pointless lawsuits and protect management from careless decisions. Management might be reluctant to implement *Shreni* dharma in the absence of such insulation. This is due to the fact that management only reaps a small portion of the benefits of *Shreni* dharma enforcement and, if they bear culpability without any protection, most of the costs as well. The rule limiting royal interference to cases of malice may aid in calibrating management's cost–benefit analysis for upholding *Shreni* dharma. With the exception of duty of loyalty violations, which are more similar to the examples of ill intent mentioned above, this argument is basically the same one used in modern times to shield directors from culpability (e.g. via the business judgment rule).

Shreni: Formation and Organization Process

The process of creating a *Shreni* seemed simple, despite the fact that the governance regulations were fairly complex.

A *Shreni*'s foundational components, such as its *Shreni* dharma, had to be established by the members first before being authorized by the king.

Second, according to some sources, a *Shreni* was required to register with the state after receiving approval and deposit its *Shreni* dharma there for use in future dispute resolution. Of course, establishing the entity formally is only the first step. The major task lies in increasing membership and maintaining the *Shreni*'s vitality and expansion.

It is crucial to explain how members were admitted to the *Shreni*, how they may leave, and what rights and obligations they bore upon both entry and exit to have a clearer understanding of how the *Shreni* membership developed. First, let's talk about the procedure for entering the *Shreni*, which was often laid down by the *Shreni* dharma. The potential member would first need to develop trust with current members. There were several ways to do this, such as agreeing to the *Shreni* dharma (*lekha-kriya*); going through a particular type of "ordeal" (*kosha*), which might not be physically taxing but had random elements to it; or having someone of high standing (possibly an arbitrator) vouch for a new member and act as guarantor (*madhyastha*).

Second, some sources claim that after mutual trust had been built, the *Shreni* assembly voted to admit the new member. If accepted, the new member would frequently have to contribute financially to the *Shreni* general treasury. Additionally, all assets and liabilities would be automatically shared by the member and all other *Shreni* members upon admittance. According to some sources, the assets and liabilities were to be distributed equally, while according to other sources, the distribution should be based on contributions made to the public treasury or perhaps on the capital and expertise offered. It seems that, at first, equal division was the rule, and as the *Shreni* developed and became a staple of society, increasingly intricate division practices proliferated.

In addition, there needs to be a way to train people in the abilities necessary to operate efficiently in some *Shreni*, particularly the craft-based ones. This type of training was permitted by a complex system of apprenticeship. There's little doubt that much of the training would have been passed down from father to son, and certain occupations were in fact mostly hereditary, but this wasn't the only way to learn the skills necessary to be a useful *Shreni* member.

The apprenticeship seems to be a very detailed contract between a teacher and student, governing professional training. For our purposes, it is necessary to note that the *gurukula* method of education typically required the student to live with the teacher, and the contract's duration could span a number of years (for example, 12 years). Once the apprenticeship period was over, the student was qualified to start working in the field. The apprenticeship program served the purpose of maintaining a continuous flow of individuals into the professions, notwithstanding its shortcomings. So, once established and staffed (in a number of ways), the *Shreni* was in operation.

The *Shreni* was, of course, not always a lifetime commitment. In general, if someone wanted to leave the *Shreni*, they could do so without the assembly's consent. After leaving, the member would no longer be entitled to any of the *Shreni*'s assets or obligations. The departure of a member, however, can have other repercussions. For instance, it appears that a member could be penalized if they left the *Shreni* after work on a project had started. Moreover, the repercussions were typically more severe if a member of the *Shreni* was expelled (for example, for violating the *Shreni* dharma). Given the reputational repercussions of such an ignominiously removed person, it would have been challenging for him to enter another *Shreni*.

The issue of transferring one's interest to the *Shreni* comes up when a member leaves, whether voluntarily or involuntarily. One is left to speculate on this part for an economic *Shreni* because little is known about it. However, it seems that in the *Shreni* used by the local government (municipal *Shreni*), a member could sell his share of the *Shreni* to another person. The duties and responsibilities (especially the voting rights) associated with these shares in administering municipal affairs are, in fact, described in very specific rules. Because liquidity is likely to be a more crucial consideration for someone in an economic *Shreni* than for someone who owns a share in a municipal *Shreni*, it appears logical to assume that if a municipal *Shreni* would permit the transference of interest, then an economic *Shreni* would as well. However, it is impossible to know for sure, and we also have limited information about how such a transfer might take place in an economic *Shreni*. In fact, one may assume that transferring one's interest would require the same kind of vote or consent, given how one is admitted to the *Shreni* (by vote of the members). It could be preferable to approach the situation as something that is warranted and is open to further inquiry.

The *Shreni* allowed people of many castes to enter it and engage in the same profession. It also allowed people to quit the *Shreni* of their own free will and enroll in another *Shreni* if they so desired. The process for entering and leaving a *Shreni* suggests a degree of social mobility, which contrasts sharply with the caste system's popularly held belief that it is fixed.

Segregation, Usage, and Accumulation of Wealth

When a *Shreni* is established and running, the next concern is how to capitalize on it and how those funds are utilized. The *Shreni*'s resources come from a variety of places. No matter the source, they were all seen as belonging to the *Shreni* as a whole rather than to particular individuals. Members who received something for the entire *Shreni* but did not distribute it to the *Shreni* were subject to severe sanctions.

Individual contributions (in cash or kind) made by members to join the *Shreni* or own *Shreni* "stock" were one source of assets. Gifts that the queen gave to certain *Shreni* members for a variety of reasons were another source, and one that was rather considerable. These presents, which belonged to the *Shreni*, would have been substantial. The profits from *Shreni*'s many projects' would have been yet another source of income. Profits from the *Shreni*'s activities that resemble banking would be a linked source of assets. It is necessary to state that the *Shreni* offered various services, including royalties, to members, as well as later non-members, and that this was a sizable source of assets and profits, even though this is covered in greater depth in the work of Shah & Agarwal. Last but not least, the Shreni assets also contained the fines that were collected from *Shreni* members who broke *Shreni* dharma. This demonstrates that *Shreni* dharma was upheld and that there were methods for separating the assets of individual *Shreni* members from those of the *Shreni* as a whole.

The *Shreni* had a lot of expenses that would drain its funds even if it would accrue assets from various sources. Specifically, the costs of making products for sale (for craft *Shreni*), buying products for subsequent resale (for merchant *Shreni*), transporting and protecting products during travel (for example, paying guards), and the costs connected with maintaining a *Shreni*.

There were other notable costs and expenses, though. First, the *Shreni* typically held back a certain sum of money to protect their members from legal action. Examples of *Shreni* arranging bail for its members are given in several sources. This is somewhat analogous to how contemporary firms fund the legal defense of executives through the indemnity of legal fees or liability insurance.

Second, *Shreni* funding might be used to give its members more incentives. In some cases, a *Shreni* will compensate its members for defending its property from bandits and criminals traveling on trade caravans. This might be seen as an early type of incentive payment to encourage the *Shreni* members to put forth more effort. Additionally, if a member disobeyed the advice of other members and produced a loss, that member was responsible for the full loss; however, if the activity resulted in a profit, that member was also compensated with an additional one-tenth of the profit.

This subsequent incentive device's asymmetry is an intriguing characteristic; if the activity created losses, the member bore all of them, but if it was lucrative, he received his share as a *Shreni* member as well as an additional one-tenth of the profits. In other words, he was responsible for all losses and only received a small fraction of gains. This shows that while the *Shreni* offered some incentives for innovation, the *Shreni* members had to have a strong conviction that gains would outweigh losses or that earnings were very likely. In other words, if he could not persuade other *Shreni* members of the importance of the activity, he would have to believe that the predicted gains (of which he would receive just a fraction) were large enough to justify taking the risk of suffering all the losses. Such an unbalanced incentive system does not seem unrealistic given that, even now, the majority of innovative activities do not result in marketable products.

After accounting for assets and liabilities, the question of how the *Shreni* members' claims to these assets and liabilities were decided arises. Equal sharing was one strategy, but there were others as well. For instance, some people proposed that sharing be determined by the *Shreni* dharma or, in the absence of one, by the amount of capital that each member contributed. On the basis of the contribution of talent and technical knowledge, some more suggestions for division were made. One has a suspicion that the algorithms for sharing became trickier as the *Shreni* expanded over time.

In fact, some of the more recent sources point to a very specific sharing structure that varied depending on the activity type, among other factors. So, according to some sources, partaking in a craft *Shreni* might be determined by seniority and skill, with the ratio for each being 4:3:2:1 for the leader of a program, the master craftsman, a person who has received all necessary training, and an apprentice. In another situation, the share given to the head who collaborates with another person can be doubled. The range of alternative sharing formulae with a higher portion for the more senior, possibly supervising, person shows that incentives have been carefully considered and would vary depending on the situation.

Conclusion

India has a long and prosperous history of trading and is a nation with significant historical antiquity. This makes it an ideal platform for researchers to research the growth of corporate organizations, including the *Shreni*. We discover that its growth fits well with more contemporary theories about the development of the company when we look at the specifics of its formation, governance, and regulation. The *Shreni* expanded as trade increased and as the supply of the monitoring techniques required for its development increased. Furthermore, there are many similarities between the characteristics of the *Shreni* and those of more contemporary Anglo-American enterprises. The *Shreni* people had many of the same issues that we do today, and they came up with many of the same solutions.

However, we discover a number of intriguing findings when we look at *Shreni* development in greater detail. The state structure, with an intermediate level of centralization and significant deference to the *Shreni* in running its internal affairs, was where the *Shreni* grew the fastest. The Gupta Empire saw the greatest growth in trade, despite the fact that trade expanded under other institutions as well. Even if other factors undoubtedly played a role in the growth of trade in ancient India, these findings are nonetheless intriguing. Additionally, the growth of the *Shreni* adds to the discussion of route dependence versus convergence in corporate governance.

Overall, the *Shreni*'s tenacity and adaptation may be shown in their capacity to endure and grow in a predictable way through so many centuries and diverse habitats in ancient India.

References

Agrawala, P. N. (2004). *A Comprehensive History of Business in India.* McGraw-Hill.

Allen, W. T., Kraakman, R., & Khanna, V. S. (2021). Commentaries and cases on the law of business organization. Aspen Publishing.

Altekar, A. S. (1944). *Education in Ancient India.* Nand Kishore & Bros. Varaneshi, 1965.

Cioffi, J. W. (2000). State of the Art: A Review Essay on Comparative Corporate. *Am. J. Comp. L.*, 48, 501.

Clark, R. C. (1986). *Corporate Law.* Aspen Publishers. Little, Brown, US.

Cowell, E. B. (2000). *The Jataka or Stories of the Buddha's Former Births* (Vol. 1). Asian Educational Services.

Cowell, E. B. & Francis, H. T. (2014). *The Jataka or Stories of the Buddha's Former Births.* Motilal Banarsidass.

Dass, A. & Deulkar, S. (2002). *Caste System: A Holistic View.* Dominant Publishers & Distributors.

Donald, R. & Tauber, L. Y. D. (2002). *Executive Compensation.* Bureau of National Affairs, Bna Books.

Hopt, K. J. (2011). Comparative corporate governance: The state of the art and international regulation. *The American Journal of Comparative Law*, 59(1), 1–73.

Jaiswal, S., (1998). *Caste: Origin, Function and Dimension of Change.* Manohar Publishers and Distributors.

Kangle, R. P. (2010). *The Kautilya Arthashastra Vol 2: Translation with Critical and Explanatory Notes: Pt2.* Motilal Banarsidass.

Khanna, V. S. (2005). *The Economic History of Organizational Entities in Ancient India.* Michigan Law and Economics Research Paper, University of Michigan.

Majumdar, R. C. (1922). *Corporate Life in Ancient India.* Calcutta University.

Mandlik, V. N. (1982). Vyavahara Mayukha, Or, Hindu-law: Including Smrities of Yajuavalkya. Asian Publication Services.

Mookerji, R. K. (1920). *Local Government in Ancient India.* The Clarendon Press.

Muller, F. M. (2001). *Sacred Books of the East.* Psychology Press.

Muller, M. (1965). *The Sacred Books of the East.* Motilal Banarsidass.

Muller, M. (2021). *The Sacred Books of the East: The Sacred Laws of the Aryas, Part II: Vasishtha and Baudhayana.* Gyan Publishing House.

Pandey, R. (1986). *The Caste System in India: Myth and Reality.* Criterion Publications.

Ross, S. A., Randolph, W., Westerfield, W., & Jaffe, J. (2005). *Corporate Finance.* McGraw-Hill Press.

Ross, S. A., Westerfield, R. W., & Jaffe, J. (2005). *Corporate Finance*, International Edition, 7th ed, McGraw-Hill, New York.

Shah, M. & Agrawal, D. P. Shreni (Guilds): A unique social innovation of ancient India. Infinity Foundation. https://www.infinityfoundation.com/mandala/ h_es/h_es_shah_m_shreni.htm.

Shavell, S. (1995). The appeals process as a means of error correction. *The Journal of Legal Studies*, 24(2), 379–426.

Sirkin, M. S. & Cagney, L. K. (2023). *Executive Compensation*. Law Journal Press.

Thapar, R. (1987). *Ancient Indian Social History: Some Interpretations*. New Delhi: Orient Longman.

Thapar, R. (2012). *Aśoka and the Decline of the Mauryas*. Oxford University Press.

Thaplyal, K. K. (2017). Guilds in ancient India. https://iks.iitgn.ac.in/wp-content/ uploads/2017/01/Guilds_in_Ancient_India.pdf.

Chapter 16

The Management and Organizational Paradigm of Chaitra Parva and Its Role in the Sustenance of Chhau

Nitin Mane[*,‡], Ruhi Lal[*,§], and Satyabrata Rout[†,¶]

[*]*Amity School of Communication, Amity University, Noida, UP, India*

[†]*Hyderabad Central University, Hyderabad, India*

[‡]*nitinmane@s.amity.edu*

[§]*aryavruhi1@gmail.com*

[¶]*satyabrata@uohyd.ac.in*

Abstract

In the eastern region of India known as Chhota Nagpur, a diverse community comprising people from different tribes, economic backgrounds, and beliefs come together to organize a festival called Chaitra Parva. This festival serves as a platform for various folk dances, including the captivating and skillful Chhau dance.

The purpose of this study is to examine the management and organization of Chaitra Parva and its significance in sustaining the art form of Chhau. It specifically explores the role of encouragement, innovation, and the active involvement of royal families in supporting Chhau. The study also delves into the ritualistic and religious aspects of Chaitra Parva, and how they ignite passion and excitement among both the Chhau performers and the local audience.

To gather data for the study, group discussions, interviews with experienced artists and scholars, and document analysis were conducted. The data were then analyzed using techniques such as tabulation, deductive coding, axial coding, and thematic analysis. The study sheds light on the organizational skills, inspirations, motivations, and real-life challenges faced by the Chhau artists in this context.

Keywords: Chhau, Seraikella Chhau, Mayurbhanj Chhau, Purulia Chhau, Chaitra Parva, management, organization, sustenance.

Introduction

Indian culture is enriched by its folk traditions. Despite adversities such as colonialism and foreign invasions, various folk forms of India persist. Multiple indigenous economic, social, and cultural models were disrupted willingly or through the influence of Western affluent culture.

To hone the skill and talent of folk dances such as Chhau, rigorous practice over a prolonged period is required. Chhau performances also need resources besides the talent of the artists. The livelihood of these artists depends on these arts. However, due to declining popularity, artists get paid less. Hence, the continuation of this art by the artists takes a lot of commitment from the artists, and many of them devote their lives to the arts. The art of Chhau dance is not confined to certain groups, as presumed by Western scholars, but anyone who shows commitment and dedication toward the practice of Chhau is allowed to learn. While only men learned and performed Chhau in the past, such restrictions do not exist anymore.

The Chhau dance remained limited to the Chhota Nagpur region, or the "Chhau belt," for a long period, as it was developed and enriched by the local culture, music, and ritualistic religious practices of the people of that region. There was resistance from the royal patrons and the Chhau *ustads* to making the art public. But the situation changed after independence. As royal patronage was seized, the artists faced hardship in finding the required income to sustain the art. The tradition of Chaitra Parva and generous royal patronage were important pillars in the growth, development, and sustenance of the Chhau dance.

Understanding factors that lead to the innovation, sustenance, growth, and development of indigenous folk arts, such as Chhau, would help in designing models for the preservation and sustenance of dying indigenous folk arts. Schechner (2014) argues that in Indian folkloric traditions, there is an ongoing convergence of theater and religion. In Indian aesthetics, the artistic experience is treated akin to the religious experience (Awasthi, 1979, p. 83). The tendency to transform rituals into entertainment, and vice versa, is practiced in the Asian context (Schechner, 2014). The role of factors such as religious practices, ritualistic festivals, and art patronage in the sustenance of Chhau would help in creating guidelines for the sustenance of other folk arts.

These guidelines could also be applicable in the post-modern world. The association of performing arts with religious ritualistic festivals, such as Chaitra Parva, helped in broadening the audience base and popularity of the art form. The dynamic Chhau dance became part of mass culture. The learnings from its management and organizational paradigm would help form a guideline for the preservation and sustenance of indigenous folk arts.

The ritualistic festival of Chaitra Parva was perpetuated for centuries with the aid of royal patronage and the religious fervor of the local populace. These factors created a sense of dedication, commitment, and integration among the local populace of all classes, creeds, religions, and socioeconomic strata, so much so that even the royal families participated actively in every aspect of the management and organization of the Chaitra Parva. The Paik dance of soldiers was integrated with the ritualistic dances and was further developed into an aesthetically vibrant dance form called Chhau. The continuation of the Chaitra Parva and the association of the Chhau dance with the rituals of Chaitra Parva enriched the technique, repertoire, narrative content, mask making, and music of this dance. These innovations, along with the preservation of earlier practices, led to the sustenance of the Chhau dance. Figure 1 depicts a conceptual framework based on these considerations.

Literature Review

Association of Chhau with Chaitra Parva

Chaitra Parva, an annual spring festival celebrated in the Chhota Nagpur Plateau of eastern India, holds a rich tradition that spans several centuries (Pani, 1969; Kothari, 1969). This region, encompassing parts of

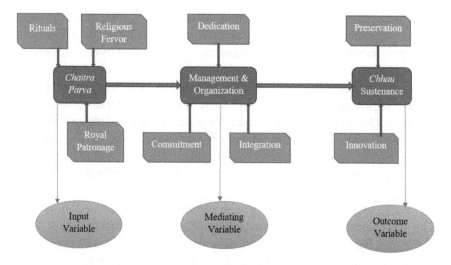

Figure 1. Conceptual framework.

West Bengal, Bihar, and Odisha, has a longstanding practice of ritualistic dance and music performances during Chaitra Parva (Awasthi, 1979).

The Chhota Nagpur Plateau is geographically situated in the south-west of West Bengal, south of Bihar, and north and west of Odisha (Bhattacharya, 1970). Scholars Gan and Mohanty (2005) suggest that the origin and growth of the Chhau dance can be traced back to the region's popular religious beliefs and ritualistic practices. The Chhota Nagpur Plateau is home to nearly a dozen styles of Chhau dance, with Mayurbhanj, Seraikella, and Purulia being the most representative styles named after the regions where they flourished (Kothari, 1969). It is worth noting that historically, these regions were part of Oudra Pradesh, with Oriya being the native language (Banerjee, 2021).

Patnaik (1997) asserts that the Chhau dance was originally associated with the Hindu festival of Dussehra. This connection persists to this day, as young boys are initiated into this dance through a sacred thread cere-mony on the day of Dussehra (p. 28). The Seraikella Dynasty, whose presiding deity is Ma Kali, celebrates the festival of Dussehra in honor of the deity. However, the major festival in Seraikella is the spring festival of Chaitra Parva, described by Singh Deo as a time when "the heart of man dances to the cosmic joy and rhythm" (Koizumi & Emmert, 1983, p. 20). During the month of Chaitra, Seraikella becomes alive with the frenzy of dance tunes, rehearsals, and performances, attracting people from all social strata (Singh Deo, 1973).

In Mayurbhanj, during the reign of Maharaja Jadunath Bhanja Deo (1822–1863), a dance form called "Raam Navami Nata" was performed on the last 3 days of Chaitra Parva (Lenka, 2001). Prior to Maharaja Krushna Chandra Bhanja Deo (1868–1882) ascending to the throne of Mayurbhanj, Chhau was not associated with Chaitra Parva (Gan & Mohanty, 2005). Patnaik (1998) explains the reasons and circumstances behind the association of Chhau with Chaitra Parva by the Bhanja rulers. When the capital was relocated to Baripada, which was a tribal area with no specific religious practices, the rulers introduced Hindu festivals and encouraged devotees from coastal Odisha to perform Danda Nata and related rituals. These devotees were then honored with land grants in Mayurbhanj. Although Danda Nata had an extensive repertoire of performances, only the mask dances of Parva and Chadaya survived. The latter eventually developed into a complete folk play and gained popularity in neighboring districts. With the acceptance of Chhau as the royal performance for Chaitra Parva, Chadaya became extinct, and Danda Nata could not survive due to its lack of regional connection. Nonetheless, devotees continued to perform the rituals, while Chhau performers did not observe the austere rituals associated with Chaitra Parva (p. 29).

The influence of tribal culture on the Chhau dance is evident, as it incorporates elements of tribal dance, music, and cultural traditions (Kothari, 1969). Patnaik (1997) discusses how the ritualistic festival of Chaitra Parva was enriched with performances such as Amadalia-Jamdalia, Sadhan, Paikali, and various mask dances. Sadhan (Pharikhanda) and Paikali, sword and shield dances performed by exuberant soldiers, share movements and formations similar to those found in the Chhau dance, such as *dula, hanumat-panikhia, bagh-dumka,* and *bagh-tabka* (p. 28).

In the past, soldiers used to practice rhythmic mock fights with weapons, including swords, shields, spears, bows, and arrows, accompanied by war drum beats (Pani, 1969, p. 35). This practice evolved into a martial art dance known as Rookmar Nacha, or Pharikhanda Khela (Banerjee, 2021). Gradually, the Chhau dance emerged from these practices and reached artistic heights with its elaborate stylization and body movement grammar.

Furthermore, Patnaik (1997) emphasizes that the tradition of mask dance based on Lord Shiva, featuring music and musical instruments similar to those used in Chhau, continues in Mayurbhanj. The Chaitra Parva celebrations honor the composite representation of Shiva and Shakti known as Ardhanarishwara (Banerjee, 2021). Ardhanarishwara holds significant importance within the Chhau repertoire, exemplifying the spirit and technique of the dance (Awasthi, 1979, p. 83).

During the ritualistic festival of Chaitra Parva, Chhau performances take center stage as a form of artistic entertainment (Kothari, 1969). The Chhau dance plays a significant role in the Chaitra Parva celebrations (Awasthi, 1979), and its evolution has been closely intertwined with the institution of Chaitra Parva (Kothari, 1969). The rituals observed during Chaitra Parva have had a profound influence on the development and performance of Chhau (Awasthi, 1979).

The deep-rooted connections between Chaitra Parva and Chhau highlight the interplay between tradition, religious observances, and artistic development in the region (Pani, 1969; Kothari, 1969; Awasthi, 1979; Patnaik, 1997).

Ritualistic Tradition of Chaitra Parva Organization

The Chhau dances, as described by Awasthi (1979), are characterized by ritualized body movements that possess an intense and trance-like quality. There exists a ritualistic association between the Chhau dances and the tribal dances of the Chhota Nagpur region, further highlighting the cultural integration and influences (p. 82).

The Chaitra Parva festival is celebrated throughout India as a springtime harvest festival. In the Chhau belt, this festival intertwines propitiation rites of tribes, religious ceremonies, harvest celebrations, and rituals dedicated to worshiping Lord Shiva (Banerjee, 2021, p. 18). Ardhanarishwara, representing the union of Shiva and Shakti, symbolizes creation and fertility, making the spring festival a celebration of new beginnings (Singh Deo, 1973).

According to Patnaik (1997), the local tribes have been celebrating Chaitra Parva for the entire month of Chaitra since ancient times. The festivities involve propitiating tribal deities through animal or bird sacrifices, accompanied by feasting, drinking, wearing new clothes, singing, and dancing (p. 30).

When the tribal culture merged with the Hindu religious practices of the ruling class, the observance of Chaitra Parva rituals extended to

13 days (Singh Deo, 1973). Rehearsals for the festival begin a fortnight in advance, lasting 12–15 hours per day, driven by the competitive spirit that inspires energetic and dedicated practice (Koizumi & Emmert, 1983, p. 20).

Patnaik (1997) elaborates on the Chaitra Parva rituals observed in Mayurbhanj, where devotees engage in austere practices. *Ghanta patuas*, the devotees associated with Shakti shrines, move through villages dancing to the beats of a brass gong (*ghanti*). They perform dances and yogic postures on stilts while balancing a holly pitcher called a *ghat*. These rituals are predominantly associated with the propitiation of deities by lower-caste Hindus and Hinduized tribes of Odisha (p. 30).

Pani (1969) highlights that the rituals begin 13 days before *Mesha*, or *Pana Sankranti*, which falls around mid-April. Thirteen devotees from various lower castes perform daily religious rites throughout these 13 days. Similar to Brahmins, the devotees wear a deep red dhoti (loincloth) and a sacred thread. They are initiated as priests and converted to Shiva-*gotra*, which signifies belonging to the clan of Lord Shiva. These devotees adhere to rules of cleanliness, follow vegetarian diets, and, in some cases, observe fasting. The focal point of the rituals is the Shiva temple, where they assemble as Lord Shiva's clansmen. Each day, the procession of devotees goes to the river for ablution, accompanied by music. The procession is led by a devotee from the Teli community, carrying a flagstaff known as Jarajara, which protects the performance space from evil, as per the *Natyashastra*. After the holy dip in the river, the procession visits important places in the city, including a temple in the palace, before returning to the Shiva temple. Throughout the procession, the devotees engage in ritualistic dances (Banerjee, 2021; Lenka, 2001; Singh Deo, 1973).

Lenka (2001) explains that a day before the festival begins, a ritual called "Asar-Mada" takes place to familiarize the dancers with the dance arena. In Seraikella, the spacious courtyard of the palace is prepared as the dance arena by spreading a mixture of cow dung and mud evenly over a 25 feet × 25 feet surface, which is then leveled using a roller (group) (p. 35).

During the nights of the festival, various rituals precede Chhau performances (Banerjee, 2021). In Seraikella, the consecutive nights are dedicated to observing rituals such as "Jatraghata," "Brundabani," "Garibhar," and "Kalikaghat" (Lenka, 2001).

On the first night, known as Jatraghata, a chosen devotee carries an earthen pot filled with holy water, sanctified through mantras, to the Shiva temple. This chosen devotee, called *ghatwali*, belongs to the Teli community. Adorned with red vermillion, the *ghatwali* wears red flowing robes, *ghungroo* (metallic bells strung together on anklets) on the feet, and garlands of Arkamali flowers around the neck. After various ritual observances, the *ghatwali* is treated as the incarnation of Shiva. Offerings are presented to the *ghatwali*, and goats are sacrificed in their presence. In a state of trance, the *ghatwali* sways fervently to the beats of drums, dancing their way to the temple on Tandva tunes. The Jatraghata dance, practiced since ancient times, is based on the concept of Ardhanarishwara, which recognizes the psychological attributes of both genders. The procession, led by a devotee carrying a flagstaff, moves from the palace to propitiate the *ghatwali*. After propitiation, performing pujas, making sacrifices, and receiving offerings from the ruler, the procession proceeds to the Shiva temple (p. 38).

In Mayurbhanj, the Jatraghata represents Maha Shakti or Mangala Gauri and is placed in the Shiva temple, remaining there for the following 4 days during the dance festival (Pani, 1969).

In Seraikella, Lenka (2001) explains that on the second night of the Chhau festival, a performance called Brundabani takes place. It portrays Hanuman's character joyfully dancing after destroying Ravana's Madhuban. The dance begins at a Shiva temple, continues to the palace, and ends at the Shiva temple (p. 39).

The third night in Seraikella is devoted to Garibhar, depicting the immortal Srikrishna-Gopi theme seen in various Indian folk forms. The chief performer carries two metal pots filled with holy water from the river, suspended from a pliant bamboo on their shoulder. Dancing their way from the river to the dance arena, the performer is accompanied by two men portraying *gopis* (milkmaids), one dressed in white and the other in black. The fourth character represents the young Lord Krishna. Upon reaching the dance arena, the performers are offered a seat, where they witness the evening's Chhau dance performances. At daybreak, they visit all households, offering the holy water they carry in the metal pots (p. 39).

In Seraikella, the fourth and final night of the festival features Kamanaghata, also known as Kalikaghata or Nishighata, which takes place after midnight. Kamanaghata symbolizes the goddess Kalika, associated with human desires. Both Kamanaghata and the devotee carrying it are adorned in black. After the performance, Kamanaghata is buried in the temple and remains there for the entire year (Pani, 1969, p. 43).

Singh Deo (1973) explains that during the final nights of Chaitra Parva, the Chhau performances and festivities continue from 9 p.m. until the morning. Pani (1969) suggests that while these rituals hold significance in Hindu religious scriptures, they do not have an explicit connection with the Chhau dance. However, Awasthi (1979) counters this view, stating that these observances create an atmosphere of religious frenzy, and the dance festival represents the culmination of these rituals. There exists a link between the Chhau dances and rituals, although further evaluation is required to understand the role of rituals in the evolution and sustainability of the Chhau dances (p. 82). Patnaik (1997) argues that Hinduism became more liberal under the influence of tantrism, leading to the development of mass cultures around the cults of Shiva and Shakti. These cults assimilated rituals from the local tribes, resulting in the organic synthesis of various belief systems within the region (p. 30).

Management of Chaitra Parva by Royal Patrons of Chhau

The Chhau dance was nurtured and developed through the royal patronage of 36 dynasties in Eastern India, particularly in and around the Chhota Nagpur area (Pani, 1969). Historical records indicate the existence of 36 Singh kingdoms in Oudra Desha, which followed Odia culture (Banerjee, 2021). The kingdoms of Mayurbhanj and Seraikella extended their patronage to these dances, playing a vital role in conceptualizing and developing them (Banerjee, 2021). As a result, these styles have highly evolved grammar and technique (Pani, 1969). On the other hand, the Purulia style of Chhau was passed down through ritualistic celebrations, characterized by a simpler grammar but intense theatricality (Bhattacharya, 1970).

The royal patronage extended beyond mere monetary donations, as the rulers actively participated in the choreography, performance, management, and organization of the festival alongside the commoners (Kothari, 1969).

Development and Sustenance of Seraikella Chhau

The regions of Seraikella and Singhbhum were originally inhabited by tribal communities until the 7th century, when they were eventually subjugated by Rajput rulers (Kothari, 1969). In 1205 AD, Darpa Narayan Singh founded the Singh Dynasty in Porahat, located in the Singhbhum district (Banerjee, 2021). This dynasty continued for 52 generations, and in the 17th century, Kumar Bikram Singh, the brother of the 46th ruler Arjun Singh III, established the Singha Dynasty in Seraikella (Koizumi & Emmert, 1983). During this time, the rulers brought in 13 castes, mostly representing Odia culture, including Brahmins, *paiks* (soldiers), and Gotipua dancers. It was around this period that the fundamental movements of the acrobatic Chhau dance began to develop, combining elements from the Pharikhanda (*phari*: shield and *khanda*: sword) practice of soldiers and the Gotipua dance (Banerjee, 2021).

Gradually, the power and prestige of Seraikella overshadowed the parent Porahat kingdom (Koizumi & Emmert, 1983). Seraikella, as a princely state, remained unconquered both politically and culturally due to the geographical advantage provided by the Saranda region's seven hundred hills. The uninterrupted rule of the Singh Dynasty, along with their patronage and participation, played a crucial role in preserving the art of the Chhau dance (Singh Deo, 1973; Kothari, 1969).

Several members of the royal family became exponents and torchbearers of the magnificent Chhau dance (Singh Deo, 1973). Bijoy Pratap Singh Deo, a royal scion, played a pivotal role in the stylization of the dance. In 1938, he established a training center called Sri Kalapith to consolidate the training and rehearsal process of *akharas* (training grounds). However, the construction of the establishment began in 1942. Bijoy Pratap Singh Deo revolutionized the masks, costumes, and choreography of Seraikella Chhau, incorporating elements of lasya, abstract ideas, contemporary thought, and Western influence. His exploration of unique abstract themes, such as *shabar* (the hunter), *nabik* (the boatman), *ratri* (night), *phoolbasant*, peacock, and *chandrabhaga* (the fictitious maiden), exemplifies this influence (Banerjee, 2021, pp. 25–26). His prodigy, Prince Suvendra Narayan Singh Deo, became a remarkable Seraikella Chhau dancer (Singh Deo, 1973). Suddhendra Narayan Singh Deo, the youngest son of the Maharaja of Seraikella, emerged as a prominent Chhau exponent, brilliant dancer, and outstanding Chhau choreographer (Banerjee, 2021).

According to Suddhendra Narayan Singh Deo, the Chhau dance during the festival involved the collaboration of princes and paupers for three consecutive days. The dance motifs drew inspiration from various aspects of nature, human emotions, and episodes from the Ramayana and Mahabharata, reflecting the rich mythology of the Hindus. Through the ages, the rulers of Seraikella preserved, developed, and extended the unique style of Chhau dance, which serves as the flowering fruit of the ancient culture of Singhbhum (Koizumi & Emmert, 1983, p. 17).

Bijoy Pratap Singh Deo initiated the tradition of 4-day Chhau competitions during Chaitra Parva. King Aditya Narayan Singh Deo further fostered the competitive spirit among Chhau dancers by organizing competitions between the akharas (groups) of Chhau dancers. The city of Seraikella was divided into Bajar Sahi, patronized by the royals, and Brahmin Sahi, patronized by eminent Brahmin families. Each Sahi was further divided into four groups, resulting in a total of eight groups participating in the competitions and annual functions. The king himself served as the *sabhapati* (chief judge) of the Chaitra Parva competitions and would honor the winner with a trophy designed in the shape of a flagstaff. This competitive environment inspired dedicated artists to devote their time, energy, and resources to create, transform, and preserve Chhau dance (Banerjee, 2021; Koizumi & Emmert, 1983).

The royal family provided patronage to Chhau dance until 1969, with partial financial aid from the Sangeet Natak Akademi after 1947 (Koizumi & Emmert, 1983).

In the new millennium, the Chhau Mahotsav (Chhau festival) initiated by local departments of tourism, youth, sports, and culture organized Chhau competitions with substantial prize money, further promoting and popularizing Chhau among the youth (Hollander, 2007).

Even when Chhau dancers perform outside the religious festival of Chaitra Parva or outside Seraikella, ritualistic elements are still incorporated. Their palms, feet, and exposed body parts are painted red with vermillion, and they traditionally begin every dance with *Jatraghata tala*. This demonstrates the lasting influence of rituals on Chhau performances (Koizumi & Emmert, 1983, p. 23).

Development and Sustenance of Mayurbhanj Chhau

Mayurbhanj, the largest of the 18 princely states of Odisha, was merged with the Indian Union on January 1, 1949 (Patnaik, 1998). The Bhanjas of Mayurbhanj had been ruling the Mayurbhanj-Keonjhar kingdom since the 4th century AD, initially as feudatories of the Bhauma king and later as feudatories of the Somavamsi kings until British occupation in 1803 (Lenka, 2001). The Bhanjas adopted the name Mayurbhanj to honor the political and cultural alliance between the ruling families of the Mayuras of Bonai and Bhanjas of Khijjingakotta in Odisha (Patnaik, 1998).

The capital of Mayurbhanj was initially located in Haripur around 1400 AD but was later moved to Baripada at the end of the 18th century, where it remained until the state acceded to the Indian Union (Lenka, 2001). The town of Baripada was divided into two parts: Uttar Sahi, located north of the king's palace, and Dakshin Sahi, located south of the palace (Lenka, 2001). Competition among the dancers of the two *sahis* (dance troupes) was common, and the younger brothers of the king, namely Krushna Chandra, Brundaban Chandra, and Gokul Chandra, were given control of the *sahis*. These brothers were not only good dancers themselves but also served as dance teachers (Lenka, 2001).

The contributions of four Mayurbhanj kings, including Maharaja Krushna Chandra Bhanja Deo, were significant in the development of Mayurbhanj Chhau (Lenka, 2001). Maharaja Krushna Chandra Bhanja Deo, who was fascinated by the Seraikella Chhau dance, played a crucial role in institutionalizing and nurturing Mayurbhanj Chhau (Mohanta, 2008). He appointed two teachers, Upendra Biswal and Banamali Das, from Dhalbhum (in Seraikella), known as Pharikhanda ustads, to train the dancers at the akharas of Dakshin and Uttar Sahi (Patnaik, 1998). In recognition of their services, he offered them handsome land grants in Kutchei and Kendumundi villages, respectively (Mohanta, 2008). These teachers, Upendra Biswal and Banamali Das, are considered the *adi gurus* (first teachers) of Mayurbhanj Chhau (Gan & Mohanty, 2005).

Under the tutelage of these Chhau masters, the technique of Mayurbhanj Chhau dance evolved from its rudimentary form (Mohanta, 2008). Mayurbhanj Chhau gradually replaced other dance performances during the last 3 days of Chaitra Parva (Lenka, 2001).

The early Chhau dances in Mayurbhanj style had a martial character, with names such as "Sandhamar" (Masculine Valor) and "Jhatak Bijuli" (Flash of Lightning) (Patnaik, 1998). Heroic characters from the epics and mythology, such as Mahadeva, Parashurama, Indrajit, and Kumbhakarna, were prominently featured in these dances (Patnaik, 1998).

After the death of Maharaja Krushna Chandra Bhanja in 1882, his eldest son, Rama Chandra Bhanja, was a minor, and the state was once again ruled by the Court of Wards (Mohanta, 2008). During this time, Chaitra Parva celebrations were barely kept alive (Gan & Mohanty, 2005). When Rama Chandra Bhanja ascended the throne in 1890, he also took a keen interest in Chhau dance and made significant contributions (Lenka, 2001). He reorganized the Sahi akharas and engaged his brothers Shyam Chandra and Dam Chandra to oversee the Chhau training in the *sahis*.

Additionally, he started a monetary grant of INR 2000 for each *sahi* (Gan & Mohanty, 2005).

The *sahis*, under the leadership of the brothers, fostered a sense of competition, with each brother spending significant amounts from their funds for preparation and rehearsals (Gan & Mohanty, 2005). They provided accommodation for star performers and personally took care of their diet and health (Lenka, 2001). The training, rehearsals, and creation of new compositions continued throughout the year, with old compositions being refined and two to three new compositions added each year, which became the highlights of the Chaitra Parva (Lenka, 2001).

In 1912, Maharaja Ram Chandra Bhanja presented the Chhau dance to the British Monarch George V and other royal guests. It was a grand performance that involved sixty-four dancers who rehearsed twice daily for six months and utilized special costumes and equipment (Lenka, 2001). This performance received universal appreciation and was considered a great spectacle (Patnaik, 1998).

Maharaja Pratap Chandra Bhanja, who ascended the throne in 1930–1931 and ruled until the merger with the Indian Union, is considered the golden era of Mayurbhanj Chhau (Gan & Mohanty, 2005). Under his reign, the rehearsal and training processes were systematized, and various upgrades were introduced. These included increased annual grants for each Sahi, the appointment of managers for each Sahi, the formation of committees to assist the managers, and scheduled rehearsals from October to Chaitra Parva in April (Patnaik, 1998). Proper physical exercises, dance practices, and a nourishing diet were provided for the artists, along with free medical aid (Patnaik, 1998).

Maharaja Pratap Chandra Bhanja also focused on enriching the technique and style of Mayurbhanj Chhau. He introduced three tempi (*vilambit, madhyama,* and *drut*) for different stages of dance, introduced mudras (hand gestures) with the help of a Kathakali guru, and incorporated classical elements into the Chhau dance (Patnaik, 1998). To compose and play music for Chhau performances, a forty-member western band with a Russian bandmaster was introduced, drawing inspiration from Hindustani and Odissi music, as well as *kirtans* and local folk songs (Patnaik, 1998).

Maharaja Pratap Chandra Bhanja's efforts resulted in the development of Mayurbhanj Chhau on classical lines, with the incorporation of classical elements and innovative practices (Mohanta, 2008). The Mayurbhanj Chhau style also began featuring Vaishnava themes, with female characters played by male dancers and abhinaya (expressive storytelling) similar to Odissi dance (Lenka, 2001). Additionally, Mayurbhanj Chhau embraced contemporary content, incorporating popular Jatra plays and presenting them in the Chhau style (Patnaik, 1998).

Development and Sustenance of Purulia Chhau

Purulia Chhau is described as a masculine dance characterized by colorful costumes and magnificent masks attached to headdresses (Bhui & Tapan, 2001). The ritual basis for Purulia Chhau is agrarian, and it is performed during Shiva-Gajan to propitiate Lord Shiva, the god of fertility. The ritualistic performance of dances such as "kap Jhap" or Tandva Nritya and six other dances, including Bhakta, Natua, Pata, Santali, Kritan, and Nachini, is part of the Shiva-Gajan festival (Banerjee, 2021).

In addition to the Shiva-Gajan festival, Purulia Chhau is also performed at the end of the Bengali month of Chaitra (Bhattacharya, 1970). While many tribal dances are performed in Purulia, Chhau stands out as it portrays themes from Hindu epics and Puranas (Bhattacharya, 1970). The majority of Purulia Chhau dancers come from villages and various agricultural backgrounds, including farmers and laborers (Lenka, 2001).

There are multiple theories about the origin of Purulia Chhau. According to one belief, it is a transformation of Lord Shiva's Tandva Nritya. People from the Kurmi caste believe that Chhau originated from the Chhowa Nach, a warrior dance that depicts fights between characters from the Mahabharata, Ramayana, and Puranas. Another belief suggests that Purulia Chhau developed as a display of martial skills by tribes living in the hills of the region, with Chhau groups performing in forest clearings illuminated by flickering firelight (Bhui & Tapan, 2001; Lenka, 2001).

Over time, Purulia Chhau has undergone transformation in its social, ritual, and performance aspects. It has evolved through three stages: Ekoira (solo performances), Mel (four to five pairs of performers exhibiting symmetry in physicality, costumes, movements, and rhythm), and Pala (the presentation of stories from the Ramayana, Mahabharata, and Puranas inspired by Yatra, a folk theater tradition). Palachhau reflects the influence of local folk traditions on the development of Chhau (Banerjee, 2021).

The adoption of Vaishnavism by the kings in the region introduced and popularized Vaishnava music, such as *kirtan* and *padavali* songs. This, in turn, inspired the development of local folk music based on

Vaishnava themes with bilingual (tribal and Bengali) lyrics, which became popular as Jhoomar. Jhoomar songs eventually became the background music for Purulia Chhau, and choreographed dances based on narratives from the Ramayana and Mahabharata were introduced (Bhattacharya, 1970).

While Purulia Chhau had relatively less royal patronage, the *jamindar* (raja) Khetra Mohan Singh Deo of Baghmundi under the Kashipur Royal Dynasty played a significant role in supporting and enriching Purulia Chhau. Padmashree Gambhir Sing Mura, a prominent Purulia Chhau exponent, ustad, and choreographer, received care, inspiration, and support from Raja of Baghmundi from a young age. Gambhir Sing Mura has played a pivotal role in reviving, preserving, and promoting Purulia Chhau and has trained numerous disciples, including Nepal Mahato (Lenka, 2001).

The modern Purulia Chhau dance in its current form evolved during the reign of King Raja Braja Bilash Singh Deo (1785–1870) and Raja Madan Mohan Singh Deo (1870–1933) of the Baghmundi estate under the Manbhum kingdom. The dance reached its peak during the reign of Raja Madan Mohan Singh Deo. Notably, unlike the royal families of Seraikella and Mayurbhanj, these kings did not actively participate in the creative process of Purulia Chhau. The innovators and contributors to Purulia Chhau were individuals such as Jeepa Singh Mura from Charida, Lal Mahato from Chhato Dava, Konka Mahato from Torang, Bhika Sing Laya from Baghmundi, and Suchand Mahato from Khudih (Bhui & Tapan, 2001).

Research Gap

As pointed out by Awasthi (1979), Chaitra Parva's contribution to the sustenance of Chhau needs thorough research. From the description of Chaitra Parva, it is evident that the Chhau dance was popular among royal patrons and the tribal populace of the region. The development and growth of Chhau dance styles happened through innovations in music, dance moves, dance techniques, dance repertoire, content, masks, and costumes. The correlation between these innovations and the popularity of the Chhau dance needs to be discussed. The interdependence between Chaitra Parva and the evolution of Chhau dance needs to be studied. The aims and objectives used to bring innovations to the Chhau dance styles in those times, need to be discussed from the perspective of creating guidelines to sustain indigenous art practices. The management and organizational paradigm that emerged from the collective efforts of the participating people and the creative passion reinforced by the religious-ritualistic frenzy need to be studied in detail.

Theoretical Foundation

Figure 2 depicts the theoretical framework of the study. In his poetics of folklore, Bakhtin classifies important characteristics of folk culture into ritual spectacles, comic verbal compositions, and various genres of bil-lingsgate (Elliot, 1999) (Figure 2). Chaitra Parva's celebration can be

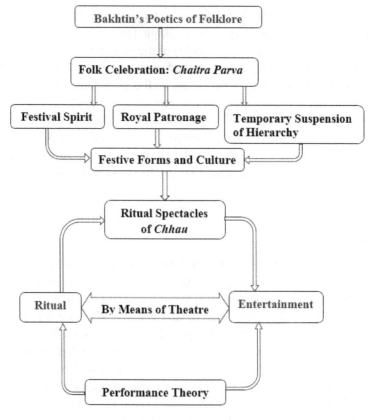

Figure 2. Theoretical framework.

understood using Bakhtin's carnival theory, which helps to explain this medieval cultural practice. Chaitra Parva is a folk celebration that creates a universal festive spirit. During the carnival, there is a temporary suspension of hierarchy, and the social hierarchy is suspended during the preparation and celebration of Chaitra Parva in the dynasties of the Chota Nagpur region. People from all castes, creeds, religions, and statuses participate in the organization and management of the festival. The tradition of engaging in ritualistic dance for 13 days during the Parva includes the performance of the Chhau dance on the last 3 days. This blending of local cultural tendencies and the amalgamation of folk arts contributes to the creation of a festive culture expressed through festive forms. The development and growth of different styles of Chhau are part of this spirited cultural process, and the aesthetically magnificent Chhau becomes the ritualistic spectacle of Chaitra Parva (Elliot, 1999).

Schechner (2014), in his book *Performance Theory*, describes Indian folkloric traditions and the notion of *maya-lila*, which refers to the playful manifestation of the divine. In Indian aesthetics, there is an ongoing convergence of theater and religion, and they are mutually supportive rather than being in opposition as in the Protestant West. The artistic experience is treated akin to a religious experience in Indian culture (Awasthi, 1979).

In the Asian context, there is a tendency to transform rituals into entertainment and vice versa (Schechner, 2014). The Chhau dance, originally practiced for the entertainment and exercise of the *paiks* (soldiers), has become associated with the Chaitra Parva. Its subsequent development and growth into distinct styles with unique grammar and a repertoire of dances represent an effort to transform entertainment into a ritual. During the last three to 4 days of Chaitra Parva, Chhau performances entertained a large audience, including both the local populace and royal families of the region. In recent decades, Chhau troupes have also been performing at other venues for the entertainment of audiences. This illustrates the transformation of ritual into entertainment, as described by Schechner, and both of these processes happen through the agency of theater.

Research Methodology

The researcher used a case study method for this study because the study could be best done in its natural environment and the researcher had no control over the key variables of the study (Yin, 2018). Bryman (2019) describes a case study as "a research design that entails detailed and intensive analysis of either a single case or (for comparative purposes) a small number of cases" (p. xv). A case study is an empirical method that does an in-depth investigation of a contemporary phenomenon in its real-world context, especially when the boundaries between the phenomenon and the context under study are not evident (Yin, 2018).

Multiple sources are used to gather information about the "case." For a careful analysis of the case, the research process includes a series of steps (Hancock *et al.*, 2021). The key aspects of the descriptive study formed a narrative report of the case. Qualitative interviews with Chhau dance scholars and exponents from the Chhau belt were done. An additional longitudinal element is added by using archival data, published interviews of Chhau exponents, research articles, books, magazine articles, newspaper articles, online audio-visual interviews, and documentaries.

The researcher has collected in-depth data through unstructured interviews and group discussions (Bryman, 2019). The case narrative was built on selected data gathered through multiple sources of evidence that converged in a triangulating fashion based on theoretical prepositions of data collection and analysis (Yin, 2018). The information gathered through the in-depth interview was used to develop a case study for analysis and finding the results (Shaika *et al.*, 2021).

The qualitative empirical study has an implicit research design. The researcher has suggested a proposition that the religious passion and ritualistic tendency of the populace, along with the royal patronage, helped in creating, developing, innovating, preserving, and sustaining a cultural legacy of the Chhau dance. The qualitative study is based on analytic generalizations (Yin, 2018). This study addresses an in-depth investigation of a particular program, namely Chaitra Parva.

Case Selection Procedure

Three cases identified are representative Chhau dance styles out of as many as 12 Chhau styles practiced in the research area. The research area is the Chhota Nagpur area in the eastern part of India, also known as the Chhau belt. Gan & Mohanty (2005) illustrate the Chhota Nagpur Plateau comprises the Purulia and Midnapur districts of West Bengal, Singhbhum, Dhalbhum, Birbhum, Seraikella, and Kharaswan of undivided Bihar, and

Mayurbhanj, Keonjhar, Nilagiri, Bonai, Talcher, and other Garjat areas of Orissa. The case selection was purposive. For case study selection, the researcher used a cross-case technique with qualitative assessment analysis. The selection was based on certain assumptions drawn from the data about key variables for accuracy and conceptual validity (Shaika *et al.*, 2021).

Case Development Strategy

The original objectives of the case study were based on theoretical propositions that led to a set of research questions. The literature review shaped the data collection plan and led to analytical priorities (Yin, 2018, p. 216). The theoretical orientation of the study helped in organizing the analysis, pointing to the relevant context, and finding explanations for the examined case (Yin, 2018, p. 217).

Research Strategy

In this research study, a systematic step-by-step case study analysis of an ongoing phenomenon in its natural context is done (Hancock *et al.*, 2021). Qualitative data was organized for clarity, thematic selection, and operationalization (Shaika *et al.*, 2021). An analysis is led by researchers' rigorous empirical thinking based on the pieces of evidence presented and consideration of alternative interpretations (Yin, 2018).

Discussion

Case Study 1: Seraikella Chhau

The current studies do not provide clear evidence of the origin of the Chhau dance, and there are differing claims among different Chhau traditions. Seraikella Chhau exponents and scholars believe that Seraikella Chhau is the pioneer of the dance form and claim that Seraikella Chhau masters and dancers were invited with honor by neighboring dynasties to teach and spread Chhau in the rest of the Chhau belt. However, Purulia Chhau exponents and scholars refute this claim.

The Singh Dynasty was formed in 1205 in Porahat, and in the 17th century, Arjun Singh III founded the Singh Dynasty in Seraikella.

The local Oriya population in Seraikella included tribals, farmers, Brahmins, Gotipua dancers, and soldiers. The soldiers used to practice rhythmic movements with weapons like swords, shields, spears, bows, and arrows to sharpen their fighting skills and entertain themselves. This practice later developed into Pharikhanda, or Rookmar Nacha. Gotipua is an acrobatic yet graceful feminine temple dance performed by preadolescent boys in the Jagannath temple to praise Lord Krishna. The basic vocabulary of Chhau started developing from the practice of soldiers mixed with elements of the Gotipua dance. The geography of the region and the political will of the kings protected the region from outside social, cultural, and political influence.

The spring festival of Chaitra is a harvesting festival in India, but the local tribal populace of Seraikella celebrated the Chaitra festival for an entire month with propitiation rites and revelry. The Seraikella rulers assimilated tribal culture with Hindu religious culture, transforming the Chaitra Parva rituals. They began observing Chaitra Parva rituals for 13 days, which culminated in 4 days of a dance festival.

The rituals are dedicated to Ardhanarishwar, a composite of Shiva and Shakti, symbolizing fertility or creation. Thirteen devotees from thirteen different castes, initiated as priests and converted to Shiva-*gotra*, perform rituals for 13 days. The focal point of the rituals is the Shiva temple, and the devotees and the local populace, including the royal family, respect the rules and regulations of the rituals and participate accordingly. These observances indicate the roots of the rituals in both tribal and Hindu traditions.

On the last few days of the rituals, the consecration of the dance arena prepared in the courtyard of the palace takes place. The rituals of Jatraghata, Brundabani, Garibhar, and Kalikaghat on consecutive four nights precede the overnight Chhau dance festival. These rituals create an atmosphere of religious frenzy in the city and grab the attention of the public with their local folk music and ritualistic dance. This atmosphere also inspires the Chhau dancers to create, execute, and shine in the Chaitra Parva competition.

The rituals, such as Asar-Mada, Jatraghata, Brundabani, Garibhar, and Kalikaghat, also have thematic associations with the Chhau dance compositions. Although the Chhau dancers do not observe the rituals, they are affected by the ritualistic and religious frenzy.

The Seraikella royal family has long offered monetary support to the Chaitra Parva celebrations, and royal family members themselves have been Chhau exponents, excellent dancers, and choreographers. For instance, Bijoy Pratap Singh, a member of the royal family and a connoisseur of dance and arts, revolutionized Chhau in the 20th century by bringing sophistication and incorporating elements of lasya, abstract themes, contemporary thoughts, and Western influences. He also established a training center named Kalapith in 1938 for Seraikella Chhau training.

Other members of the royal family, such as Suvendra Narayan Singh Deo and Suddhendra Narayan Singh Deo, have also made significant contributions as Chhau exponents, dancers, and choreographers. King Aditya Pratap Singh Deo of Seraikella encouraged Chhau exponents, dancers, mask makers, and musicians to create new dances and redefine the existing repertoire by organizing competitions. The Chhau dance competitions between eight dance groups in Seraikella used to be the most awaited event of the Chaitra Parva, attracting a wide audience, including royal guests from neighboring dynasties. After the king's death in 1969, financial support for Chhau came from the state and central governments, and in the new millennium, district Tourism, Youth, Sports, and Culture departments organize Chhau Mahotsav to promote and popularize Seraikella Chhau. Some of the rituals associated with Chhau are still followed even when the dance is performed outside the Chaitra Parva festival.

Case Study 2: Mayurbhanj Chhau

In the Mayurbhanj Dynasty, local tribesmen used to perform rudimentary Chhau dances on the last 3 days of Chaitra Parva as a way to pay respect to their king. The king, in turn, organized competitions between two groups called *sahis* and acted as a judge, awarding performers for their efforts. The conscious efforts of the rulers in the Mayurbhanj Dynasty played a significant role in the association of Chhau dance with the Chaitra Parva festival and its subsequent development. Four Mayurbhanj kings, in particular, played a crucial role in enriching Mayurbhanj Chhau.

Maharaja Krushna Chandra Bhanja Deo (1868–1882) was captivated by the Seraikella Chhau dance and hired two Chhau teachers from Dhalbhum in Seraikella, namely Upendra Biswal and Banamali Das, to train the dancers in Mayurbhanj. Under the tutelage of these Chhau masters, the technique of Mayurbhanj Chhau dance evolved from its rudimentary form. Eventually, Mayurbhanj Chhau replaced other dance performances on the last 3 days of Chaitra Parva.

However, after the untimely death of Maharaja Krushna Chandra Bhanja Deo in 1882, the patronage of Chaitra Parva was significantly reduced as his elder son was a minor and the kingdom was ruled by a representative of the British Raj.

When Maharaja Ram Chandra Bhanja ascended the throne in 1890, he, along with his brothers Shyam Chandra and Dam Chandra, took a keen interest in organizing, training, and patronizing Sahi akharas (dance troupes). They provided financial support, residence, healthy diets, and medical assistance to the star performers. Old dance compositions were refined, and new compositions were encouraged with monetary support for costumes. The brothers spent substantial amounts on the preparation, rehearsals, and shows of their dance troupes. In 1912, a performance of Mayurbhanj Chhau was witnessed by British Monarch George V and other royal guests, who praised the performance and the efforts of the royal family for their dynamic and magnificent execution.

During Maharaja Ram Chandra Bhanja's reign, Vaishnava themes were introduced, incorporating female characters performed using lasya movements. Interestingly, the female characters were portrayed by male dancers. One notable performance was a contemporary theme from a Jatra play called "Bidyasundar Pala," performed in the Mayurbhanj Chhau style. This particular love story was performed by renowned Chhau exponents Bisweswar Bhanja and Dinabandhu Behera, lasting for an impressive 4 hours. After Maharaja Ram Chandra Bhanja's death, his elder son, who was a minor, inherited the throne, leading to a reduction in the grants for Chaitra Parva to INR 250.

However, Maharaja Purna Chandra Bhanja, who ascended the throne in 1920, reinstated the grants but discontinued them a few years later when two of his Chhau ustads (teachers) were lured away by the king of Dhenkanal.

The reign of the fourth and last king, Maharaja Pratap Chandra Bhanja, marked the golden period of Mayurbhanj Chhau. Coronated in 1930, he ruled the dynasty until its merger with the Indian Union. He systematized the rehearsal and training process, increased monetary grants, and took care of the diet and health of the dancers, choreographers, musicians, and mask makers. He established committees to manage rehearsals, training, and Chaitra Parva performances. Additionally, he appointed some Chhau artists to the royal service to elevate their socioeconomic status and encouraged innovations and modifications in music, striving to develop Chhau as a classical dance form.

Case Study 3: Purulia Chhau

Purulia Chhau is characterized as a more masculine dance form, known for its colorful costumes and beautiful masks attached to magnificent headdresses. It is also performed during the Chaitra Parva festival. The rituals associated with Purulia Chhau have a tribal and agrarian basis, with Lord Shiva being propitiated through the ritualistic performance of Shiva-Gajan. In the region of Purulia, various tribal dances are performed, and the majority of Purulia Chhau dancers are villagers, farmers, agriculturists, and laborers.

The origin of Purulia Chhau has multiple interpretations. Some believe it evolved from the masculine and virile Tandva Nritya performed during Shiva-Gajan. Purulian Kurmis believe it originated from the war-like Chhowa Nach, a children's dance based on themes from epics and Puranas. Another belief suggests that it evolved from martial dances performed after seasonal hunting trips in the month of Vaishakh. There is also a belief that it originated from ghost or witch dances.

While the exact origin of Purulia Chhau remains unclear, it has undergone transformation through social, ritual, and performance-related factors. Its development can be seen in three stages: Ekoira, which involves solo performances; Mel, which features four to five pairs of performers exhibiting symmetry in physicality, costumes, movements, and rhythm; and Pala, which includes the presentation of stories from the Ramayana, Mahabharata, and Puranas. Palachhau signifies the influence of local folk traditions on the development of Chhau.

The *jamindars* (landlords) of Baghmundi played a significant role in providing opportunities to Purulia Chhau dancers. The contributions of King Raja Braja Bilash Singh Deo (1785–1870) and Raja Madan Mohan Singh Deo (1870–1933) are noteworthy in this regard. Gambhir Sing Mura, a prominent Purulia Chhau ustad, received care, inspiration, and support from the Raja of Baghmundi from a young age. Padmashree Gambhir Sing Mura has played a crucial role in reviving, preserving, and promoting Purulia Chhau in the district, training numerous Purulia Chhau exponents. Nepal Mahato is one of his notable disciples.

The influence of Vaishnava music, such as *kirtan* and *padavali*, popularized by the Hindu kings of the region, inspired the development of bi-lingual Bengali and tribal folk songs and music known as Jhoomar. Jhoomar serves as the predominant background music for Purulia Chhau.

The role of tribes and their dedication to preserving the tradition of Purulia Chhau is highly significant. For instance, villages predominantly inhabited by the Mura caste would allocate their entire year's earnings to ensure the continuation of the Purulia dance tradition.

Data Analysis and Interpretation

Data analysis was done in four phases: (1) familiarizing, (2) generating, (3) reviewing and defining, (4) reporting (Braun & Clarke, 2006). The exploratory research was guided by the conceptual and theoretical frameworks, which helped in the in-depth descriptive data collection and focused thematic analysis (see Table 1). The interpretations are drawn through a rigorous thematic analysis in which emerging patterns were identified, analyzed, and reported (Braun & Clarke, 2006, p. 79). The cyclical thematic analysis was done until saturation. The foundation phase focused on an in-depth literature review to identify cases apt for the study, and the philosophical paradigm emerged through comprehension of concepts and theories. (Lincoln *et al.*, 2011).

The researcher logically used inductive and deductive approaches. First, the inductive approach explores and gathers information and evidence, leading to a detailed research inquiry. Then a deductive approach was used to find grounds for theoretical considerations and test arguments (Shaika *et al.*, 2021). The analysis was done iteratively, gradually building more complex combinations, groups of codes, and higher-order concepts (Yin, 2018).

A rich explanation and description of the case in response to a research inquiry is part of reflexive and active analysis. The researcher

Table 1.   Phases of case analysis.

Familiarizing	Generating	Reviewing and defining	Reporting phase
1. Familiarizing with the data 2. Identifying items of potential interest 3. Relating to research focus — research questions	1. Building on codes identified in data-transcripts and/or field notes 2. Generating themes, subthemes, and codes	1. Provides the researcher with the basis for a theoretical understanding of the data 2. Reviewing the themes 3. Defining names of the themes	1. Case analysis report 2. Does a theoretical contribution to the research focus

rigorously investigated how the emerging codes and concepts reflect the meaning of the words and phrases retrieved from the data.

Based on Yin (2018), while familiarizing themselves with the data, the researcher actively and reflexively searched for patterns, insights, and concepts. They analyzed the data by adopting the following strategies:

- juxtaposing data from different interviews,
- putting information into different arrays,
- creating matrices of contrasting categories and placing their evidence along with them,
- creating event sequences,
- writing memos and notes (pp. 215–216).

Yin (2018) elaborates that the analysis strategy would be cyclical, revolving, or toggling between original research questions, prepositions, data, defensible data handling, and the ability to find and draw conclusions (pp. 215–216).

Analysis: Case Studies 1 and 2

In the case of Seraikella and Mayurbhanj Chhau, the feudatory kings had developed a composite culture, with the inclusion of tribal cultural practices with that of Hindu culture. Chaitra Parva satisfies the audience with the entertainment and ritualistic spectacle of Chhau. It also provides religious fulfillment through religious songs, dances, and the blessings of Lord Shiva incarnate. This helps in creating the popular festive culture and festive form (see Tables 2 and 3).

The display of dances in front of the enthusiastic audience and the royal guests, inclusive of the royal family, inspires the dancers, ustads, musicians, mask makers, and costume designers alike. The support and care, improved organization, and innovative inputs help in the growth, development, and sustenance of Seraikella and Mayurbhanj Chhau (see Tables 4 and 5).

Analysis: Case Study 3

In the case of Purulia Chhau, royal patronage had created the composite culture and impetus for the development of Chhau (see Tables 6 and 7). However, the tribal culture did not completely assimilate with the Hindu

Table 2. Case No. 1: Seraikella Chhau — ritual, religiosity, and royal patronage in Chaitra Parva Organization.

Initial codes	Properties	Evidences
Ritual	Propitiation of tribal deity, propitiation of Lord Shiva, harvesting rites, austere observances	Animal or bird sacrifice & revelry, Tandva *nritya*, religious rites for 13 days, cleanliness, vegetarian diets and fasting, Shiva-*gotra*.
Chaitra Parva	Asar-Mada	Consecration of dance arena
	Jatraghata	A devotee possessed by Lord Shiva, Tandva dance performed by a devotee in trance, animal sacrifice.
	Brundabani	Dance of Hanuman, Lanka destruction.
	Garibhar	Srikrishna-Gopi theme.
	Kalikaghat	Goddess of human desires buried.
Religious Fervor	Vaishnavism, Shaivism, Ramayana, Mahabharata, Purana	Possessed by Lord Shiva, trance, Tandva, Jhoomar, ki1tan, Mahishasur *vadh nritya*, Kaliya *damana nritya*, Hara Parvati *nritya*, Sarpa *nritya*, Radha Krishna *nritya*, Ardhanarishwara *nritya*.
Royal Patronage	Financial support and livelihood	Monetary grants to dance troupes, nourishing diet, residence and healthcare for dancers.
	Political assimilation	Hinduization of Chaitra Parva rituals, music and dance.
	Regulation in organization and management	Uninterrupted reign, competitions, judgement of quality, trophy, competitive spirit, increased rehearsal time, rehearsal schedules, performers practiced celibacy, establishment of Sri Kalapith, a Chhau training center.
	Active participation	Chhau exponents, brilliant dancers, and choreographers.
	Innovations	Kumar Bijoy Pratap Singh Deo transformed the masks, costumes, and choreography; stylization of Chhau; inclusion of lasya elements; themes based on abstract ideas, contemporary thought and Western influence; abstract themes such as *shabar, nabik, ratri, phoolbasant, chandrabhaga*; motifs from animate and inanimate nature.

Table 3. Case No. 1: Deductive coding — Sustenance of Seraikella Chhau through Chaitra Parva Management and Organization.

Open code	Axial code	Selective code
Animal sacrifice	Audience contentment	Popular base and support for Chhau
Revelry		
Entertainment		
Tandva dance		
Lanka destruction act		
Dance of Hanuman		
Jhoomar and *kirtan* music		
Cotemporary ideas		
Abstract themes		
Dances based on Vaishnavism and Shaivism	Religious fulfilment	
Blessings from Lord Shiva incarnate		
Dances based on episodes of Ramayana and Mahabharata.		
Ritual observances		
Kalikaghata Win over dark desires		
Religious rites		
Competitive spirit	Performer attainment	Creative environment for innovation and growth of Chhau dance
Monetary grants		
Land grants		
Nourishing diet		
Free healthcare		
Free residence		
Increased duration of rehearsals	Improved organization and management	
Rehearsal and training schedules		
Uninterrupted rein of kings		
Organizing competitions		
Encouraging winners with a trophy		
Establishment of a Chhau training center called Srikalapith		

(Continued)

Table 3.   (*Continued*)

Open code	Axial code	Selective code
Transformed the masks, costumes and choreography	Artistic Enrichment	
Refining existing dance numbers		
Inclusion of abstract themes		
Use of mudras and stages of dance		
Stylization of Chhau		
Western influence		
Inclusion of *lasva* elements		
Contemporary thought		

Table 4.   Case No. 2: Mayurbhanj Chhau — ritual, religiosity, and royal patronage in Chaitra Parva Organization.

Initial codes	Properties	Evidences
Chaitra Parva Ritual	Worship of Lord Shiva, harvesting rites, austere observances, propitiation of gods	Animal or bird sacrifice & revelry, Tandva *nritya*, religious rites for 13 days, cleanliness, vegetarian diets and fasting, Shiva-gotra, tribal dance, tribal music, tribal culture.
	Asar-Mada	Jharajhara installation beside the stage.
	Jatraghata-goddess Shakti, and Nishighata — Lord Shiva	Dance to invoke Lord Shiva and Shakti.
	Propitiation of Lord Shiva	Kanta Ghata: rolling on the thorns; Nian Pata: walking over ashen ambers; Jhula Pata: swaying over the flames.
Religious Fervor	Worship	Goddess Ambika, Goddess Kichkeshwari, Lord Bhairab, Lord Shiva, Goddess Shakti.
	Themes from Vaishnavism, Shaivism,	Trance dance, Tandva, Maha Shakti, Mangala Gauri, Ardhanarishwara, Jhoomar, *kirtan*, Kiritarjun, Tamudia.
	Ramayana, Mahabharata, Purana	Krishna, Samudra-manthan, Dashavatar, Bansichori.

Table 4. (*Continued*)

Initial codes	Properties	Evidences
Royal Patronage	Financial support and livelihood	Monetary grants to dance troupes, land grants, regular salaries to dancers, musicians and ustads, nourishing diet, residence and healthcare for dancers, inclusion in royal service: Ananja Charan Sai, in charge of palace lights; Sambhunath Jena, caretaker of the Queen's Garden' Hem Behera, head of agricultural operations.
	Political assimilation	Hinduization of Chaitra Parva rituals, music and dance.
	Regulation in organization and management	Uninterrupted reign, Chhau dance competitions, trophy, manager for Sahi, competitive spirit, committees for Chaitra Parva, increase rehearsal time, rehearsal and training schedules, performers practiced celibacy.
	Active participation	As dancer, choreographer, innovator.
	Innovations	New dance choreographies, refining existing dances, live music with a 40-member Russian band.
	Classicize Chhau	Use of Hindustani and Odissi classical music, *layas*, *mudras* and stages of dance, enactment to background song.
	Introduction of social themes	Jatra, Bidyasundar Pala.

Table 5. Case No. 2: Deductive coding — Sustenance of Mayurbhanj Chhau through Chaitra Parva Management and Organization.

Open code	Axial code	Selective code
Animal sacrifice	Audience contentmen	Popular base and support for Chhau
Revelry		
Entertainment		
Tribal dance and music		
Ritual act of rolling over thorns		
Ritual act of swaying over the flames		
Jhoomar and Kirtan music		

(*Continued*)

Table 5.   (*Continued*)

Open code	Axial code	Selective code
Ritual act of walking over ashen ambers		
Tandva dance		
Mangala Gauri	Religious	
Blessings from Lord Shiva incarnate	fulfillment	
Ritual observances		
Invoke Lord Shiva and Shakti		
Worship of Hindu deities		
Competitive spirit	Performer	Creative
Monetary grants	attainment	environment
Land grants		for innovation
Salaries		and growth of
Jobs in royal service		Chhau dance
Nourishing diet		
Free healthcare		
Free residence		
Increased duration of rehearsals	Improved	
Rehearsal and training schedules	organization and	
Uninterrupted reign of kings	management	
Organizing competitions		
Encouraging winner with a trophy		
Committees to manage Chaitra Parva		
Manager for Sahi		
Conception of new dances	Artistic enrichment	
Refining existing dance numbers		
Forty-member Russian band		
Hindustani and Odissi classical music		
Lavas, mudras and stages of dance		
Classicize Chhau		
Enactment with background songs		
Social themes		
Artistic exchange with renowned masters of other dance forms		

Table 6. Case No. 3: Purulia Chhau — Ritual, religiosity, and royal patronage in Chaitra Parva Organization.

Initial codes	Properties	Evidences
Chaitra Parva Rituals	Propitiation of tribal deity, propitiation of Lord Shiva, harvesting rites, austere observances, sacrificial communal rites.	Animal or bird sacrifice & revelry, religious rites for 13 days, Shiva-gotra, tribal dance, tribal music, tribal culture, Shiva-Gajan, Sun-God worship, Jatraghata and Kalikaghata.
Religious Fervor	Vaishnavism, Shaivism, Ramayana, Mahabharata, Purana.	Jhoomar, kirtan, dance drama based on Ramayana and Mahabharata.
Royal Patronage	Raja of Baghmundi	Dance and music learning center; Purulia Chhau exponent, ustad and choreographer, Gambhir Sing Mura was provided care, inspiration and support; Encouraged mask making in Charida; Modified masks from wooden masks to paper and clay masks, Durga Puja, Dussera celebration, Worship of Sri Lakshmi, Saraswati, Vishnu, Thirthankaras.
	Malla King-Vir Hambir	Adoption of Vaishnavism, Hindu religious rites, Hindu image-making.
	Feudal chiefs from tribes	Ceremonial worship of Hindu deities, musical recitation of epics and Purana, ceremonial worship of goddess Durga, sacrifice of buffalo.
	Themes	Episodes of the Ramayana, Mahabharata, and Purana.
Contribution from tribes	Bhumij	Feudal chiefs worshiped of goddess Durga and Kali; farmers worshiped animistic gods.
	Mura	Worship Sun-God called Sing Bonga, Priests, annual hook-swinging ceremony, ustads of Chhau, Chhau performance is sacred duty, sacrificed hard-earned resources to continue tradition of Chhau.
	Dom	Soldiers, war drums, music, country-made liquor.

Table 7.   Case No. 3: Deductive coding — Sustenance of Purulia Chhau through Chaitra Parva Management and Organization.

Open code	Axial code	Selective code
Animal sacrifice	Audience contentment	Popular base and support for chhau
Revelry		
Entertainment		
Tribal dance and music		
Sacrifice of buffalo		
Jhoomar and Kirtan music		
Musical recitation of epics and Purana		
War drums		
Shiva-gajan	Religious fulfillment	
Sun-God worship		
Ritual observances		
Propitiation of tribal deity and Lord Shiva		
Durga Puja		
Worship of Sri Lakshmi, Saraswati, Vishnu, Thirthankaras		
Dussera celebration		
Ceremonial worship of Hindu deities		
Religious rites		
Themes from episodes of Ramayana and Mahabharata	Performer attainment	Creative environment for innovation and growth of chhau dance
Sacred duty to perform chhau		
Care and support to chhau ustads like Gambhir Singh Mura		
Encouraged mask making in Charida		
Dance and music learning centre	Organization and management	
Tribes sacrificed hard-earned money		
Community participation		
Modified masks from wooden masks to paper and clay masks	Artistic enrichment	

culture. The dance form, once codified by the feudatory kings, was later passed on from generation to generation as a sacred duty by local tribes and passionate ustads of the region. The ritualistic commitment of the populace and their religious fulfillment inspired them to continue the practice.

Conclusion

The study indicates an association of the Chhau dance performance with the Chaitra Parva rituals helped in popularizing the art form. The efforts made by the local populace and the royal families in organizing the Chaitra Parva and managing the rehearsal and training process of the dance troupes helped in the growth, development, and sustenance of Chhau.

(a) **Cultivating a composite culture:** The popularity of Chaitra Parva and the inclusion of Chhau dance helped create a sense of cultural communion among a diverse population belonging to different castes, tribes, and religions. The ritualistic nature of the spectacle and the incorporation of religious themes contributed to this composite culture.

(b) **Religious frenzy and entertainment:** The religious fervor surrounding Chaitra Parva attracted the audience, and the use of popular folk and tribal music as the background for the Chhau dance rooted it within the local culture. The visualization of exciting episodes from Hindu scriptures not only entertained but also provided a spiritual experience to the audience.

(c) **Ritualistic energy and social consciousness:** The rituals preceding the Chhau festival gathered audiences and built expectations. The themes, music, and passion of the performances reflected the ritualistic energy, and the festive nature of Chhau became part of the social consciousness. The careful association of festive culture and ritualistic sensitivity with Chhau performances deepened the spiritual connection.

(d) **Encouragement and recognition:** Recognizing the contribution of performers through awards and praise augmented their passion for the art form. This support and appreciation motivated the artists to excel and continue their artistic endeavors.

(e) **Financial support and well-being:** Provision of monetary grants and salaries and taking care of the artists' health and diet freed them from economic concerns, allowing them to focus on their art. The financial support provided artists with more time and energy to innovate, refine their skills, and strive for perfection. Royal grants enhanced the quality of work by supporting ustads, dancers, musicians, and mask-makers.

(f) **Institutionalization and creative environment:** The institutionalization of Chhau *akharas* (training centers) improved the quality of performances. Measures such as increased rehearsal duration, proper scheduling, advanced training, communal living arrangements, and proper healthcare created a creative environment. This facilitated artistic exchange, experimentation, and skill enhancement among the performers.

(g) **Contemporary innovations:** The Chhau dance benefited from contemporary thoughts, a liberal exchange of artistic ideas, and inspiration from other dance forms. Constant innovation and growth played a significant role in enhancing the dance form.

(h) **Socio-cultural integration:** The royal patrons aimed for socio-cultural integration through the festival, and the Chhau dance proved effective in achieving this goal. Chaitra Parva provided a platform for Chhau dance performances, and the emphasis on the ritual spectacle supported the development and popularity of Chhau.

Overall, the study highlights the importance of audience support, careful planning, financial assistance, encouragement, artistic exchange, innovation, and socio-cultural integration in the growth and sustenance of the performing arts, including Chhau.

Performing art relies heavily on the presence and support of an audience. Without an audience, the art form cannot thrive or sustain itself. Therefore, efforts should be made to attract and engage audiences for the continued existence of performing arts. With careful effort and planning, popular support for art can be cultivated. By creating platforms, events, and rituals that incorporate art forms and resonate with the cultural sensibilities of the audience, the popularity and acceptance of the art form can be enhanced. Providing financial support, encouragement, and artistic input to artists creates a conducive and creative environment for their work. This support allows artists to focus on their artistry, innovate, and refine their skills, ultimately contributing to the growth and development of the art form. Encouraging a liberal exchange of artistic ideas and embracing constant innovation in the arts are vital for their sustenance. By incorporating new perspectives, influences, and techniques, the art form can remain relevant, dynamic, and appealing to the audience.

In conclusion, the study highlights the significance of the audience base, cultivating popular support, financial assistance, encouragement, artistic inputs, liberal exchange of ideas, innovation, and growth for the sustenance and development of the performing arts such as Chhau.

References

Awasthi, S. (1979). Seraikella Chhau: Talking to Guru Kedar Nath Sahoo. *The Drama Review*, 23(2), 77–90.

Banerjee, U. K. (2021). *Chhau Dance: Traditional to Contemporary*. Gurugram (Haryana): Shubhi Publications.

Behera, L. (2017). Major festivals of Mayurbhanj. *The Researchers' International Research Journal*, 3(2), 32–38.

Bhattacharya, A. (1970). Chhau Dance of Purulia. *Journal of the Indian Musicological Society*, 1, 1.

Bhui, S. & Tapan, P. K. (2001). *Chhau Dance: An Anthology* (1st edn.). B. R. Rhythms.

Bryman, A. (2019). *Social Research Methods*. Oxford University Press.

Braun, V. & Clarke, V. (2006). Using thematic analysis in psychology. *Qualitative Research in Psychology*, 3(2), 77–101.

Elliot, S. (1999). Carnival and dialogue in Bakhtin's poetics of folklore.

Gan, P. K. & Mohanty, S. K. (2005, April). The Chhau dance of Mayurbhanj: Its growth and royal patronage. *Orissa Review*, April, 46–50.

Hancock, D. R., Algozzine, B., & Lim, J. H. (2021). *Doing Case Study Research: A Practical Guide for Beginning Researchers*. New York: Teachers College Press.

Hollander, J. (2007). *Indian Folk Theatres*. New York: Routledge.

Koizumi, F. & Emmert, R. (1983). *Dance and Music in South Asian Drama: Chhau, Mahakali pyakhan and Yakshagana: Report of Asian Traditional Performing Arts 1981*. Tokyo: Academia Music Ltd., The Japan Foundation.

Kothari, S. (1969). The Chhau Dances/Les Danses Chhau/Die Chhau-Tänze. *The World of Music*, 11(4), 38–55.

Lenka, B. P. (2001). *Chhau, the Shining Ornament of Eastern Art and Culture* (1st edn., pp. 1–221). Baripada, Orissa: Rajashree Prakashan.

Lincoln, Y. S., Lynham, S. A., & Guba, E. G. (2011). Paradigmatic controversies, contradictions, and emerging confluences, revisited. *The Sage Handbook of Qualitative Research*, 4(2), 97–128.

Mohanta, B. K. (2008). Growth and development of Chhau Dance in Orissa. *Orissa Review*, June 27–32.

Pani, J. (1969). *Chhau: A Comparative Study of Sareikela and Mayurbhanj Forms. Sangeet Natak.* 13, 35–45.

Patnaik, D. N. (1997). *The Chhau Dance of Mayurbhanj: I, Sangeet Natak,* Vol. 125–126, 19–30.

Patnaik, D. N. (1998). *The Chhau Dance of Mayurbhanj: II, Sangeet Natak,* Vol. 125–126, 59–74.

Schechner, R. (2014). *Performed Imaginaries*. London: Routledge.

Shaika, S., Lal, R., & Jonjua, M. (2021). Sustainable development goal 3: Case study of using folk media as a potent tool in India. *Journal of Contemporary Issues in Business and Government*, 27(1), 4426–4443.

Singh Deo, J. B. (1973). Chhau, Mask Dance of Seraikella, Cuttack: Jayashree Devi (exclusively distributed by Murishiram Manohartal, Delhi).

Yin, R. K. (2018). *Case Study Research and Applications*. Delhi: Sage.

Epilogue

Samir Chatterjee

Emeritus Professor, Curtin University, Perth, Australia

Samir.chatterjee@cbs.curtin.edu.au

Several far-reaching insights from the exposition presented in this volume have the potential to broaden and enrich the theoretical and practical perspectives of the area of organizational architecture in the Indian context. As the preceding chapters reveal, the emergent issues and trends in Indian organizational dimensions are complex and manifold, as well as being deeply rooted in the cultural context of the country. Just as revealing is the point that this contextual evidence needs to be explored through the multilayered and cross-verging dynamics of global imperatives. The balancing of traditional value frames with global pressures has become one of the main challenges facing organizational realities (Chatterjee, 2009a).

The breathtaking pace of transformation in technology and innovation as well as the emerging domination of market culture have profoundly impacted various areas of organizational functioning. For example, the speed of technological innovation, the imperatives of sustainability and social responsibility, and the challenge of finding local solutions at global interfaces create very different structural and process challenges in organizations. The underlying assumption of the chapters in this volume has been that, in the Indian context, the pursuit of maximization of shareholders' economic and financial value has never been fundamental to business. Instead, the integrative theme binding the chapters included in this volume is centered on the creation of social and human centric values. The emphasis on ethics, social responsibility, ecological sustainability, and local innovations has been explored as deeply rooted priorities linked to traditional frames. Leading among the many Indian organizations is the example of Tata Group, incorporated in 1868, with a revenue of US$132 billion in 2022. Tata's vision espouses its core mission in terms of the embodiment and application of traditional Indian values. The company spends approximately US$500 million annually on social causes. Beneficiaries include educational, health, and scientific research institutes.

This volume is part of the World Scientific book series titled *Emerging Issues and Trends in Indian Business and Management*. The chapters in the volume focus on the key challenges outlined above. Previous volumes have covered technological as well as entrepreneurial challenges. The discussions in this volume have raised several significant "holistic" issues confronting the design and dynamics of modern work organizations in India.

The key aspects of the organizational dimension have been categorized into five groups, namely functional, responsibility, ecosystem, subaltern, and historical considerations, under the title "FRESH." These themes have been researched and investigated in the chapters that followed, as the chapters unfolded attempt to advance knowledge for scholars, administrators, and policymakers. It is hoped that this approach, labeled "FRESH," would assist readers in identifying the priorities that underline the organizational challenges from a new perspective. However, it must be noted that India and Indian organizations present considerable contradictions for investigators, given the complexities and multilayered nature referred to earlier. On the one hand, the Indian Space Research Organization (ISRO) has astounded similar organizations around the world, including NASA, by their excellence in matching their organizational capabilities with the unpresented demands of innovations needed in space science and technology. On the other hand, many industries, such as agribusiness and mining, have yet to reach their potential in responding to the nation's needs.

As the discussion in Chapter 1 has elucidated, differences in the perceptions of organizational governance have been mostly attributed to the "historical" and "subaltern" perspectives. Hofstede's classic study categorized India as having "high power distance," collective emphasis with high masculinity, and low uncertainty avoiding culture. As the subtopics of subaltern and historical aspects discussed in Chapter 1 suggest, the collectivism of culture in the general society is not necessarily transferred to the organizational context, as in Japan. Though Indian employees share many similarities with their Japanese counterparts in terms of transferring many social attributes to the organizational life, a typical Japanese employee is still totally and primarily dependent on their organization for social identities. Unlike Indian employees, Japanese employees' primary kinship is to other employees and the organization rather than their respective families. Japanese employees need to be loyal to their group and consider their work role often as "duty," unlike in the Indian context where primary kinship is still rooted to families. In addition, the governance culture in India has remained patriarchal and hierarchy-driven, unlike the Japanese "bottom up" systems.

The organizational dimension in India has also undergone changes brought about by the dramatic shifts in workforce characteristics. For example, in the 1960s, blue-collar jobs comprised 88% of the workforce in India, which is predicted to decrease by more than 5% by 2030. The rise of gray-collar workers with the emergence of BPO services and call centers was a feature of organizations working in global time zones. The advent of AI and other technologies is also impacting organizational functioning. However, the rise of green-collar workers described in this volume under the "sub-altern" category is expected to increase exponentially over the coming decades.

It may be of interest to note that, of the six points highlighted in the volume, five chapters included in the final two parts demonstrate how remarkable the footprints of an ancient civilization remain immersed in contemporary organizations. As Chapter 15 espouses, the Shreni system of management was widespread in India by 800 BC, and this system guided the institutional managerial frameworks not only in government, religious, and military organizations but also in all types of trade and commerce (Chatterjee, 2009b). The first known treatise on management in the world, called *Arthashastra*, written around 300 BC by the legendary scholar, teacher, policy adviser, and political mastermind Kautilya Chanakya, formulated a series of principles of good governance that are still latent in many organizational ideas in India (Chatterjee, 2013). It may be noted that Kautilya's book on public management was well known in India 1,000 years before Machiavelli's *The Prince*. *Arthashastra* provided guiding philosophies as well as tools and techniques for managing all types of organizations.

The arrival of Islam in the 10th century AD as well as multiple conquests by Persians, Afghans, and Turks, brought about new directions in organizational philosophies. Notable from this era may be that of the Mughal emperor Akbar, who made attempts to revive indigenous concepts and practices in his administration (Sen, 2005). The subsequent British rule for more than two centuries transformed the organizational frameworks of traditional India, where Western ideas became dominant in structures and processes in all types of organizations. Indian businesses paid a heavy price in terms of the destruction of successful local industries during this colonial transition. For example, a ban was imposed on the import of cotton and silk from India during the 1700s. This was accompanied by the popularization of importing products and services, as well as organizational ideas, from the British system. However, the cast-based family system of business survived the colonial system and reemerged powerfully after independence in 1947. For example, the houses of Tata, Birla, and others marked their domination in the economic sphere until the economic liberalization of the 1990s (Chatterjee, 2013).

An emerging group of organizations is leading India in a diverse range of human endeavors; in addition, many multinationals from the US, Europe, and Asia also dominate the Indian corporate landscape. A growing number of Indian organizations have become global and are experimenting with cross-verging organizational cultures and processes in their attempts to adjust to local imperatives.

India's space research institute ISRO, business conglomerates such as Tata Group and Reliance industries, and global software consulting companies such as Infosys and Wipro are some of the examples of these new types of organizations. It may be of interest to note that one of the major successes of India in the past couple of decades has been the export of global managers. Many excellent global companies around the world have India-trained CEOs running their organizations. It is true that India has not been able to match China's massive dominance in the creation of global companies, but the former dominates the global scene in managerial talent ahead of all other Asian countries. Overall, there is a perceptible shift in managerial leadership capabilities and organizational excellence in many areas of corporate, governmental, and social life. As was pointed out in their book, *The India Way*, by Cappelli and his colleagues, "These differences help explain why India way companies focus on long term customers because those relationships are at heart of the organization, why they see themselves as extended families with mutual organizations and why

they bang away at hard, persistent challenges until they crack them"
(Cappelli *et al.*, 2010, p. 206).

References

Cappelli, P., Singh, H., Singh, J., & Useem, M. (2010). *The India Way: How India's Top Business Leaders are Revolutionizing Management.* Boston: Harvard Business Press.

Chatterjee, S. R. (2009a). Managerial ethos of Indian tradition: Relevance of a wisdom model. *Journal of Indian Business Research*, 1(2/3), 136–162.

Chatterjee, S. R. (2009b). From Shreni Dharma to global cross-vergence: Journey of human resource practices in India. *International Journal of Indian Culture and Business Management*, 2(3), 268–280.

Chatterjee, S. R. (2013). Cultural and traditional legacies, leadership values and human resource management principles. In A. Nankervis, F. Cooke, S. Chatterjee, & M. Warner (Eds.), *New Models of Human Resource Management in China and India* (pp. 27–45). London: Routledge.

Sen, A. (2005). *The Argumentative Indian: Writings on Indian Culture, History and Identity.* London: Penguin.